WARNING

Do not attempt to read this book if you are a Manchester United supporter.

Any Manchester United supporter who causes wilful damage to property after reading this book cannot use the contents of this book as a defence in law.

If you have read bad reviews of this book, they will have been written by Manchester United supporters. Bad word of mouth will have originated from the same source.

Manchester United supporters are to be found in all walks of life. They may smile at you in newsagents' shops or in bus queues. You can find them on parent-teacher associations or in local amateur dramatic societies. They will not be found in the environs of Manchester.

Their opinion about this book is highly untrustworthy. Please ascertain your interlocutor is not a Manchester United supporter before listening to any adverse judgment.

Thank you.

The Author

MANCHESTER UNITED RUINED MY LIFE

Colin Shindler

HEADLINE

First published in 1998
by HEADLINE BOOK PUBLISHING

10 9 8 7 6 5 4 3 2 1

British Library Cataloguing in Publication Data

Shindler, Colin
    Manchester United ruined my life
    1.Shindler, Colin - Childhood and youth
    2.Manchester United Football Club
    3.Soccer fans - England - Manchester -
    Biography
    I.Title
    796.3'34'092

    ISBN 0 7472 2174 X

Typeset by
Letterpart Limited, Reigate, Surrey

Printed and bound in Great Britain by
Mackays of Chatham PLC, Chatham, Kent

HEADLINE BOOK PUBLISHING
A division of Hodder Headline PLC
338 Euston Road
London NW1 3BH

DEDICATION

This book is for my son, David Shindler
In partial expiation for the guilt I have suffered since
inflicting my love for Manchester City on him when he was
still secure in the womb.

ACKNOWLEDGEMENTS

Although this is a book of personal reminiscence, it could not have been written without the help of others. I should like to record my thanks to Jeffrey Cohen, Michael Chadwick, David Green and Howard Davies, with whom I have shared joys and sorrows in our march along the Maine Road.

I am grateful too to Colin Barlow, who afforded me access to Manchester City, and to Ian McShane, whose unlimited fund of stories gave me a good picture of what life was like when his Dad, Harry, played for United.

My brother, Geoffrey Shindler, is responsible for having started the whole *mischegass* forty-five years ago and though his heart belonged to United from an early age, he is too much of a gentleman to exploit the vulnerability of my feelings for City.

In particular I should like to thank Jack Rosenthal, the most talented writer and the kindest man I know, for encouraging me to embark on the journey and sustaining me when I had doubts. Having to sit with him on my sofa while he watches another Manchester United victory on Sky Sports is a small price to pay for a friendship I value so highly.

Finally I must acknowledge my debt to my wife, Lynn, and my daughter, Amy. They have never really understood what it is that turns me into a furniture-kicking, door-slamming, growling bear most Saturday evenings during the football season. This book may provide a partial answer.

Chapter One

In 1961, after the transfer of Denis Law to Torino, Manchester City signed Bobby Kennedy from Kilmarnock for a then record fee for a half-back of £45,000. Kennedy was a strong, aggressive defender in the mould of Dave Mackay. Since Mackay had just helped Tottenham Hotspur to win the Double, it was hoped that Kennedy might prove a similar catalyst for us. He didn't. However, in the 1967–68 season in which Manchester City won the League Championship, he was a useful utility defender.

Less than a month after City's heroic 4–3 victory over Newcastle United at St James' Park which clinched that Championship, to be precise, on Wednesday 5 June 1968, I went to my first May Ball in Cambridge. I staggered back to my room (alone, I might add) at about 6am. Two hours later there was a perfunctory hammering on the door and my neighbour Martyn Jones burst into the room, yelling, 'They've shot him! They've shot Bobby Kennedy!' Wakened from a deep sleep in this manner, my brain wasn't at its most agile but the news caused me to sit bolt upright in bed. 'Why the hell would anyone shoot Bobby Kennedy?' I asked. 'We've just won the League.'

'They've killed him!' Martyn shouted, even more loudly.

'Well, he was only a reserve,' I responded reasonably, still puzzled as to why Martyn should be so concerned, let alone what crazed Manchester United fan could have committed this extraordinary murder. Had he shot Colin Bell or Mike Summerbee, the action would have been tragic but comprehensible. But to shoot Bobby Kennedy! Perhaps the mad marksman had been at Stamford Bridge and seen that terrible mix-up between Kennedy and City goalkeeper Ken Mulhearn. There were thousands of us who would happily have pulled the trigger at that moment. Slowly, as the buzzing in my head started to subside, I gathered that a lone gunman had assassinated Senator Robert F. Kennedy in the Ambassador Hotel in Los Angeles moments after the announcement of his victory in the California Democratic Primary. Although America and much of the world was to be plunged into mourning by this tragedy, I was comforted by the thought that the real Bobby Kennedy would be fit to start the 1968–69 season and went back to sleep.

My first days at university coincided with my need to shave regularly. Faced therefore with the need to choose a razor blade, I immediately decided on Gillette, for the simple reason that they had become the first sponsors of the knockout cup in cricket and my beloved Lancashire had reached the semi-finals in the first two years of the competition. In the late 1960s, under the captaincy of Jack Bond, Lancashire were maturing into the best one-day side in the country, becoming the first winners of the John Player Sunday League in 1969 and 1970 and eventually claiming the Gillette Cup in finals at Lord's in 1970, 1971 and 1972. Gillette and I shaved in total harmony.

In the mid 1970s, Manchester United underwent a revival after their relegation to Division Two in 1974 (famously helped on their way by a 1–0 defeat at home to Manchester City in the penultimate match of the season). Gillette responded by producing a television commercial showing

Tommy Docherty, the United manager who had taken them down before bringing them back up, and his left-winger, Gordon Hill, in the act of shaving. I was appalled. From the moment that commercial appeared, I swore a Gillette blade would never touch a hair on my face again. It hasn't; my commitment to Wilkinson Sword has been absolute. And Gillette's replacement as sponsors by NatWest enabled Lancashire to keep winning at Lord's without causing any heart-searching on my part.

In the 1997 general election, each of the parties complained about their rivals' negative advertising, as in 'New Labour: New Danger.' To me, Manchester United have perfected the real art of negative advertising. The more the faces of David Beckham and Ryan Giggs and Eric Cantona adorn merchandise, the more I feel I can resist the lure of the product. I suspect I shall never travel by Eurostar or purchase any goods made by Nike, but I don't feel unduly deprived.

My dislike of Manchester United and all its works, and my devotion to Manchester City despite the Job-like nature of the travails they have inflicted on me, are unshakable passions. This book is an attempt to understand why a rational man should be reduced to such a level of irrationality by sport. In particular, it is the wail of a man who has suffered silently under years of overweening Manchester United arrogance. I have seen too much of that dour, humourless Scottish manager and the bullet-headed, condescending kung-fu practitioner to withstand any more of the fawning media adulation of Manchester United. In the movie *Network*, Peter Finch, as the disaffected newsreader, complains about the state of television and hence the world by advocating that fellow sufferers stick their heads out of the window and shout, as loudly as they can, 'I'm mad as hell and I'm not going to take it anymore.' I know there are millions of people who feel about Manchester United as I do. Well, like Finch and his supporters, we too are mad as hell and we aren't going to take it anymore.

For better or worse, my life has revolved around Manchester sport. This book charts the progress of my early life not just in the traditional milestones of professional accomplishments or family triumphs and tragedies but through my battles with the two football teams in Manchester. City and United have given me some of the greatest highs and lowest lows that can be gained without recourse to narcotics. I am convinced that there is nothing you can stick up your nose or inject into your veins that can possibly match the joy of beating United at Old Trafford.

Even if City haven't done so since 1974 (did I mention that before?), I can take almost equal pleasure in the achievements of others who do. On television I can look beyond the foreground figures of the celebrating opponents and pick out the stunned faces of the United supporters in the background to give myself a positively religious glow of warmth. 'Cut to Ferguson,' I shout at the screen, 'please!' And when that miserable face duly appears, unable to comprehend the latest Schmeichel lunacy or Pallister idiocy, I feel as a Crusader knight must have felt when he first looked upon Jerusalem. Yes, this is why God created the earth and all who dwell thereon. 'Come on, you Galatasaray!'

I will do anything within my power to create a defeat for Manchester United. In 1992, the last year of the old Football League, United were favourites to take the title from the pursuing but inferior Leeds United. On Easter Monday, Ferguson's team gave away two silly goals at home to Nottingham Forest. When the second goal went in, I was sitting in the garden with my right ankle resting on my left thigh. I was reading page 23 of the book that was open on my lap. I was aware that I had done something right, but I didn't know what precisely. All I could do was to remain in exactly the same position for the next twenty-five minutes.

The book remained steadfastly on page 23. I pretended to read, but not a word sank in. My leg was attacked by cramp. Still I wouldn't surrender. The agony became almost too much to bear, but there were now only five minutes left. Wracked by pain, I kept that right ankle firmly planted on the left thigh. United battered away at the Forest goal but I held on. When the final whistle went, I rolled off the chair onto the grass, clutching my leg in agony. When the feeling in it came back an hour or so later, I considered it well worth that Herculean effort, although I was a little disappointed not to get so much as a phone call from Brian Clough. Incidentally, in case you didn't know, United lost the Championship to Leeds that season. I claim a modest share in their failure.

Passion for sport defies logic. Thanks to the innovation of football fanzines, Nick Hornby's book *Fever Pitch* and Danny Baker's phone-ins, millions of us now know that we are not alone in our obsessiveness. The interesting thing is that every story is the same and yet every one is different. Most of us have a pre-match ritual. Mine involves brown socks. I don't wish to elaborate on this. Those of you who understand will simply nod approvingly, 'Brown socks, I see'; those who don't see can stop reading here.

There is a particularly mad Manchester United supporter whose pre-match ritual, he admitted in a call to Danny Baker on the radio, involves pulling the toilet chain, washing his hands (thus destroying some of my belief in the primitive nature of United supporters), drying them on a towel and running down the stairs to touch the front door before the toilet has stopped flushing. If he manages it, United will win that afternoon; if the toilet stops flushing first . . .

'What do you do before a really big match?' asked Danny.

'I throw meself down the stairs,' replied this sage individual. United's failure to win the League Championship between 1967 and 1993 was attributed to his family's removal to a bungalow, and their resurgence to his purchase of a house on two floors. Needless to say, the caller did not come from Manchester.

I do, which is why I claim the privilege of writing about United as well as City. How does it start, this passion, this insanity? Why does it take such a hold that twenty years of misery and the finest education in the land cannot diminish its power? At this point, my voice slowly starts to fade and the colour pictures dissolve to sepia and then to black and white.

Appropriately, my initiation began with a Manchester derby match played at Old Trafford. There were 60,956 locked into the ground that last day of 1955, and a further 20,000 locked out. I had never seen so many people in the whole of my six and a half years on this earth. It was my first real football match, my first Manchester derby and I was about to learn one of life's great lessons.

It all started so well. Jack Dyson, the inside-left, put City ahead in the first half, to the dismay of most of the ground and all of the people sitting around me in the Main Stand. (Dyson had the job I coveted – playing for City in the winter and bowling off-spin for Lancashire in the summer. Who could ask for anything more?) United were unbeaten at home with the 1955–56 season more than halfway through, and they were on their way to another League Championship. They had, however, already lost at Maine Road, 1–0 to a Joe Hayes goal in the first derby match of the season. Then, Bert Trautmann, the German ex-paratrooper and the greatest of heroes to this tiny Jewish City supporter, had stood like Horatius on the bridge repelling the barbarian Red hordes. Trautmann's presence had been so dominant that Matt Busby had reputedly instructed his forwards not to look where they were shooting, so that Trautmann couldn't anticipate the shot.

Now, on New Year's Eve, he threatened to repeat his heroics. United's Tommy Taylor soared to meet the pinpoint crosses of the wingers, Johnny Berry and David Pegg, but always those ubiquitous hands of Trautmann were there first. Duncan Edwards thundered in shots from twenty-five yards out, but Trautmann was equal to them.

The Old Trafford faithful began to stir restlessly. To lose once to Manchester City in the season was regarded as unfortunate. To lose both derby matches would be a Greek tragedy. To me, God was in his Heaven and all was right with the world. Wrapped in gloves, scarf and coat, but wearing short trousers because I wouldn't be barmitzvahed for another seven years and hence was not allowed to wear long trousers (I have searched the Torah from start to finish for any evidence of this Divine Commandment but failed to find it), I was nevertheless glowing inwardly.

City wore pale blue shirts (officially Sky Blue); United wore blood red ones. Like the colours, somehow the very arrangement of letters on the page still seems to me to symbolise their different virtues. 'Manchester City' looked then, and has remained, attractive, euphonious but somewhat fragile. 'Manchester United' looks aggressive, monolithic, devoid of poetry and humour. I would accept that this is a subjective viewpoint, but to me City v United was like Saxons v Normans, Cavaliers v Roundheads. City might have been, in Sellar and Yeatman's famous phrase, 'Wrong but Wromantic', but United were undoubtedly 'Right but Repulsive'.

The last day of 1955, the pre-Raphaelite Manchester City fielded two tiny forwards in Joe Hayes and the supremely gifted, frequently drunken, Scottish inside-forward Bobby Johnstone against the full might of the magnificent 'Busby Babes'. The baying of the Old Trafford crowd was overwhelming as the Reds strove forward in search of an equaliser, only to

7

sink back exhausted as they failed to find a way past the inspired Trautmann.

But there was another reason why City were going to win that game. Even at the age of six, I had already seen enough movies and read enough stories to glory in the deeply held belief that virtue was always triumphant in the end. City were going to win this game because they were my team and (therefore) morally superior – hence the inner glow.

And then it happened – the cruellest of blows from an uncaring Fate. Ray Wood, the United goalkeeper, who had been booting the ball upfield all match only to find the commanding presence of City centre-half Dave Ewing's receding hairline, tried again. This time a gust of wind caught the ball on its descent, floating it over Ewing's head and into the path of Tommy Taylor, who hammered it past the advancing Trautmann and into the net.

As Old Trafford erupted, a tiny doubt crept into my mind. Technically it was now possible that City might not win this game. It was a feeling shared by sixty thousand others as United increased the fervour of their attacks. Still Roy Paul, Ewing and Trautmann marshalled the brave City defence. Only ten pale-blue shirts and Trautmann's roll-neck green jersey now stood between a small boy's belief in the essential fairness of the world and the hordes of Babylon.

United won a corner. The crowd bayed. David Pegg swung his left foot and the ball floated into the City penalty area. Trautmann strove manfully for it through a crowd of desperate players, but Dennis Viollet got there first and glanced it into the net with his head. The world was filled with a mass of waving red scarves. I clung resolutely to the belief that all might still be well and, spurred on by the manifest unfairness of the scoreline, the City forward-line launched a series of counter-attacks.

Now it was United's turn to look strained and uncertain,

the Red crowd anxiously whistling for the end. Roy Clarke, the City left-winger and future manager of the Manchester City Social Club, burst through the United defence and hammered a shot past Wood – and against the crossbar whence it rebounded to safety. The final whistle blew shortly afterwards; family and friends gathered up the children, returned to their cars and drove back happily enough to north Manchester.

For them it was a day out, the annual trip to mingle with Manchester *goyim*, a matter of no great significance. For me it was a bitter lesson. It's an unjust world, as the Mikado points out, and virtue is triumphant only in theatrical performances. That match was the start of a trauma for which the only cure could never be obtained on prescription. Joe Mercer and Malcolm Allison would find it briefly, but it dissipated almost as soon as it had taken effect.

Despite the existence of the vast proportion of Manchester Jews who support Manchester United, I have always believed that City, with their lovingly preserved penchant for self-destruction and self-deprecating humour, were the only team for a Jew to support. United's achievements have always placed them in the heart of the Establishment – the one place Jews should never be. This view of the world grew out of an upbringing in a middle-class Jewish household in Manchester during the 1950s and 1960s, influenced by one remarkable man.

His name was Laurence Weidberg and he was my maternal uncle. He was, by any standard, an eccentric man. In 1960, when I was eleven years old, he moved from Manchester to London. I was profoundly upset. He told me very seriously that he no longer found it possible to reconcile his deeply held love of cricket with the economic necessity for it to rain hard and often, since he owned a factory which manufactured raincoats. It was like Edward VIII intoning with equal solemnity that he could no longer bear the onerous burden of ruling the country without the support of the woman he loved.

Uncle Laurence was the son of a penniless immigrant from Galicia (an area of Eastern Europe then under the hegemony of the Habsburg Empire) who arrived in this country in 1905. Grandpa Weidberg started Eltite Raincoats Ltd, the factory in Bury, Lancashire, which Laurence inherited. He moved to Bury from the Strangeways area of Manchester, where he had begun manufacturing caps, in order to avoid the attentions of the trade union officials in the big city. Grandpa was an unreconstructed capitalist who forbade Laurence the chance of a university education. Laurence became a socialist in revenge.

He was not what you might consider to be a conventional socialist. For a start, his raincoat factory paid the workers peanuts. When he moved to London he owned a hire-purchase company, exploiting the desire of the working classes to enjoy their part in the Macmillan boom years. He took offices in the Finchley Road above the North Thames Gas Board showroom, confiding in a burst of Baldrick-like inspiration that he had chosen this location in the belief that since heat rises, and since the showroom would be demonstrating gas fires all day, it followed logically that his offices would be heated for free. The fact that this didn't happen never caused him to doubt the essential brilliance of this cunning plan.

Uncle Laurence also drove a Bentley (and a bubble car) and lived in one of the most exclusive roads in Hampstead. He was a mass of contradictions. He mistrusted people with a university education yet he also envied them. He was a Jew who opposed Zionism, a trade union supporter who didn't necessarily want them in his factory. He was a Marxist of the Groucho persuasion – unwilling to join any club which might accept him as a member, whether it was the Socialist Party of Great Britain, on whose behalf he wrote daily letters to the editor of the *Manchester Guardian*, or the MCC.

The MCC brought out the most mischievous side of Uncle Laurence's nature. He would sit with his shirt off at the front of the balcony at the Nursery End at Lord's – now known as the Upper Compton Stand – in the days when gentlemen at cricket matches still wore hats and ties even when they weren't sitting in the pavilion. The purpose was partly his own comfort but mostly to arouse the ire of the authorities. It succeeded triumphantly. Convinced that there was no bye-law to stop him baring his chest, he continued to do so despite the imprecations of the MCC stewards until a notice was formally displayed, officially stating that shirts must be worn at all times. It was signed 'By Order of the Secretary of the MCC' himself. That was enough to provoke a response. Uncle Laurence took his shirt off and draped it carefully over the notice.

Eventually, after lengthy correspondence with the MCC – which Laurence enjoyed more than the secretary, the former Sussex and England wicketkeeper S.C.Griffith – a compromise was reached. Laurence would be allowed to remove his shirt at Lord's on condition that he sat quite still while naked to the waist. Laurence likened himself to a statue by Rodin rather than one of the nudes at the Windmill Theatre. Once that battle had been won, he moved on to other pressing matters which necessitated similar amounts of correspondence with the long-suffering MCC authorities. Diligent campaigning eventually wrung an admission that they would display the first-innings totals of the teams on the scoreboard. Before my Uncle Laurence took up the cudgels on their behalf, spectators had to rely on memory, the daily paper or the purchase of a scorecard.

Uncle Laurence died before he could win his final battle.

11

At the bottom of the scoreboard was a row of numbers from 1 to 11, usually with an 'S' at the end to denote substitute. Above each number was a light which flashed when that player, whose number corresponded to the batting order as printed on the scorecard, fielded the ball. Laurence became particularly agitated when he realised that the light never flashed for the poor fielder who had to retrieve the ball after it had crossed the boundary. If the ball stopped a foot short of the rope, was fielded and returned to the wicketkeeper, the fielder was rewarded with the display of his lightbulb; but if the ball beat him to the boundary, he suffered the ignominy of eternal darkness. Laurence fought long and hard on behalf of the despairing fielders but he never managed to convince the authorities to fill this yawning void. To this day, scoreboard operators continue to maintain their tradition of neglect, unaware of how close Uncle Laurence came to causing them to change the habit of a lifetime.

Laurence had a number of pet theories, much like the North Thames Gas Board cunning plan, all of which sounded plausible to a child of five and indeed could very well have been invented by a child of five. One of them was a belief that a car responded best if driven only in second and fourth gears. He never volunteered an opinion as to why, in that case, first and third gears were available – perhaps this was another capitalist/Gentile plot. Not even a trail of broken transmissions and wrecked gear-boxes was sufficient to dissuade him from this firmly held belief. To this day, whenever I hear the sound of gears crashing I assume my Uncle Laurence is in the vicinity.

Among the sage advice he gave to this five-year-old scion of the respectable Jewish bourgeoisie was to carry a ten-shilling note inside your driving licence. If you were ever stopped by the police and they demanded to see your licence, this was a foolproof way of preventing whatever traffic violation had been detected from being taken any further.

His flirtation with the law was two-edged. When the 70mph maximum speed limit was imposed, Laurence decided to travel down the M1 in the outside lane at exactly 70mph. Anybody who overtook him *ergo* was breaking the speed limit. Inevitably, he was pursued down the motorway by an army of outraged, horn-blaring, lights-flashing drivers, who were forced to overtake on the inside, since Laurence remained unmoved by their evident road rage. Indeed, he duly noted the registration numbers of the offending vehicles and passed them on to the police, expecting, knowing him, at least an OBE in the next Honours List – which he would have taken great pleasure in refusing, then writing to the newspapers to let them know of his sacrifice. Instead of the official gratitude he anticipated, however, he was himself prosecuted by the police for driving without due care and attention. Laurence was outraged, fulminating against another example of the fascist police state he believed we all lived in.

Ironically, though Laurence adored cricket, he hated football and yet he was responsible, as for much else in my life, for my original decision to support Manchester City. In 1952, when I was aged three, he decided it was time for me to be introduced to one of his great passions – rugby league. The initiation was to take place on a patch of East Manchester urban decay known as Belle Vue. The home team, Belle Vue Rangers, had been the recipient of my uncle's support since they had originally played as Broughton Park Rangers. Laurence lived in the Broughton district of Manchester. Within seconds of arriving at the ground, I was a die-hard Belle Vue Rangers supporter.

Die-hard was the appropriate term because I am unreliably informed that Belle Vue Rangers lost that match 52–0. Unfazed, I asked when we could see my heroes again, only to be brutally informed that the match I had seen was the last one ever to be played by Belle Vue Rangers, who at the moment of the final whistle had gone out of existence. I cried the bitter tears of a three-year-old. I could only be comforted by the prospect of supporting another team which played in blue. 'Swinton,' said Uncle Laurence, assuming my allegiance, like his, was to rugby; 'Manchester City,' whispered my brother Geoffrey, surreptitiously. He had already been a supporter of Manchester United since the season of their FA Cup triumph in 1948. Laurence's eldest son, my cousin Ronnie, was a supporter of Salford Rugby League Club because Broughton was technically addressed as Salford 7. Since I lived in Prestwich and blue was now confirmed as my colour, I was already set in opposition to my closest relatives.

Most people have relatively straightforward reasons for choosing a football team to support. Usually it is because a particular team has been recently successful (Manchester United) or because it has been handed down like a tribal ritual from father to son (everyone else). I have always taken a perverse pride in the fact that my addiction grew out of failure – well, not just failure, obviously, more in the nature of a team so inept that they courted and achieved total extinction. It was, though I did not appreciate it at the time, an excellent preparation for future events.

The 1954–55 season was a wonderful time to be a Manchester City supporter though, sadly, I remember absolutely nothing of it. The record books tell us that City won a pulsating derby 3–2 at Maine Road, went to Old Trafford in the return match and won, incredibly, 5–0 and then to round it off neatly, beat United yet again in the fourth round of the FA Cup in front of a crowd of 74,723. That was the year City reached the final for the first time since 1934.

My only memory of this triumphant season is the first minute of the Cup final against Newcastle United. I remember settling in front of the television set, devouring live moving pictures of my heroes. Newcastle's first attack ended in a corner on their right wing. Over came the cross and Jackie Milburn, who rarely scored with his head, glanced the ball in at the near post. Forty-five seconds had elapsed since the kick-off.

My mother marched into the room, instantly spotted the danger, turned the television off smartly and in one fell swoop put on my coat and dragged me out of the front door for a walk round Prestwich Park. This was a woman who had been raised on tales of valiant Jewish mothers and how they protected their offspring against pogroms. True, I was not in great physical danger in the lounge of a semi-detached house in the suburbs of Manchester in May 1955, but events outside my control 200 miles away were threatening to cause me the sort of pain from which my mother had shielded me since birth. When we returned from that enforced walk, Newcastle had won 3–1. The City right-back Jimmy Meadows had been carried off injured in a continuation of what became known as the Wembley hoodoo, and they had been forced to play most of the match with only ten men. It was not much consolation but at least I had avoided actually seeing the humiliation, thanks to my mother's swift action.

I should at this point introduce three of my friends who will feature in these pages. Jeffrey Cohen was born two days before me and has remained two days older for the past forty-eight years. We have worn the age gap lightly. Jeff was a goalkeeper by vocation, not, as usually happened at the age of six, by bullying. His allegiance to Manchester City began around the time of the FA Cup final appearance in 1955, but it was a desperately capricious start. He simply asked his father, 'Which team do we support?' and his father, remembering that City had just got to the Cup final and that it was the year of the three derby victories, answered, 'City.'

Looking back on it from a distance of forty years is like

recalling a narrow escape from a car crash on the motorway. A fraction the other way and life could have been changed forever. There certainly would have been no need for Jeff to redesign the first car he ever bought as a student. In 1968, he resprayed his Morris Minor sky blue on the bonnet, roof and boot, but red and black along the rear and front wings to match the away strip. The latter has since been more widely replicated by the AC Milan shirt which, seen from a distance, appears to belong to a fellow City fan of similar vintage to our own. On closer acquaintance it always tends to be a disappointment.

Jeff's somewhat fortuitous decision to support City in 1955 was reinforced by the legendary performance of Bert Trautmann in the FA Cup final the year after the defeat by Newcastle. For City reached the final again in 1956, determined to rectify the failure of the previous year. 'We'll be back next year to win it,' allegedly said skipper Roy Paul to the Queen as he collected his loser's medal in 1955. ('If I had a pound for every time I've heard that one,' presumably muttered the Queen under her breath, 'I wouldn't need the Civil List.') As it so happened, City *were* back next year to win it. The reliable Joe Hayes put them ahead in the third minute and, though Kinsey equalised for Birmingham City ten minutes later, Dyson restored the City lead midway through the second half and a presumably sober Bobby Johnstone wrapped things up for a satisfyingly symmetrical 3–1 victory.

That 1956 FA Cup final, however, is remembered as Trautmann's match. The City goalkeeper dived at the feet of the onrushing Birmingham inside-forward Murphy with fifteen minutes left, grabbed the ball safely but, we later found out, broke his neck doing so. Knowing what was at stake, Trautmann played on for the final quarter of an hour, unaware that he was jeopardising his life in the process.

Perhaps fortunately, after the event he remembered nothing of that final pulsating quarter of an hour. As Trautmann staggered up the steps to the Royal Box to collect his winner's medal, the BBC commentator, Kenneth Wolstenholme, offered the view: 'He's probably already forgotten about that bang on the neck.' Trautmann didn't play again for over six months.

Trautmann's bravery made City supporters out of little boys all over Manchester that day. Jeff certainly dates his conviction from that moment, as does his best friend at the time, our class-mate Michael Chadwick. Mike lived near Bury Old Road, a long distance from our school, Park View County Primary. From where Jeff and I lived this was hundreds of yards and almost out of the self-regulating Jewish ghetto. Nevertheless, Mike was hugely popular because he was the most talented dribbler of a football ever to stride the earth.

Wider experience suggests this title should more accurately be bestowed upon George Best or Diego Maradona, but my memory of the six-year-old Michael Chadwick was that here was the best footballer in the world – he was certainly more skilful than I was, although I had other attributes which made me a classic right-half, much influenced by City's Ken Barnes, popularly tagged the best uncapped wing-half in England.

Michael Chadwick was fast and tricky. He would have been at his peak aged twenty-four in 1973, but he was overlooked by Sir Alf Ramsey as England went crashing out of the World Cup after a 1–1 home draw with Poland. Ramsey might have pointed out with some justification that by this time Mike was selling women's lingerie, but I can only reiterate that had Sir Alf seen Mike in the playground between the ages of six and eleven, he couldn't fail to have picked him for England. Indeed, Mike should have been

17

playing for England at the age of ten, but his career was abruptly halted by his father.

He was selected for the Prestwich & Whitefield Boys team but because their matches took place on Saturday mornings, Mike was forbidden to play. His barmitzvah was only three years away and the neighbours might not approve of the sight of Mike dashing out of the house on the Sabbath carrying his football boots, when social conformity dictated that he was more appropriately seen in an uncomfortable suit carrying his prayer shawl on the way to the synagogue. His father, needless to say, like mine, worked on Saturdays and was in no position to go to synagogue himself. I was never selected for Prestwich & Whitefield Boys. I seem to remember proclaiming that a similar religiously inspired prohibition had prevented me from playing in the trial matches. If only.

The playground is frequently the venue for immutable sporting judgments. Ian Aston, who was a year older than I was, is without doubt the fastest bowler in the history of the world. Armed only with a tennis ball and bowling at a set of chalked stumps, his pace was terrifying. Admittedly the length of the pitch was dictated by the distance between the playground wall and the school building and was probably only about fifteen yards, but he was even more terrifying in the nets off his full run-up and with a significantly harder red ball. Stories of Ambrose and Marshall, Croft and Garner, Lillee and Thomson are all very well in their way, but, like Mike Chadwick's dribbling skills, in my mind Ian Aston's brute pace, which must have ranked with that of the fastest bowlers in cricket history, will never be surpassed in the annals of professional sport.

The fourth member of the early City quartet was an interloper from London by the name of David Green. He moved to Manchester aged nine, having seen Trautmann's Cup final on television. This established his allegiance to Manchester City, but by then it was already too late to prevent a fondness for Essex County Cricket Club taking root. Thus, whereas with most schoolfriends the bitter antagonisms of the winter were replaced by a solid alliance for Lancashire in the summer, David Green managed to remain at odds with his immediate surroundings throughout the year. This alienation was intensified by the London accent which was found to be incomprehensible in Bury. In the days before *The Bill* and *EastEnders*, a Cockney accent had the mystique and impenetrability of a foreign language.

I first came into contact with David Green in the playground at Bury Grammar School, on our first day at secondary school in September 1960. The contact was in the form of a bad foul perpetrated by him on me. It somehow symbolised the nature of a relationship that would encompass both a friendship and a rivalry so deep that nobody, including ourselves, could really work out where the one began and the other finished. We have made television programmes and feature films together for nearly twenty years, engaged in an odd quadrille like two sumo wrestlers shuffling round the ring, searching for a hold on each other's nappy.

David's fouling was promiscuous in that it was dispensed without concern for race, religion or ability. Famously, he once kicked a boy called David Harris so high up that he got his foot caught in the other boy's blazer pocket. In trying to extricate it, he managed to tear the blazer pocket open. We were all impressed – except David Harris and, presumably, David Harris's mother. There was another boy called Harris in the same class – Laurence Harris, no relation to the aforementioned David Harris. David Green broke this other Harris's ankle in the playground one lunchtime with an especially vicious tackle. There was less sympathy for the

19

latter victim, who had proclaimed his support for Manchester United.

The climax to David Green's career came when he was sent off in a house match. He had taken a particularly strong dislike to the marking attentions of Baz Treanor, the opposing centre-half, and retaliated to what he considered a push in the back by stamping on Treanor as he fell to the ground after a clearance. Treanor rolled over in agony, clutching his right shin, yelling, 'You've broken my leg, you've broken my leg!' Had David been a true professional, turned round in surprise and helped up his opponent, offering words of commiseration, the incident would no doubt have been forgotten quickly. This was never David's way. 'Good,' he replied instead, 'now I can break your other leg.' Whereupon he kicked the prostrate Treanor hard on the left leg, and trotted off to the dressing-room before the master in charge could point the finger.

David, Jeff and I went to Bury Grammar School together. Jeff, Mike and I had started out at Park View Primary School together. We weren't the only City supporters we knew; it just seemed that way to us. In the years from 1957 to 1965, when we were at the impressionable age from eight to sixteen, City faced a yearly battle against relegation, a battle that was to be lost in 1963. United won the League Championship in 1957 and would arguably have won the Double that year if Ray Wood, the goalkeeper, had not been incapacitated in the Cup final by a dubious shoulder-charge from Aston Villa's outside-left Peter McParland. After the calamity of Munich, Busby famously resurrected United to win the FA Cup in 1963 and to weld the side of Best, Law and Charlton into the League Champions of 1965. The bonds that still bind the four Jewish friends were forged in those years of painful adversity.

I mention Munich deliberately because it may be difficult

for City supporters who have arrived recently on the scene to understand fully what happened in Manchester in February 1958. The day after United had drawn 3–3 at Red Star Belgrade to progress into the semi-finals of the European Cup, the aeroplane carrying the team, officials and press crashed in taking off from Munich airport. Seven United players, Roger Byrne, Geoff Bent, Eddie Colman, Mark Jones, Billy Whelan, Tommy Taylor and David Pegg, died instantly. Duncan Edwards, whose brave struggle for life won him admirers outside the football-supporting community, died fifteen days later. Johnny Berry and Jackie Blanchflower never played again. Busby hovered near death, but eventually returned to England to see United reach their second successive Cup final.

I was devastated by the news of the crash. Everybody in Manchester was. I am informed that the nation wept, possibly wherever football was played tears were shed – but not like they were in Manchester. It was a death in the immediate family. Most of the young men killed were local. Tommy Taylor and David Pegg came from across the Pennines, Duncan Edwards from Dudley in the Midlands and Billy Whelan was Irish, but the rest of them and the very heart of the team was Manchester.

There was no City/United divide on this. The great City and England goalkeeper, Frank Swift, died at Munich, but our tears were shed for us – the city of Manchester. Nothing better illustrates the despicable bile which has entered the game in recent years than the unpleasant song references to Munich chanted now by rival fans. I yield nothing to any of them in my desire to see Manchester United in their rightful place, rooted firmly to the bottom of the GM Vauxhall Conference, with the added bonus of seeing the price of their shares slip so low that trading is suspended in them on the floor of the Stock Exchange, but any adverse reference to

21

what happened at Munich that day moves me to their instant defence.

Such references invariably stem from those idiots who were not alive in 1958 to recall the mood of a city in mourning. In my class, we were instructed to write diaries of our lives, under the influence of a grey-haired woman called Mrs Newlands, to whose idiosyncratic but inspired teaching methods I have remained in debt for forty years. Using real ink and a cracked nib, I scrawled page after page detailing the latest medical bulletins from the Isar Hospital where the survivors of the crash were being treated. The day Duncan Edwards died, I could scarcely write for tears. His last reported words were apparently enquiring about the time of the kick-off for Saturday's match and the likelihood of his being passed fit to play in it. It upsets me still.

Mrs Newlands was a fierce critic of our work. Failure in the weekly spelling tests would lead to the culprit being hit on the hands with a ruler or bent over a wicker basket and smacked with a plimsoll, not on the bottom but more devilishly on the unprotected back of the thigh. I hate to say it, because I have been an unreconstructed liberal since I first read the *Manchester Guardian*, but I have always been an excellent speller, so I must regretfully conclude that her methods worked.

Certainly I remember failing to spell 'television' correctly in one test, the humiliation of which was far greater than the pain that was inflicted as a consequence. Her reliance on the plimsoll and ruler was complemented by her ability to inspire a love of learning and a respect for the basics of grammar, spelling and punctuation, which I shudder to hear Sir Rhodes Boyson echoing. In February 1958, Mrs Newlands listened in silence as the class recorded their individual reactions to the Munich air disaster, making no attempt to correct anything. It was a masterly stroke of psychology which would have been applauded by today's trauma therapists as much as her sporadic violence would have been condemned. To me, it was the ultimate confirmation of how deeply Munich had affected us.

To this day, I cannot sit in an aeroplane without instinctively recalling that the surviving heroes of the crash, Bill Foulkes, Harry Gregg and Bobby Charlton, sat at the front of the plane playing cards when the plane attempted its final, fateful takeoff. Whether I look out of the window or bury my head in a book, not once have I ever been able to experience a takeoff without thinking about Munich. Twice a trip the same images flash through my mind – the broken plane lying crazily askew the ice and snowbound runway, combined with the picture of the Munich Memorial at Old Trafford.

I make no apologies for intensely disliking Manchester United, the club, its manager, its chairman, its board of directors, its ludicrously widespread fan base or, most particularly, its bloody souvenir megastore. Why don't they cast a glance at the City souvenir shop to see how a genuine club operates? At Maine Road, the shop is firmly bolted at most times when fans might want to purchase something. Reluctantly, at 2pm on match days, it opens its doors and its fifteen square feet of space to serve the regular 25,000 to 30,000 who still turn up. The only replica shirt everyone wants to buy, of course, is that worn by the team's best player, Georgi Kinkladze. On the last day of the 1995–96 season, with the match against Liverpool sold out, the City souvenir shop discovered it had run out of the letters 'K' and 'Z'. It isn't so much that we City supporters of a certain age are trapped in a timewarp of the 1970s. It is that we are trapped in a bad *situation comedy* of the 1970s. *Terry and June*, I think.

Although I used to go to Old Trafford almost every other week in the 1960s (see Chapter Six), I haven't been back

23

there since 27 April 1974. That match ended Manchester United 0 Manchester City 1. The winning goal was scored by Denis Law with a casual backheel past Alex Stepney. The United crowd invaded the pitch in an attempt to cause the game to be abandoned; it was, but the result stood anyway and United were relegated to the Second Division. Some memories are too precious to risk being destroyed by traversing the same ground. I have to say, however, even on that day I did not fail to make my pilgrimage to stand in front of the Munich Memorial and read again the names etched as deeply on my mind as they are on that stone tablet.

The approach to the Memorial is now dwarfed by that gigantic souvenir superstore, a clear demonstration of Manchester United plc's belief in the subservience of God to Mammon. When Alex Ferguson finally clears his desk, it is more likely to be at the behest of the chairman of the Stock Exchange than the traditional choir of disaffected supporters. Again, United have only to look across Manchester to see how these things should be done. City's revolving door in the manager's office gives the fans a sense of involvement in the club's affairs. What can United fans do but buy the shares, buy the season ticket, buy the cheap-day return to Manchester from whichever remote part of Europe they live in? The fact is that I, who despise Manchester United, feel an affinity for that club that the County Down Reds, the Cherbourg branch of the Manchester United Supporters' Club, the Ryan Giggs duvet-purchasers, the David Beckham pyjama-wearers, can never match. The soul of Manchester United has nothing to do with public flotations or executive boxes. It is about Matt Busby's dream as he stood in the bombed ruins of Old Trafford in 1945.

Manchester has changed since 1958. So has the country, so has the sporting culture. For a lad who grew up with Bert Trautmann and timed his adolescence to coincide with the arrival of Lee, Bell and Summerbee at Maine Road, it is not easy to feel similarly passionate about Ged Brannan and Gerry Creaney. I live in London now, a consequence of my professional life working in television, making films for as wide an audience as possible. I spend time in Los Angeles, like any writer with a suitcase full of movie scripts. When they ask me where I live, I have to reply, 'London.' When they ask me where I come from, I always say, 'Manchester.'

Chapter Two

It is indicative of the poverty of their imagination that Manchester United named their ground after the home of Lancashire County Cricket Club. In ancient times, the number 48 bus used to stop where Lou Macari's fish and chip shop now stands. If you turned right down Warwick Road North, you wound up at the football ground; but if you turned left and walked past Barlow Road (named, I later discovered, after a nineteenth-century opening batsman rather than Colin Barlow, the speedy Manchester City forward of the late 1950s), you arrived at my other temple of worship.

I knew this was a temple from an early age, because God had left a message outside the turnstiles. It read: 'PLAY NOT GUARANTEED. NO MONEY RETURNED. BY ORDER.' Since the weather in Manchester hasn't changed much in forty years, the notice is probably still there, though possibly couched in language more suited to the age of the Citizen's Charter.

Naturally Uncle Laurence had his own response to what he perceived as another fascist/Gentile pogrom aimed specifically at him. For this, Laurence collected around him a group of acolytes. They were mostly, but not exclusively, Jewish (I seem to recall the names of Sidney Weintraub and Eric Cohen) and their professions were varied, but what they shared was an adoration of Laurence's wit. On a good day there would have been about twelve of us – three children and nine adults. We would sit in the Hornby Stand (now unimaginatively renamed Stand D North) and we would all laugh at his jokes, sometimes dutifully but mostly genuinely.

Most but not all of the adults were members of Lancashire CCC and had little coloured, stiff-backed membership cards containing that season's fixture list to prove it. Women had a different colour (reduced tariff because, despite their membership, they couldn't sit in the pavilion) as did children, known as Junior members, who shared the same disadvantages of apartheid as the Lady members. The Hornby Stand, situated in a prime spot behind the bowler's arm, was open to members only. Laurence, in classic socialist mode, wouldn't be seen dead sitting with the proletariat in the 'free seats' on the popular side.

As a child of parents with no interest in any kind of sport whatsoever, nobody was going to waste two guineas on providing me with the privileges of Junior membership. In addition, nobody was too keen on forking out for admission to a performance that might at any moment be abruptly terminated by the funereal clouds which always seemed to hover over Old Trafford. The ominous 'BY ORDER' notice lent added weight to the belief that watching cricket was a futile and unrewarding pastime.

Laurence's response was to put his own unique brand of socialism into operation. It was based on the accepted idea that the workers' strength lay in their solidarity, which meant that none of the group was to move anywhere except as part of the group. Laurence's strategy was that groups of twelve were an intimidating presence even to gatekeepers wearing peaked caps – an awesome symbol of power to one of my tender years. So my uncle would hold out his hand and a collection of membership cards would be deposited in it. Holding them in a large multi-coloured display like a royal flush, Laurence would then stride purposefully through the membership gate at the entrance to the ground and past the man at the foot of the Hornby Stand, waving the multi-coloured fan at him. Laurence would make momentary eye contact with the cowed official as if daring him to stop us and ask why nine adults and three children were bearing a total of only eight membership cards, but to the best of my memory there was never a confrontation.

There was an easier way. Two men would enter while the ticketless one hovered in the toilets. When the two had secured their seats in the stand, one of them would retreat to the urinals carrying both membership cards, handing the spare one to the one loitering who, it was to be hoped, hadn't been arrested for importuning in a public convenience. This procedure could be repeated indefinitely until the entire group had been legally admitted, but in many ways it was too easy. It lacked the gladiatorial bravado which Laurence found so attractive and the implicit challenge to authority, which he always won. It also took about half an hour, and the last one into his seat might have missed the sight of the first three batsmen as they were clean bowled by Brian Statham.

My first match at Old Trafford (the real one) was the Whitsuntide 'Roses' clash with Yorkshire in May 1955. Laurence took me to pay a grudging respect to Len Hutton, who had recently captained England to a glorious 3–1 victory in the Ashes series in Australia. The reason for the grudging nature of the respect was that Hutton was a Yorkshireman, and our delight in the triumphs of Yorkshiremen, even when their sweaters were adorned with the three lions of England, was always tarnished by a recognition of the fact that since they were Yorkshiremen, they were inherently the enemy and all too soon the three lions would be replaced by the white rose, and traditional enmity restored.

Nevertheless, I am pleased to record that I did see Len Hutton batting in his last match against Lancashire. I am even more pleased to record that he was ignominously bowled for 2 by K.B.Standring, a local grammar school boy who played for Clitheroe in the Ribblesdale League. Standring bowled at a brisk fast-medium pace and faded from view after just six Championship games, but his place in history was secured with that one dismissal. It was one of the few moments of joy in a match which Lancashire were to lose by five wickets. Yorkshire, I was soon to discover, were to assume the role of Manchester United in my cricketing universe.

A few weeks later, Hutton retired from the game due to chronic lumbago. My mother, who also suffered from the same complaint, continued to play beach cricket into her forties and I was puzzled as to why Hutton didn't just get up in the morning and moan then get on with life, as my mother did. My mother exotically also suffered from fibrositis in the shoulder, just as Bert Trautmann was reported to have done. In addition to her being the fount of all medical and nutritional knowledge, as I supposed most mothers probably were, these remarkable coincidences merely intensified my love for her.

I have always felt there is something admirable in acquiring sporting injuries. In 1994 I was producing *Lovejoy* for the BBC. Ian McShane, the United-supporting eponymous hero, fell off a wall during a stunt and 'did a Gazza', as he explained to an admiring audience, which meant tearing the anterior and posterior cruciate ligaments – a typically sexy injury. In the early 1980s I was producing a love story for the BBC, set in the world of the ballet, and was intrigued to discover that though the reputation of the male ballet dancers for being not entirely heterosexual was perfectly well-founded, their injuries evoked entirely different responses.

Damaged knees were the worst because they were career-threatening – which I knew because Bob Willis and Graham Dilley were constantly dropping out of the England Test team for the same reason – but the dancers were also afflicted by those other familiar sporting ailments, groin strains, pulled hamstrings and calf-muscle injuries. As they danced on through pain, my respect for them increased rapidly. There was no gesturing to the wings pointing at the source of the pain, and their directors did not hold after-performance press conferences to announce the state of their dancers' bodies in order to mitigate the probability of a bad review. Dancing at Sadler's Wells or Covent Garden was like playing for Liverpool under Kenny Dalglish. If you acknowledged your injury and dropped out, the chances were that Darcey Bussell would take your place and you'd never get it back. Wasn't that what happened to Jan Molby?

My second match at Old Trafford in the summer of 1955 was more memorable. The occasion was the third Test between England and South Africa. This was before the Sharpeville massacre and Laurence's increasingly vocal campaign against apartheid, so we were still allowed to eat South African oranges and watch their cricketers. The Hornby Stand was packed and the children were deposited on the grass between the boundary rope and the fence. It was a wonderful Test, won by the South Africans by three wickets with minutes to spare on the last afternoon.

Frank Tyson, Lancashire-born and rejected by his home county as a youngster, was playing his first domestic Test of the summer after having destroyed the Aussies Down Under during the winter. Early on, he induced an edge from the opener Jackie McGlew which was safely caught behind the wicket by Godfrey Evans. The umpire gave the batsman not out and McGlew went on to make a century. Tyson's wild anger caused him to pitch the ball shorter and shorter, which was meat and drink to a cutter and puller of McGlew's quality.

At the other end, the Middlesex off-spinner Fred Titmus,

in only his second game for England, was being hit out of Test cricket for seven years. A tall, gangling, unprepossessing batsman called Paul Winslow, coming in at number eight, scored the third century of the South African innings in a style never bettered even by Ian Botham. Sixes went crashing to every part of the ground. Tony Lock bowled the ball off which Winslow went to his hundred. It soared majestically over the television commentary stand and into the neighbouring practice ground, the ball disappearing into the distance like a shell from a cannon.

Uncle Laurence had been observing this mayhem with a certain amount of anxiety as Winslow continued his assault on the hapless spinners. The boys behind the boundary ropes had collected a number of small glass lemonade bottles which doubled as makeshift cricket bats during the lunch and tea intervals. Inevitably these bottles were the unwitting target of Winslow's straight drives, and after another one had landed a few feet away, smashing into a bottle and scattering a trail of glass, Uncle Laurence thought it time for action.

In those far-off days of Churchill's final term as prime minister, when sweets had just come off the ration, it was accepted custom not to move when sitting behind the wicket from which the bowler was operating. Showing splendid disregard for this custom, the 'Hey, you!' from the steward and the 'Siddown!'s from everyone else, Uncle Laurence began fighting his way desperately towards me as Winslow deposited another Titmus delivery into the ranks of the delighted small boys. He scooped me up and shoved his way back into the relative safety of the Hornby Stand, where I spent the rest of the day perched on his knee. Winslow was finally out lbw to Alec Bedser for 108, made out of a stand of 171 with the wicketkeeper John Waite, who had also reached his century when South Africa finally declared at 521 for 8. Nobody who saw that innings by Winslow would ever forget it. After the tour had finished, and in accordance with time-honoured selectorial wisdom, Winslow never played for his country again.

Between the entrance gate on Warwick Road and the steps leading up to the Hornby Stand was the bar. I needed no second urging to hurry past the serried rows of men in flat caps drinking beer. It's hard to tell which came first – an instinctive belief that such an activity was inherently wrong, or a deep and ineradicable loathing of the smell of beer. I was never told Jews didn't drink, merely that Gentiles did. 'A *shikker* is a *goy*,' was the Yiddish expression. 'A Gentile is a drunkard.' Charming. Except . . . in my limited experience, it was true. The *goyim* also gambled away the housekeeping money, and a Jewish girl who fell for a Gentile's charms could expect to be smacked around when he rolled back from the pub. That would be after her family had said prayers for her as if she were dead. The influence of Louis Golding's novel *Magnolia Street*, in which all these events are described, was never very far away.

The only alcoholic drink to be consumed in our house was the extraordinary kosher wine used for religious services. I say extraordinary because it tastes like alcoholic Ribena and defies analysis as a wine. There was one bottle of sherry in the house and a bottle of cherry brandy – bought, I dare say, in honour of Prince Charles's notorious encounter with a glass of it during his wild, tearaway teenage years. I don't remember either bottle ever being opened, though they were housed in a glass-fronted drinks cabinet which mostly contained cut-glass drinking goblets – also never used.

Matches at Old Trafford and Maine Road constituted my first real exposure to the non-Jewish world. Park View County Primary School certainly contained a proportion of non-Jews but, because it served the middle-class Jewish ghetto in which my home was situated, there seemed to be as many Jews as non-Jews in my class. Just as the boys instinctively herded together for protection against the massed ranks of little girls in flower-print dresses across the room, so each gender group sub-divided itself along religious lines. Out of the thirteen boys in the class in my last year at Park View, ten were Jewish.

Rather like the unspoken state of prohibition in which I lived, this wasn't like the sectarianism of Belfast or Jerusalem. Though at root, like most religious wars, it was based on fear of the unknown, I don't remember a direct lecture to beware the evil Gentile and to seek out the company of fellow Jews – but the ideology was absorbed just as effectively. My father never trusted the non-Jews he worked with, although ironically it was his Jewish accountant who went to prison for embezzlement; my mother was convinced that the non-Jewish shopkeepers were always trying to shortchange her. The fact that by far the most expensive item in her household budget was the extortionately priced kosher meat was greeted with a resigned shrug. As with inflated transfer fees in football, the extra outlay was justified because it kept the money circulating in the game.

Uncle Laurence's unique brand of socialism was entirely compatible with this fear of the Gentile masses. Although he reacted against his father's traditional Orthodox Judaism, that was mostly because he was against almost everything on principle if it wasn't carrying a rugby ball or bowling a cricket ball. Laurence's companions were witty Jews who read the *Manchester Guardian*, debated political issues and told jokes sitting in the sun watching the cricket during the day, and could be found in the Free Trade Hall after the close of play listening to the Hallé Orchestra conducted by Sir John Barbirolli.

Saturday mornings while Uncle Laurence was still living in Manchester were reserved for the ritual surrounding the start of play on the first day of a County Championship match at Old Trafford. My father worked on Saturdays, so although I frequently saw my neighbours dressed in their Sabbath best walking to synagogue, I was waiting for the arrival of Uncle Laurence's Daimler (the Bentley came later) and the trip down Bury New Road, along Deansgate, through the centre of Manchester, out onto the A56 in the direction of Altrincham and finally into the Lancashire CCC car park opposite the Stretford Town Hall.

'Carduptodatescorecard,' shouted the vendors of scorecards which printed the names of all the players. It was worth sixpence just to study the initials. Even now, I can close my eyes and see A.C.Walton of Middlesex, Halfyard D.J. of Kent. Amateurs were permitted to have their initials first; professionals must have them printed after their surnames. Thus, it was always P.B.H.May and M.C.Cowdrey but just as surely it was Statham J.B. and Trueman F.S. This led to the infamous proclamation over the tannoy in the cultured voice of the Lord's secretary, announcing a correction to the names as printed in the scorecard. 'Instead of F.J.Titmus, please read Titmus F.J.'

I could never understand why it was desirable, as it clearly was, to be an amateur rather than a professional. How could it possibly be better *not* to be paid for playing a game you loved than to receive a nice fat cheque for the same wonderful activity? My sympathies were always with the professionals and the more I discovered of the history of humiliations imposed on them, the more that sympathy increased. 'Amateur' strikes me as being as much a word of abuse as 'professional' seems to be a mark of commendation. If something is described as 'amateurish', it surely means something not to be admired. My reservation with the term 'professional foul' is hence that it is an oxymoron. A truly professional defender does not need to hack down the opposing forward on the edge of the penalty area. A true professional ushers his opponent towards the

35

corner flag, where he can't do any damage.

Just as I couldn't understand why anybody would want to play cricket without payment if money was on offer, so I couldn't understand why the northern counties, in particular, should be so assiduously still seeking the Holy Grail of the amateur captain when even the MCC had offered the professional Len Hutton the captaincy of England in 1952. To a true northerner, the very term 'amateur captain' was a contradiction. In the 1920s, Yorkshire's nominal captain was Major Lupton; the real captain was Wilfred Rhodes. On the final day of one match, Yorkshire were progressing comfortably enough towards a declaration when a wicket fell. Major Lupton disappeared into the amateurs' dressing-room to pad up. When he emerged, the grizzled veteran Emmott Robinson looked at him sadly: 'I shouldn't bother if I were thee, Major. Wilfred's declarin' end of t'next over.' Ironically, at the same time that Lancashire dismissed their last amateur captain, at the end of the 1962 season, the distinction between amateur and professional was officially abolished and all players became cricketers.

Perversely, Len Hutton later wrote that he welcomed the old division when the professionals could safely slag off the amateur captain in the privacy of their own dressing-room. Let us not forget that it was Yorkshire's long-serving captain and later president Lord Hawke who prayed God that he wouldn't live to see the day a professional captained England. He didn't. He died in 1938, a few weeks after the man who was to fulfil his nightmare scenario had scored 364 against the Australians at The Oval. Still, what can you expect of Yorkshiremen?

The Lancashire v Yorkshire Roses fixture was still a pretty big deal when I first started going to cricket matches in the 1950s. By the summer of 1960, when I had just passed the Eleven Plus and was about to follow my brother into Bury Grammar School, I was travelling to Lancashire matches at

Old Trafford with my friends on the number 48 bus. This may sound like a fact of no innate importance, but in my sheltered background, to be allowed to travel by myself on public transport was like allowing Edwardian debutantes to smoke, drink alcohol and engage in sexual activity at their coming-out ball in Buckingham Palace.

The very first time I can remember being allowed to walk anywhere by myself, other than between home and school, was when I went for a haircut after school in Sedgley village, a good mile from the house. I was nine years old. The barber was a malicious and ironically bald man called Frost, who appeared to want to wreak vengeance on the rest of the world for the cruel jest God had played on him. Presumably when he began in his profession he boasted a fine head of hair, but as the years rolled on the hair fell out and with it went his professional standing. The clippers with which he attacked the back of my neck seemed to be specially blunted, causing him to tear the hair out by its roots.

The fact that Frost supported United merely confirmed my view of the inherent viciousness of all Reds. This belief was intensified when he made me sit on a plank of wood stretched across the arms of the barber's chair. This invariably left me with a splinter in the back of my bare thigh which my mother had to remove with a needle later that day. His Bury-supporting partner was a gentle man called Albert (Albert and the Lion I always used to think) who had clippers which worked. Unfortunately, they took it in turns to serve the next customer, so I was always desperate for Albert to get there before Frost could attack me. However, the downside was that Albert was an even worse barber than Frost, and for the seven days after the haircut it was advisable never to look in the mirror or at your reflection in a shop window. Some boys were reduced to remaining in the house until their hair had grown back to a level of respectability. In later years, I wondered why Frost and Albert hadn't been turned in to the authorities – if not the Office of Fair Trading, then certainly the police. As I turned proudly into our street with the identical short-back-and-sides those Army-trained barbers gave everyone, no matter which style they might have requested, I saw my mother, like a caged lioness, prowling up and down the pavement outside the house. I felt like Dr Vivian Fuchs, who had recently crossed the Antarctic.

By now I had developed an obsession with cricket history and statistics and was aware I had a pretty good memory, so that I could spout seemingly learnedly about matches I had never seen. This stemmed from burying my head in the minutiae of the county cricket scoreboard printed in the *Manchester Guardian* during the summer, and reading my prized annual *The Boys' Book of Cricket* as soon as it was published.

The August Bank Holiday match of 1960 saw one of the great finishes in Roses history. In bald statistics, with Lancashire needing one off the last ball, it could be argued that it was no more exciting than their magnificent last-ball victory in the semi-final of the Benson and Hedges Cup in 1996, when Peter Martin scooped Craig White away past point for the two winning runs. Certainly that match, although spread out over two days because of rain, deserves its place in the pantheon, but I opt for the 1960 match because a game which is fought over three days and two innings, and which still comes down to the final ball, seems somehow worthier than one which evenly apportions fifty overs to each side.

Seventy-four thousand people watched that classic 1960 encounter. Barber and Wharton carried Lancashire past the Yorkshire first-innings score with only one wicket down, but Trueman and Ryan restricted the eventual lead to 72. When Statham and Higgs then removed half the Yorkshire side for

36, it seemed likely we would be celebrating a rare innings victory. Led by Philip Sharpe, the best slip-catcher I ever saw, Yorkshire recovered to 149, but that still left Lancashire to score a mere 78 in over two hours. Time to unravel the bunting? In your dreams!

Lancashire wickets seemed to fall more regularly than runs were scored, and after an hour and a half they were marooned on 43 for six. As so often, the Australian Ken Grieves marshalled the desperate Lancashire rearguard action and the score crept agonisingly up towards the target. At 60, Grieves miscued Trueman straight to Vic Wilson at deep mid-off. Wilson was the Yorkshire captain and one of the safest catchers in England. We groaned as the ball dropped safely into those massive hands of his – and out again, to a triumphal roar. Trueman's grand tragic gesture of despair only increased our happiness.

However, with only two overs left we still needed 18 – laughable in the context of today's one-day cricket, but a veritable mountain on that hot August day. Geoff Clayton, known as 'Chimp' because of his monkey-like crouch behind the wicket, fluked two edgy fours off Ryan, but the cries of ecstasy were stilled as Grieves nicked one to Jimmy Binks and was caught. At the start of the final over by Trueman, there were three wickets left and six runs needed.

Clayton was left with the dilemma of protecting the tail or taking every run on offer. Off the first ball, he pushed a single and opted to take it. A wise decision, we thought. Tommy Greenhough could handle a bat and it was one less to get. Off the second, Trueman uprooted Greenhough's leg stump. What an idiot Clayton was to have taken that single, screamed 12,000 Lancastrians. Jack Dyson, the off-spinner and Manchester City forward whose job I coveted, came in to join Clayton and scrambled two improbable leg-byes off his first ball. Three to win, three balls to go; two wickets left.

Dyson just dug Trueman's fourth ball out of the blockhole, looked up expecting to see Clayton's beam of approval, only to find his partner galloping towards him, screaming the same words as everybody else in the crowd. Dyson just made his ground in a flurry of bodies, bats and broken stumps. Clayton drove a single off the penultimate ball which meant that we couldn't lose. That wasn't much comfort since for all but the last two hours, Lancashire had been winning the match since 11.30 on Saturday morning. A draw now would be desperately disappointing.

The fielders closed in. Trueman stamped back to his mark. Dyson looked round the field. It was hard to see where that run was going to come from. There seemed to be no gaps anywhere. Contracts with God were being rapidly made all round the ground as Trueman steamed in for the last ball. Gathering pace, he launched himself at the popping crease, the ball aimed unerringly for another middle-stump yorker. At the last moment, it started swinging to leg, Dyson got a thick inside-edge and the ball shot away past backward short-leg and over the boundary at deep fine-leg. The crowd erupted and spilled onto the pitch. The stentorian voice of the Lancashire secretary issued his traditional but now futile demand over the loud-speaker – 'Would the little boys please keep off the pitch' – but he was just, as an American would have said, 'whistling Dixie.' I was eleven years old and I had found my drug of choice.

At school, this obsession with cricket was fortunately translated into prowess on the field. I was generally reckoned the best cricketer in my year, much as Michael Chadwick, with stronger competition, was acknowledged as the premier footballer. In those days, the 'best' meant anyone who could bowl straight, stay in for more than two overs, and catch a hard ball if it went into the air. Then, as now, sporting skills compensated for many other deficiencies in the popularity stakes. And I had plenty.

I was a softie, physically quite frail with a fragile health which caused me to be absent, according to one school report I still possess, no fewer than forty-six days. This was the term I was finally taken to Blackpool by my mother for six weeks, to recover from the sinus problems caused by the smog which polluted the Manchester air in the days before the Clean Air Act began to have a slow impact. The dirt and grime which covered all the buildings must at some level have been present in our lungs. It was in the television lounge of the Hazeldene Hotel on the sea front in Bispham, north of Blackpool, that I saw Manchester City win the FA Cup in 1956.

The more I reflect on those primary school days, the more the fragility shows itself. Not that I was alone. One of the playground football matches was between the Toughs and the Softies. No surprises for guessing which side I and my co-religionists were on. This was one of Jeff Cohen's inspired, Trautmann-like displays, and in contrast to the usual playground result of 15–12, there were no goals for the entire eleven minutes the match lasted. With the last kick of the game, the softies scored the only goal as the bell rang for the end of break.

Nevertheless, the school team was a different proposition altogether. I couldn't tackle, so I couldn't play in defence, and I wasn't good enough, strong enough or charismatic enough to claim one of the coveted attacking forward positions, which was why I was safely ensconced at wing-half. But at least I was in the team. Poor Jeff Cohen was replaced in goal by Jeffrey Edis, to his everlasting humiliation. Forty years after this tragedy, Jeff remembers it as the heaviest blow life has dealt him, staring grimly ahead as Mr Williamson, the master in charge, known familiarly as Williebobs, slowly wrote out the names of the Chosen on the blackboard. Vivien Burns, who was sitting next to Jeff, tried to comfort him, but we were considerably more naive than today's nine-year-olds and

41

there was nothing she could possibly say or do that could console the weeping victim.

Jeffrey Edis's sole merit was his height. At well over four feet high, he towered over the rest of us. He also had a tendency to catch the ball by using his hands like the vertically snapping jaws of a crocodile. However, on the day of the big match there seemed to be a divine intervention. Someone dropped out at the last moment and Jeff was asked to play. He raced home to get his boots and cycled desperately to the ground where he thought we were playing.

Unfortunately, the ground was not visible from the road and by the time Jeff got there, Elliott Lennick, who was a worse player but had the merit of living close to the pitch and could find his boots in five minutes, had taken the field in Jeff's place. I suppose the only possible measure of satisfaction Jeff could find was in the result. We lost 8–2. Apart from the small matter of a difference in ability, we always felt that the result was a direct consequence of what became known as Williebobs's famous pre-match tactical talk. 'Some of you,' he mused while sucking on his pipe, 'are finally beginning to learn which side of the ball is round and which side square.' We were 5–0 down before we could clear our heads.

Williebobs was an improvement on Mrs Newlands, however. She was convinced that the rules of football were similar to those of hockey, and would give long corners and short corners when the ball rolled out of play behind the goal-line. A few of us were unconvinced, but Mrs Newlands had successfully taught us long division, multiplication, the capitals of the world and how to parse a sentence. At the age of eight, it took more courage than we possessed to challenge her knowledge of the Laws of Association Football, however dubious we felt.

Whereas Mrs Newlands was a gifted teacher, Williebobs was not. I always felt he must have been issued with a teaching credential on being demobbed from the army. He had absolutely no sense of vocation and could as easily have become a barber or a car salesman if that's what he had been told. He once regaled us with a story of a Victorian birching. I can't for the life of me remember from what possible context this story arose, but he held the class of pre-pubescent nine-year-olds in rapt attention.

Michael Chadwick remembers him with great affection because Mike had endured two years of misery under Mrs Newlands, who had a very low tolerance for his inability to concentrate for more than two minutes at a time. Williebobs rated Mike and sent me home at the end of term with a report claiming I was fifteenth out of the thirty-eight kids in the class. My mother regarded this as a sure sign I was on my way to borstal, so I was never particularly fond of Williebobs.

Fortunately, the following year normal service was resumed under Mrs Burns. I moved swiftly back up the batting order and Michael Chadwick reverted to type as the naughty boy of the class. The usual punishment imposed for all infractions was invariably to write out Psalm 121: 'I lift up mine eyes unto the hills/From whence cometh my help.' As a self-confessed pedant, I was delighted to discover in later years that this particular psalm was grammatically incorrect. I desperately wanted to write to Mrs Burns to tell her that the 'From' in 'From whence' is redundant. It would have been small compensation for the humiliation she heaped on me.

It was the day of the 8–2 disgrace which brought me this further shame. For weeks I had been obsessed with wanting a tracksuit like a real footballer's. There was one on sale in Lupton's, the local sports shop, priced at 37/6, or nearly two pounds in contemporary parlance. In these days of the £50 replica shirt, it is hard to convey quite how magical the apparition of that tracksuit was. After weeks of intense campaigning, my mother bought it, triumphantly relating to

43

my father her success at knocking a further half-crown off the price. I think they both regarded it as a terrible waste of money. Since our family was in the business, buying clothes retail was considered an offence against centuries of Jewish tradition.

I wore the tracksuit to school on the day of the big match with the sort of pride displayed by Olympic athletes who are chosen to carry their country's flag. I don't think I was seeking the envious glances which my expensive, distinctive attire inevitably attracted. No doubt I didn't exactly reject the attention, but I never thought I was being deliberately provocative. Nevertheless, at the start of afternoon school I was summoned to the front of the class. I don't know quite what I was expecting, possibly some kind of commendation since my school career had been relatively successful to this point.

I was therefore deeply shocked to be told in no uncertain terms by Mrs Burns that the tracksuit I had dreamed of, campaigned for and worn with such high hopes was a deliberate flaunting of wealth in front of the poorer children whose parents could not afford such largesse. I could articulate neither the agony my mother had gone through before she agreed to buy that tracksuit, nor the precarious finances of my own family. At the age of nine, I knew that 37/6 was a veritable fortune for my mother to spend on an item of clothing that was regarded by the family as essentially frivolous.

I had nothing but the noblest of intentions in wearing that tracksuit but my public dressing-down, and, I suppose, the essential rightness of the philosophy behind it, made such a profound impact that it removed all the pleasure I had expected wearing that tracksuit to give me. To this day I have never again given a toss about clothes, and my wife has to buy them for me and then spend hours convincing me that I need them. Left to my own devices, I would need a couple of comfortable shirts and alternative pairs of trousers and that would be it. I have always rather admired Alfred Hitchcock's method, which was to have seven identical dark-blue suits, seven white shirts and seven dark ties. It certainly takes the pain out of worrying what to wear when you get up in the morning, and I don't suppose he was ever torn off a strip for flaunting his wealth.

With my limited cricketing ability, but with a passionate interest in the game which had communicated itself to colleagues and teachers, I was made captain for the first match against Higher Lane Primary School. Travelling there, I sat on the front row of the double-decker bus, planning my tactics, as I knew from my reading all great captains did. It was therefore with a sense of stomach-churning horror that I discovered, as we got off the bus, that I had forgotten to bring my plimsolls. I was now committed to opening the bowling and the batting in my open-toe sandals. My team would lose all the respect I had so patiently built over the years in the playground.

My *faux pas*, however, was as nothing compared to that of Williebobs, the man who had dropped Jeff Cohen. I didn't make the breakthrough with the new ball I had been expecting, though the new ball had probably been new when Montgomery was chasing Rommel round the North African desert. Eventually, with the opening stand approaching double figures, the batsman on strike edged me to long-leg and ran. His partner had dutifully watched the ball as it trickled down the leg side, but had been so transfixed by the sight that he had forgotten to run – as a consequence of which, both little boys were now standing next to me at the bowler's end. Long-leg, meanwhile, had picked up the ball and the game simply stopped. Nobody seemed to know what to do.

45

Umpiring at square-leg, Williebobs came to the rescue. Staring at the boy holding the ball, he shouted very loudly, 'Throw the ball underarm to the wicketkeeper. Macdonald, get up to the stumps, boy, and catch it. Then knock the bails off.' The manoeuvre was eventually completed. A shout of 'Howzat?' went up. The umpire at square-leg deliberated without having recourse to a third umpire, but eventually gave out one of the boys standing in the crease at the bowler's end. The opposing umpire, the Higher Lane sports master, who had watched proceedings unfolding with horror, then had to decide which of his boys was out. The unfortunate boy departed with many a lingering look back to the serene Williebobs.

The match finished amid some controversy. After Jeff Cohen and I had been bowling without further success for an hour, we started to complain that there was something wrong. The ball seemed to take minutes to get to the other set of stumps. Eventually, the home side's umpire was prevailed upon to measure the pitch. It turned out to be twenty-four yards long. Even Brian Statham would have struggled to beat the bat from that distance. I remember nothing more of this match. The humiliation of the open-toe sandals and the great Williebobs scandal has obliterated every other detail. I suspect, however, that we were eventually rained off. We usually were.

Chapter Three

There is a certain irony in the fact that the only match I ever wanted Manchester United to win, they lost. It was the 1958 FA Cup final, and while I had been ambivalent about United's Cup run, particularly the two exciting semi-finals with Fulham (the latter of which United won 5–3), I harboured no such doubts over the final itself.

My brother went to the delayed fifth-round tie after Munich, at home to Sheffield Wednesday. He showed me the famous programme with eleven blank spaces where the United team-sheet should have been printed. Waves of emotion swept down the Old Trafford terraces and overwhelmed the opposition. To have beaten United at this point would have been like dancing on the graves of the Munich martyrs. It didn't need intimidated referees, or a manager with a stopwatch, to make Old Trafford into a fortress. United won 3–0. In the next round, after a 2–2 draw at the Hawthorns, they beat West Bromwich Albion in the replay with a goal in the last minute. Colin Webster's shot was almost sucked into the net by the mass will of the assembled multitude. United were no longer just playing football or performing in a theatre of sport. They were the object of an almost religious fanaticism. Their Cup run to the final was pre-ordained.

I was certainly conscious that something happened in those weeks after Munich which turned United from being the other team in Manchester to the object of pity and affection in the hearts of people all over the country, all over the world. I didn't like this. I didn't like United much, but I regarded this new interest as unwelcome at best, prurient at worst.

The First Division at this time contained not just the two Manchester teams but Everton, Burnley, Blackburn Rovers, Blackpool, Bolton Wanderers and Preston North End, all within a thirty-mile radius of Manchester. I would have regarded it as strange if people from any of these towns supported United rather than their own local club. When it became clear that United were drawing support from way beyond the confines of Lancashire, a sense of outraged ownership came over me. They weren't my team, but in a strange way I felt as if United belonged to me, not these interlopers, and I determined to support them in the Cup final, in which they were due to play Bolton Wanderers. Besides, City had finished fifth in the First Division that season, four places above United. I could afford to be magnanimous.

Like everyone else, I was caught up in the saga of whether Matt Busby would have recovered from his injuries sufficiently to lead the side out at Wembley. In the end, the honour was fittingly left to Busby's second-in-command, the much underrated Jimmy Murphy (who was also manager of Wales in his spare time). This was attributed to Busby's nobility of spirit, a desire to ensure that Murphy received due acknowledgement of his achievement in keeping United afloat after Munich. In the light of Eamon Dunphy's biography of Busby, it appears that the great Sir Matt was far less generous towards Murphy than had been previously assumed.

Bolton scored early in the game and United never looked like getting back into it. The knockout blow was literally delivered by Nat Lofthouse, the brave Lion of Vienna, who barged Harry Gregg, the United goalkeeper, into the back of the net. There was something about that Bolton team which never appealed to me. They had, notoriously, the two hardest full-backs in the history of the game in Roy Hartle and Tommy Banks. Ian McShane recalls the story told by his father, the United winger Harry McShane. After one particularly violent tackle which left the flying outside-left in a crumpled heap on the cinder track, he could hear the voice of the other full-back calling, 'Roy, when tha's finished with 'im, kick 'im over here, will tha?' The true significance of the remark is only apparent when you learn that at the time Harry was playing *for* Bolton not against them. The incident occurred in training.

United's defeat taught me not to interfere with the laws of nature. I was a Manchester City supporter, I had enough troubles of my own; I didn't need to assume United's as well. For this was the time of the infamous Marsden Plan. Les McDowall, the City manager, had helped to devise the Revie Plan a couple of years earlier. This involved Don Revie wearing a number 9 on his back but playing in midfield, confusing the opposing centre-half, who didn't know whom to mark. It was not dissimilar to the way in which the great Hungarian side of 1953 had played Hidegkuti in a deep-lying role.

The Revie Plan got off to a sticky start with a 5–0 defeat at Preston North End, but the team stuck with it and, aided by the fact that Revie, Ken Barnes and Bobby Johnstone, on whom it largely depended, were skilful players, it was the basis of the two great FA Cup runs in 1955 and 1956. Three months into the 1956–57 season, Revie, who had been Footballer of the Year in 1955 but whom McDowall reckoned was a bolshie individual in the dressing-room, was transferred to Sunderland, and Roy Paul, captain of City and Wales, left the club shortly afterwards for the new pastures of non-League Worcester City. A team which had threatened to challenge the might of the Busby Babes now couldn't give a decent game to the survivors of Munich. So McDowall came up with the Marsden Plan.

Keith Marsden was a workaday inside-forward who couldn't hold down a place in the first team in his proper position. Why McDowall thought this made him the perfect candidate to perform as a flexible centre-half was beyond anyone's comprehension – not least that of Marsden himself. The experiment was clearly seen to be flawed when City were beaten 6–1 at Preston North End. Nevertheless, the following week McDowall persevered with the new plan for the match against West Bromwich Albion at the Hawthorns. I suppose you could say that it worked better for the first hour or so, because fifteen minutes into the second half City were trailing by three goals to two. This could only be accounted a tactical triumph because the match finished with the scoreline West Bromwich Albion 9 Manchester City 2.

Keith Marsden, along with the eponymous Plan, slid ignominiously back into obscurity, from which he emerged briefly in November 1964 when he appeared in court to answer police charges of keeping a disorderly house at the Empress Cabaret Club, Manchester Road, Stockport. Mr Marsden was further charged with owning the establishment which allowed unlawful gaming and an indecent strip-tease performance. The performance in question, according to the police constable giving evidence, had induced in the audience a state of frenzy and cries of 'Get 'em off!' The policeman added that he personally had not joined the demands, but the girl had complied with the audience's wishes. It occurs to me that getting them off is the basis of a strip-tease, but in the 1960s it was all far too much for Manchester in general and for the ill-fated Keith Marsden in particular.

Les McDowall never stopped experimenting. He was clearly dissatisfied with the classic 'WM' formation played by nearly all British teams, and he seems to have spent long nights alone in the manager's office under the Main Stand tinkering with blueprints that would revolutionise football. Undaunted by the Marsden fiasco, McDowall carried on selling all his good players and acquiring incompetents in their stead – a policy reintroduced with startling success by Malcolm Allison in the days of his Second Coming, and more recently by Alan Ball.

In the 1962–63 season, as City stared relegation in the face like an impoverished housewife opening the door yet again to the rent man from the council, McDowall invented yet another plan. He had two exciting young wingers at his disposal: the seventeen-year-old, hopelessly left-footed Neil Young, whom McDowall played at outside right, and David Wagstaffe, whom City sold to Wolves at the height of his career. McDowall's plan was to withdraw both wingers into defence to help out the full-backs. The new plan was abandoned at half-time as City slid out of the FA Cup, beaten 2–1 at home by Norwich City.

It won't have escaped your attention that McDowall actually invented the wing-back thirty years before anyone else in football caught on. Like a mad scientist constantly blowing up the laboratory while searching for the right formula, McDowall was a man out of his time. I don't know when his time was, exactly. It's just a shame he couldn't have been persuaded to swap jobs with Matt Busby. He would have sold Duncan Edwards to Swansea Town and played Bobby Charlton as an overlapping left-back, and saved me a lot of the aggravation and heartache McDowall was to impose on me.

It was on one of these awful Saturday evenings, after I had listened in wretched misery to *Sports Report* on the Light Programme bringing news of a 7–2 win for Manchester United and a 5–1 defeat for the Blues, that my mother finally lost her temper. This might arguably count as child abuse because I was in the bath at the time, wailing at the insupportable miseries of life being heaped on this innocent little boy. Naked as I was, with soap running into my eyes, I was uniquely vulnerable to my mother's imprecations. 'It's the same every Saturday night,' she moaned. 'You're always upset. Why don't you support a decent team, like your brother? They win all the time and he's always happy. Why don't you support United?'

I had to admit there was a certain sense of logic behind the appeal. My mother wiped the soap out of my eyes with the flannel. I looked bravely up at her anxious face. Since the day I started supporting Manchester City, it seemed as if it had brought her nothing but misery. (Boy, if she only knew what was coming up!) By a simple arrangement of words, I could make the two people I cared about most in the world – her and me – happy. 'OK, Mum,' I said, mustering as much courage as I knew how, 'I'll support Manchester United.' You should have seen the smile on the woman's face. It illuminated the whole of Prestwich and Whitefield, to say nothing of vast areas of Asia.

In bed that night, I felt like Joan of Arc rehearsing her recantation before the Inquisition in Rouen. The words were easy but nobody was fooled. I could stand in front of the mirror in the bathroom and smile and say to the reflection, 'Hello, I'm a Manchester United supporter' – but like Joan, I feared that I would wind up burned at the stake for being a Blue anyway. 'What shall it profit a man if he gain the whole world yet lose his soul?' asks the Bible. Could I really answer, 'It would stop me feeling miserable on Saturday evenings'?

The following Saturday provided the answer. I think this was in the days before David Coleman, *Grandstand* and the teleprinter, which made Eamonn Andrews, *Sports Report* and the first reading of the Classified Football Results the sole arbiter of fortune. As John Webster solemnly intoned, 'Arsenal 0, Preston North End 0' and so on down the list, my heart began its familiar rapid pattern of beating. When it got to 'Manchester City 1,' I knew by the inflection of Webster's voice that the other half of the equation would be 'Nottingham Forest 1.' The disappointment of dropping a home point was more than compensated by the recognition that the heart had returned home.

The irritation at hearing 'Aston Villa 1, Manchester United 3' merely confirmed what I had known all along. Changing one's footballing allegiance is as impossible as changing one's religious affiliation. Of course, it happens, but one has to question quite how deeply held were the original beliefs of the Anglicans who have been accepted into the Church of Rome. Supporting a football team is not a question of expediency, of convenience.

If favourite players are transferred elsewhere or supporters move house to a different part of the country, that hardly constitutes reasonable grounds for changing teams. You can add a local team as an adjunct to your primary purpose, but you can no more stop supporting your first love then than you can stop when they go through months or years of bad results. Nobody said it was going to be easy, but it is the very longevity of the struggle which ultimately rewards the fleeting moments of triumph.

Recent Manchester United converts will have closed the book at this point, unable to comprehend the logic. What we are faced with here is the classic confrontation between Faith and Reason. 'Reason,' as John Osborne's Luther points out, 'is the devil's whore, born of one stinking goat called Aristotle which believes that good works make a good man. But the truth is that the just shall live by faith alone.'

Luther's faith was severely tested by the widespread political upheavals in Europe, a response to a reformation he believed was essentially a reform of religious practice. He died, unfortunately, before he could test his theory by supporting the local Borussia Dortmund team rather than the Bayern Munich glory boys. He therefore restricted his activities to nailing 95 theses for disputation against indulgences to the church door in Wittenberg, rather than spray-painting obscene references to Jürgen Klinsmann.

There is a reason why Manchester United, like any successful club, have accumulated a vast army of camp followers. Their supporters have only to look in the Old Trafford trophy room, or, more easily, into the eyes of colleagues and friends who don't share their affiliation, to confirm why they have chosen to festoon their living-rooms, bedrooms, bathrooms and wardrobes with overpriced tat from the United megastore. Supporting other teams, particularly Manchester City – whose geographical proximity to their Cheshire-based rivals makes them uniquely fitted to indulge in this exercise – is a test of blind faith. It has been ever thus.

In 1960, United were in transition from the Busby Babes to the Law, Best, Charlton side of the 1960s. Busby seemed to be a shadow of his former self, still mourning the loss of his Babes and the destruction of the side he had spent ten years constructing. In November of that year he signed Noel Cantwell from West Ham for £30,000, seeing in him a replacement for Johnny Carey and Roger Byrne, who had previously been his representative on the field.

Cantwell, who was part of the famous West Ham Academy of the 1950s (notable graduates who all, coincidentally, ended up in Manchester included Malcolm Allison, John Bond and Frank O'Farrell), was disappointed with the atmosphere he found at Old Trafford. In his first season, United finished seventh in the First Division, just as they had in 1960. In 1962 they slipped to fifteenth and in 1963, as we shall see later, despite their FA Cup triumph they finished just three points and two places above City, who were relegated.

Even the signing of an ex-Manchester City player failed, initially, to spark a revival. Denis Law is uniquely a hero on both sides of Manchester. Although he is primarily associated with United in their glory days of the 1960s, and with the infamous postscript backheel which sent United down in 1974 (that incident has a remarkable way of popping up at the slightest provocation), Denis Law's first introduction to Manchester was in March 1960 when Les McDowall signed him from Huddersfield Town for a then British record fee of £55,000. Law was to City in 1960 what Kinkladze became in 1996. Everyone knew he was the best player in the team, including the other players, which isn't always helpful. The tendency was to give him the ball and let him weave his magic. Eventually, even the other side tended to get the hang of this plan, and the result was invariably brutal treatment and a creeping sense of futility.

Nevertheless, Denis Law's First Coming gave the blue side of Manchester a new hero to supplement the decade-long worship of Bert Trautmann. Law was quite brilliant as he scored ten times in his first nineteen games. Technically it was eleven, but the goal against United in the Maine Road derby on 29 August 1960 was wiped out after the game was abandoned because of rain. Rain itself, even rain in August, was hardly an unusual occurrence in Manchester, but referee Arthur Ellis didn't appear to understand that the points City gathered at the start of the season, when all the other teams were still metaphorically putting away the Nivea cream, were usually the points that saved them at the end of it.

Denis suffered an even greater misfortune in the fourth round of the FA Cup that year when he scored all six goals as City led at Luton by 6–2. With twenty minutes left, the referee abandoned the game and City inevitably lost the replayed game the following Wednesday, 3–1. Guess who scored for the Blues? The only possible comfort was a sense of *schadenfreude* as United were walloped 7–2 by Sheffield Wednesday on the same day.

Even that small comfort disappeared a couple of weeks later as, true to form, City also lost the replayed derby match, and I was in the Platt Lane Stand to witness one of those injustices which rankle forty years after the event. After twenty minutes of the first half which even match reports agreed that City had totally dominated, a harmless-looking centre from the right wing was about to be collected by the City reserve goalkeeper Steve Fleet. Alex Dawson, the bustling United centre-forward, challenged for it but was being well marked by City's latest Scottish signing, Jackie Plenderleith. Having no chance of reaching it with his head, Dawson simply fisted the ball into the net. With that 'Don't you talk to me like that' attitude that is beloved of referees the world over, the best referee in England, Arthur Ellis, pointed to the centre-circle.

A slight doubt must have crossed his brain, however, because three minutes later he gave us a penalty that never was. Outside-right Clive Colbridge fell over in the penalty area and Ellis pointed to the spot. Even aged ten, I knew this was what cricket umpires call 'the adjuster'. City right-back and captain Barry Betts, clearly an honourable man, smashed the penalty-kick as hard as he could against the crossbar. United went on to win 3–1, to add to their emphatic 5–1 win at Old Trafford earlier in the season. That old all-pervading sense of injustice and futility enveloped me. If it wasn't Bobby Charlton, it was the bloody referee. How were we ever going to win one of these damn matches?

By the end of the season, Denis Law had had enough and he was transferred to Torino for £125,000. Like Kinkladze now, and like the fans then and now, he didn't trust anyone on the side but himself to do anything. You couldn't blame him, really. He was playing in the same team as John McTavish, a centre-half whose principal claim to fame is that he hammered a hat-trick of own goals past Bert Trautmann in successive matches. It was hard enough for Bert to keep out the opposition by himself; it was asking a bit much for him to tackle his own players as well, especially since they had the vital element of surprise on their side.

Football teams, like governments, usually have periods of around five or six years when they can be defined by results, and a particular collection of players, as successful or otherwise. Occasionally, the start of a decade links with a change of government and can help characterise a new era. The coalition National Government formed by Ramsay MacDonald in 1931 certainly heralded the Depression, just as the war cabinet of Winston Churchill announced in May 1940 signalled the end of the misery perpetrated by the Tories in the Thirties. Churchill's return to power in 1951 at the expense of the tired Labour government of Attlee was the start of the infamous thirteen years of Tory misrule, and Harold Wilson's defeat by Ted Heath just four days after England's crushing 3–2 loss to West Germany in the 1970 World Cup was certainly the start of the Seventies, as surely as Margaret Thatcher's triumph in 1979 was the end of it.

The Sixties, it could be argued, didn't start until 1963–64. It wasn't just the Labour victory, it was the explosion of pop music and fashion, and the recognition of new ideas in all walks of life, that marked it as a different decade from the previous one of stifling conformity. Tories will argue, with some justification, that it was the gathering strength of the economy in the Fifties, after the wartime and post-war austerity, that permitted the extravagance of the Sixties, but I was part of that teenage explosion and the desire to cast off the restrictive, stifling prejudices of the Tories and their discredited ways was almost tangible.

Does this help an appreciation of sport in Manchester? Well, yes, in a funny way, it does. The years of the Macmillan government, of 'You've never had it so good' and the start of ITV and the opening of the M1, were very clearly defined for me by a particular Manchester City team. It was essentially composed of Trautmann, who wasn't getting any younger, and Denis Law, who was never going to stay with us. The skilful and successful team which had reached successive Cup finals in 1955 and 1956 was broken up far too quickly, and a series of incompetent ones assembled in its place.

The names are a litany of misery – useless wingers, Sambrook and Colbridge; hopeless half-backs, Benson and Chadwick; forwards who couldn't score and defenders who couldn't tackle.

In the annual struggle against relegation, one year was particularly close. On the last day of the 1958–59 season, City were due to play Leicester City while their rivals for the drop, Aston Villa, were at home to West Brom. The two clubs marked for death were equal on points, but Villa had the superior goal average; so if the two results were the same, City would go down. After conceding a goal after ten minutes, City, encouraged by three brilliant saves from Trautmann and the support of a crowd of over 50,000, fought back with passion and skill – the two elements which had been in singularly short supply since the previous August. Although City finally won 3–1, attention had long since switched to Villa Park. Villa had kicked off fifteen minutes before us, and all through that dramatic second half we knew that they were leading 1–0. With just over ten minutes to go at Maine Road, the news came through that Ronnie Allen had equalised for West Brom with almost the last kick of the game. That last-gasp goal sent their West Midlands rivals down instead of us, and it was party time at Maine Road.

The newspapers had headlined the day of these matches

as 'D-DAY'. Puzzled, I asked for clarification and was told that D-Day meant Decision Day. I didn't seek to question the statement, but when, a few years later, I learned about the Allied invasion of Normandy in June 1944, I couldn't shake the original concept from my brain. In the years since 1959, any subsequent reference to D-Day has always called to mind not the heroically taken beachheads of Gold, Sword, Juno, Omaha and Utah, but the dramatic finale to the 1958–59 Football League season.

The revisionist historians of Manchester United see the years of Matt Busby's reign the way Tory historians view the reign of Queen Victoria – as an unbroken series of imperial triumphs and economic expansion. In reality, they conveniently ignore the salient fact that United went through similar turmoil to City during these years.

Busby had ruled United since 1945 with a quiet autocracy that brooked no dissension. Harry McShane tells of reacting adversely to being dropped from the first team by complaining to the manager. Busby just listened, saying nothing at all. Eventually, after a minute or two of total silence, McShane got up and left. 'After all,' he pointed out, 'it was his office. What else could I do?' The net result of McShane's complaint was that he didn't play for the reserves on Saturday – or the first team, or any other Manchester United team for ten weeks. Shortly thereafter, Busby placed him on the transfer list. No doubt the manager's intransigence was bolstered by the knowledge that there was a seventeen-year-old left-winger called David Pegg who was now ready to take McShane's place.

United's indifferent form in Cup and League seemed to be a reflection of Busby's own doubts about his ability to build a third great team. Much of his motivation appeared to have died with the players on the runway in Munich. Instead of Mark Jones or Jackie Blanchflower, there was the uninspired

59

Ron Cope at centre-half. The purchase of Albert Quixall from across the Pennines was not the success that Tommy Taylor's move had been. Maurice Setters was no Eddie Colman. The youth team provided Nobby Stiles and Tony Dunne, but George Best was not yet ready for first-team action and United were simply not firing with any purpose. Bobby Charlton ploughed a lonely furrow out on the left wing, leaving the central midfield role to a combination of Setters, Stiles and Nicholson – not a creative corpuscle among them. The key signings were Crerand and Law but they, too, were a couple of years away.

The decline of the two great clubs mirrored a sense of foreboding in my own life. In 1957, my father sold Northern Raincoat Ltd, his chain of undercapitalised raincoat shops, and negotiated a service contract for himself to stay on as managing director. Within six months the contract was broken and my father removed from office. An unsatisfactory court case followed, in which the hostility between my father and my mother's side of the family broke out into open warfare. I later discovered that my Uncle Laurence had taken to a study of the law as something to do in his spare time. After he moved to London, when there was no cricket to be watched at Lord's or The Oval, Uncle Laurence would visit his bank in Southampton Row, then wander down to the Law Courts where he would sit happily all day listening to the arguments – though with his shirt firmly buttoned. He liked arguments, particularly of the legal kind, and when they were not forthcoming he couldn't resist the temptation to initiate them himself. In this spirit of legal curiosity Laurence immersed himself in my father's case, offering his many opinions as well as the services of his own solicitor.

Although my father won an initial judgment, his opponents took the case to the Court of Appeal and when negotiations for a compromise settlement were underway at the court door, both Laurence and his solicitor were conspicuous by their absence. My family never trusted the *goyim*, weren't too sure about fellow Jews and wanted everything kept inside the family. The trouble was, they didn't trust each other either, all of which led to a distinctly confusing adolescence.

It was never clear to me, after Northern Raincoat Ltd was sold, quite how my father managed to earn a living. One day, I was playing in the drive, chipping the ball against the side of the house and volleying the return into the garage door – a move recently copied with success, I note, by Gianfranco Zola – when a man drove up and asked if I knew 'a Mr I. Shindler'. Receiving an affirmative reply, he thrust a brown envelope into my hands and drove away.

Since these were the days before bungs in motorway cafés and cash-for-questions sleaze, I thrust the envelope into the pocket of my trousers and returned to the volleying routine. That night, as I hung up my trousers, the brown envelope dropped out. I took it downstairs to my mother, who almost fainted at the sight of it. It turned out to be my father's wage packet. Apart from the fact that Jews who owned their own businesses didn't deal in wage packets, except those of their employees, my mother was appalled at the casual and insulting manner in which my father had been paid. I'm still unclear as to what sort of a job he was doing at the time. It was the beginning of a long downward spiral for us into genteel poverty.

Although financial problems soon followed the loss of the business, my days at primary school seemed in retrospect to have been lived in a John Major-like world of Fifties security and respectability. As I progressed through the school, I knew I was no good at Maths, Nature Study and Art, but more than competent at English, History and Geography. I never fought this early analysis. I felt it was probably genetic, a feeling confirmed when, at the age of eleven, my daughter Amy was accepted into her new school by the headmistress with praise for her English but a grim prognostication for her future Mathematics career which strongly echoed my own.

The Eleven Plus examinations hung over my generation as the spectre of the Depression and the Second World War hung over that of my parents. It is very hard to be nostalgic over a system which reduced children, teachers and parents alike to mass neurosis. At one end of the spectrum of choice stood Manchester Grammar School, then, as now, the 'best' school in Manchester. Next rung down on the ladder of desirability was Bury Grammar School, where my brother had been safely installed for five years, followed by Stand Grammar, a grammar school, certainly, but there was a general acceptance that you only went there if you had 'failed' the other two. At the opposite end of the spectrum was the terrifying prospect of the Secondary Modern School, known as 'Heys Road' because of its location.

Heys Road was for us what Hell must have been to mediaeval peasants. I had no vision of Heys Road as a school. There were no classrooms, dining hall, changing-rooms or football pitch. It was a place where children went and were never seen again. Parents whose children failed the Eleven Plus and had to go to Heys Road removed themselves from polite society. For all the many achievements of R.A.Butler's 1944 Education Act, Heys Road and its fellow institutions were its inevitable by-products. When I first read of Dotheboys Hall and the rest of the horror stories about Victorian schools, the image of Heys Road as some kind of modern Dante's Inferno was reinforced. Heys Road lay between Park View School and Michael Chadwick's house, the other side of Bury Old Road. Even cycling up there, I skirted Heys Road. It was just remotely possible that I could be knocked off my bike, kidnapped and forcibly imprisoned in the Heys Road school. Why any political party should wish to restore this mental torture is beyond my comprehension. Have they all forgotten what it was *really* like?

To forestall the deathly prospect of Heys Road, I was tutored privately after school. Inevitably, my English was good but the Maths showed no sign of improvement, and besides, I was really only interested in playing football after school – for hours, if possible. Even by myself with only a tennis ball and a garage door for company, there was plenty to hold my interest: a derby match in which I was playing centre-forward for City, an international against Scotland in which I was playing centre-forward for England, a World Cup final against Brazil. Coincidentally, every match ended with my scoring the winning goal with the last kick of the game. The repetition never paled. I'm always surprised when I hear of fellow anoraks whose solo games of Subbuteo end in defeat for their own side. Being the sole arbiter of the laws, you had to be very incompetent indeed to lose in such a controllable situation.

In the summer, the chalk came out and three stumps were drawn on the long-suffering garage door. Throughout the long overcast summers of the late Fifties and early Sixties, I wheeled away, holding my fingers religiously down the non-existent seam of the tennis ball and landing it as near as I could to a chalked circle on a line of the off-stump. I knew from a voracious reading of ghosted sporting autobiographies that this was how all famous sportsmen started. I have to own up to the fleeting thought that a stranger who would turn out to be Matt Busby (a more charismatic figure altogether than Les McDowall) might possibly be driving up our cul-de-sac and be impressed enough at my control and dedication to offer me a trial. In fact, the only stranger who ever drove up in such fashion was the bloke delivering my father's wage packet.

The cul-de-sac gave us a wonderfully privileged space in

which to play. Admittedly, on one side the ball ran away down an unforgiving hill, but on the other it simply rebounded off a curved wall. In the summer, if we used my gatepost as the wicket, I could drive the tennis ball in the arc between point and mid-on without causing the fielders to do anything other than fetch the ball back from the flower beds. In the evening, the men returned and inconsiderately left their cars in the street. We reckoned that was an outright provocation. They knew perfectly well that the street was now a cricket pitch, and we had no moral qualms about hammering the ball into the side of their cars with a satisfying thud. The sound of a front door opening shortly thereafter was the cue for the game to be temporarily abandoned, as every player fled for sanctuary.

The first of the Eleven Plus exams was the Manchester Grammar School Entrance Examination. This was in two parts – a written test and an interview. One dark January morning, fortified by extra tutorials, I was driven miles across Manchester to begin a process which, like passing from page boy to squire to knight, took a further fourteen years to complete. Earning a doctorate was marginally less glamorous than being ritually clothed in chain mail, but there was Latin spoken at each ceremony . . .

The English was easy, the Maths probably very difficult. What I remember is the essay subject, which was something like 'Describe what happens on a Tuesday'. I'm sure there were slightly more abstract topics which could have been chosen, but I seized on this one because Tuesday happened to be the day on which my favourite magazine, *Charles Buchan's Football Monthly*, arrived through the letterbox. It was the work of a moment to twist the whole essay into a eulogy of Manchester City, about which I am sure I wrote with a zeal and a fluency which must, as they used to say, have 'caught the eye' of the examiners.

Well, yes, it probably did, and since Manchester Grammar School is almost in Cheshire, where Manchester United play, it requires very little deduction to work out that the reason I failed the first part of the entrance exam to Manchester Grammar was that the essay was almost certainly marked by a Manchester United supporter. The idea of my coming to their Red-loving institution and polluting the atmosphere was clearly too much for him to stand, and I was labelled a 'failure' at the age of ten. It can't be entirely coincidental that Michael Atherton and John Crawley, who opened the batting for Manchester Grammar School in the 1980s, are self-confessed United supporters. So no problems for them.

Despite the fact that I later passed the exams for both Bury and Stand, I was much traumatised by this early rejection. I knew I wasn't strong or fast or tall. I was somewhat feeble, well-read, and had been told I was clever. This was a statement of fact, not a means of praise or encouragement. Therefore the rejection by Manchester Grammar, like City's defeats by United, was another indication that sometimes the world didn't behave as it ought. The cleverness got knocked out of me in the first few weeks at Bury Grammar School, which meant I floundered for years. It was City and football, Lancashire and cricket, which came to my rescue, as they always have.

Before Bury, though, there was the final year of primary school which, notwithstanding the dreaded Eleven Plus and the even more dreaded Heys Road, was a glorious year of sporting achievement and *Swallows and Amazons*-type friend-ships and adventures. The Park View school football team, an object of scorn and derision the previous year, matured into our own version of the Busby Babes. Jeff Cohen, a ten-year-old Bert Trautmann, was restored to his rightful place between the posts; Michael Chadwick, trickier than Ray Sambrook or Clive Colbridge, tormented full-backs the length and breadth of Prestwich; Roger Lane, a big, strong lad, gave us some badly needed stability at centre-half; and I finally recovered from my series of debilitating illnesses long enough to clock up a term with fewer than twenty absent days.

The key to our success, however, was an impish midfield genius called David Gadian. David was younger than the rest of us and didn't join us till the penultimate year. Though a United supporter, he shared my interest in football and the detail that could be gleaned from the daily perusal of the sports pages. He was also easily the cleverest boy in the class and, infuriatingly, the most modest, though he had little to be modest about. There was absolutely nothing you could dislike about him. Needless to say, he passed the Manchester Grammar exam easily and our devoted lifelong friendship was split asunder. We sat next to each other on the combined double desk and seat, whispering about matches past, present and future, particularly that amazing 7–3 victory by Real Madrid in the European Cup final of 1960, a game that influenced everyone who saw it live on television.

The local equivalent of the European Cup was the Crofton Cup and that year we made it to the final, where we were due to play Butterstile Lane. I can't remember being so nervous before any of the Eleven Plus exams as we all were before this game. Fortunately, on the big occasion we didn't freeze. Mike Chadwick scored twice in the first half and we led 4–1 at the interval. In the second half, David Gadian simply tore the opposition apart and we finished 8–2 winners. Clearly the previous year's 8–2 defeat had been God's way of making us appreciate our famous victory all the more. I'm not sure that anything in later life ever gave me more complete satisfaction than that crushing win over Butterstile Lane. There was a simplicity about it which later triumphs never attained. It was our destiny.

Amazingly, there were seven Jews in that side. Like the

Israeli Army under Moshe Dayan which had raced across the Sinai to the Suez Canal, we were demonstrating that the popularly held belief that Jews were wimps was now out-dated. United supporters Peter Jacobs, our forceful centre-forward, and Jeffrey Edis, whose tackles made us wince almost as much as the poor sods on whom they were inflicted, asked no quarter and certainly gave none. Their general filthiness allowed Michael Chadwick, David Gadian and me to pretend we were the footballing aristocrats of North Manchester Under-11s.

The key event was that Williebobs, our master strategist, had resigned and we no longer had to worry about which side of the ball was round and which side square. Instead we were playing football like Busby used to advocate: 'Go out and enjoy yourselves and give the ball to a red shirt.' You remember the Hungarian side of 1953 which beat England 6–3 at Wembley? Well, that was Park View County Primary School Under-11s in 1960. Except, unlike Ferenc Puskas, David Gadian could kick with both feet.

Chapter Four

The summer term of 1960 which had ended in a blaze of glory was followed, like a Biblical plague, by three years of tragedy. It wasn't just the football, although it soon became clear, when despite the presence of Denis Law we lost the next four derby matches to United, that supporting City wasn't going to help my assimilation into Bury Grammar School. The world was becoming a cold and unwelcoming place, and I felt myself being edged towards the margin.

I can still remember lying in bed one Monday night in the first week of September 1960, knowing that tomorrow morning I was starting secondary school and it was a significant moment in my life. After that, it all got much worse. Park View had been a school of T-shirt and shorts, first names and kids who lived round the corner. It had been built in the 1930s and was modern enough to contain 'prefabs' for extra classrooms. They were known as 'The Huts'.

Bury Grammar School was an imposing redbrick building with two hundred years of history behind it. It was an institution which used only surnames. It had a school uniform of grey shirts, grey short trousers, tie in the house colours, blazer with the school crest – also in house colours – on the breast pocket, and, most humiliating of all, a school cap. I took a particular dislike to that cap; it became a symbol of the new rigid authoritarianism which I felt was strangling me. We were told that to be seen in the streets of Bury without that cap meant an automatic caning, if we were so observed by a prefect or master. The injustice of it rankled. The accepted practice was to wear the cap so far back on the head that the peak was pointing almost vertically. During the cricket season it was entirely different. I could then use the cap to look like Cyril Washbrook or, since Washy had just retired, the new Lancashire hero, Geoff 'Noddy' Pullar.

Jeff Cohen, who felt similarly about the cap, was so traumatised by it that even today, nearing fifty, he still dreams that he has to wear it on his way to his job as policy co-ordinator with the Mental Health Act Commission. When his clients point out to him that he is wearing a cap, size 6⅞, with a school crest on the front, and that he is due to take a meeting with the Minister for Social Services in five minutes, he is, of course, very embarrassed.

It wasn't just the uniform that I found oppressive; there was also the history. The Park View 'spirit' was only manifested on days of school matches, when it just bonded the players ever tighter. This new school spirit was a foreign substance imposed on us without explanation. The Roger Kay Hall, where we trooped for morning assembly, was a cavernous place occupied by tall, strong boys with deep voices. Even among our own first-year intake, there was a proportion of boys who had attended Bury Grammar Junior School and were already wise in the ways of what to expect. I felt small, insignificant and very unhappy.

There had been so many Jewish kids in Park View that we never felt like a minority. On the High Holy Days in September, the school virtually closed down. On Friday afternoons during the winter months, we all went home at lunchtime to prepare for the arrival of the Sabbath – or in my case, to play hours of Subbuteo with Michael Chadwick and Jeff Cohen. During prayers in assembly, it was the accustomed practice for the Christian children to clasp their hands together in front of them, like we had seen in the drawings in mediaeval history books. The Jews put their hands behind their backs, and at least one of them tried to memorise the order of the Lancashire batsmen in the first-class averages.

At Bury Grammar School, the Jews were admitted for the General Announcements but then ejected from the assembly and sent off to a classroom where a Jewish prefect conducted Jewish prayers. During the recitation of the daily prayer to God, 'Shema Yisroel Adonai Elohenu Adonai Echad', we could hear the sound of hymns drifting down the corridor from the main assembly. At Park View, they had been rather cheerful songs like 'All Things Bright And Beautiful' and 'We Plough the Fields and Scatter', but now they seemed to be tuneless dirges about crucifixion and resurrection – scary concepts at the best of times, but in this new context they sounded like ancient calls to arms for a pogrom against the Jewish infidel. I hasten to add this was a personal response, and that the majority of the boys in Jewish assembly were either catching up on homework or throwing paper darts dipped in ink at the unsuspecting necks of the smallest boys in the front rows.

If there was anti-semitism in school, it was negative rather than positive, a sense of prejudicial ignorance rather than ideological distaste. It was believed that the headmaster, a militant Methodist, imposed an unofficial quota on the Jewish intake, in case too many of them got in. Jeff Cohen remembers being asked in his interview whether he was an Orthodox Jew, which he assumes was a way of checking whether he would be available to play for the school teams on Saturdays. There was a particularly eccentric Physics teacher called Duncan, who had a shock of bright-red hair and was familiarly known as 'Max Planck', not because he bore any relation to the distinguished

71

German physicist but because it sounded like the name of a mad scientist. The Bury Max Planck was a profound pessimist, always predicting failure for any boy who couldn't come up with the right answer to a question in class. The bench where David Green and Jeffrey Cohen sat was always the noisiest. Planck would spend much of the lesson shouting at 'the Jewish Bench' to shut up. It was a vain call.

Next to Cohen, Green and Edis sat Michael Alexander, another Jewish graduate of Park View, whose father was a bookie and who had developed an inordinate interest in money and betting from the age of six. At Bury Grammar he had a finger stall for counting money and would ask us to test him as he counted the right number of pages in a text book. All our French text books became dog-eared as he practised his money-counting technique. Today, strangely enough, he is a successful accountant living in south Manchester.

My whole world seemed to darken that autumn. The usual escape routes were all blocked. For all my physical fragility, I had always been acknowledged as a bright kid. Indeed, my very first memory of my first term at primary school is of being dragged kicking and screaming into school and left on display at the front of the class with tears streaming down my face while the teacher, Mrs Brennan, intoned solemnly to a class of wide-eyed five-year-olds, 'Look at him. He's the cleverest boy in the class and the biggest baby.' At Bury Grammar, my propensity for bursting into tears gained few admirers.

More serious for me was the newly expanded syllabus. Latin and French were cautiously approachable, but Maths now expanded into geometry and algebra, which left me confused. Physics was like a language I couldn't speak, and for one hour and twenty minutes each week we were submitted to a double period of torture, known as 'Woodwork', by a psychopath called 'Johnny' Grundy, whose psychotic ravings were usually saved for the most helpless, incompetent child in the class – me.

To this day, even the smell of wood shavings causes a Pavlovian response of incontinence. The lesson would begin with the ritual disrobing of the blazer and the unfolding and donning of a white overall. We looked like a meeting of eleven-year-old Freemasons. I spent as long as I could on this, as it was the only part of the lesson I was any good at. Grundy would then inspect us as we stood to attention by our work benches, private parts squeezed up against the vice. Sometimes I felt that inserting my private parts into the vice might be less traumatic than what was inevitably to follow.

The purpose of the lesson was . . . well, to be honest, I never really knew, because at the end of two years I was still working on the first exercise. Others in the class were making tables and chairs and three-piece suites, but I was still hacking, chiselling and sawing away at a rectangular block of wood. Every week the torture would begin anew as Grundy handed out the refined Chippendales to the others, saving his most withering contempt for me as he hurled the block of wood across the room at my head, to the accompaniment of widespread sniggering.

As the class began their planing of wood into something that might stand proudly in their living-rooms, Johnny Grundy would be regularly rung on the telephone. This was particularly impressive as the only other telephone in the school was in the headmaster's office. Surely he couldn't be talking to the headmaster ten times each lesson.

One day, caught short by a call of nature, Grundy left the room. One of the more foolhardy souls started to examine Grundy's desk, under which he discovered a button. He pressed it and the phone rang. We shrank back in terror, like natives in an old Hollywood film confronted with their first experience of technology. The foolhardy one picked up the phone. There was no one there. He replaced the phone and pressed the button again. Same routine. The secret was out. The psychotic Grundy was clearly ringing himself on the phone and talking to the dialling tone.

I was equally inept at Art, but the master, 'Paddy' Perham, was a warm, humorous man and despite finishing in last place, as I did in Woodwork, I was never humiliated and at least he left me with a love of art, provided it wasn't my own. Finishing 32nd out of 32 was not an enjoyable experience, but Art and Woodwork were non-academic subjects and as such not entirely relevant to my future career and, more to the point, they were only once a week.

I also finished 32nd out of 32 in Physics, which was originally presided over by a bullet-headed lunatic whose real name was Ibbotson but whom history and tradition had denominated 'Joe Plug'. Plug's favourite instrument of instruction was an old plimsoll, which was applied with considerable force to the posterior of any boy found playing with the gas taps on the benches. He gave Jeff Cohen 0 out of 10 for a diagram which was immaculate but was drawn in ink rather than pencil. Jeff's Physics career followed mine down the toilet. Plug retired at the end of our first year, but he left a residue of fear and loathing.

There was an intake of almost a hundred boys at the age of eleven. At the end of the first term, after the Christmas exams, the top eleven from each class were merged to form the 'Rapid' stream who would take the GCE 'O' Levels in four years. The remaining sixty-four would be divided into two classes of thirty-two who would take five years to get to 'O' Level stage. Both Jeff Cohen and David Green were kept in one of the latter classes, despite David Green's finishing third in his class in those exams. His temperament was clearly suspect, although he later attributed the decision to anti-semitism.

David Green's real problem was that he was constitutionally incapable of giving the teachers what they wanted to read. Instead, he preferred to demonstrate his own unique cleverness. In the Sixth Form, he was supposed to write an essay on the industrial revolution. We were particularly proud of the revolution in Bury; the Crompton 'Mule' was invented near Bolton, Hargreaves's Spinning Jenny came from Blackburn, and John Kay's Flying Shuttle was devised in Bury itself. Instead of celebrating Lancashire's contribution to the technological revolution in the textile industry, David Green wrote an essay celebrating Manchester City and how a glorious football club was born out of the back streets of the industrial revolution. The essay was marked as D++ rather than a straight D. When pressed as to what the double plus represented, the teacher admitted: 'I liked your style.'

In the Christmas exams of that first year, I finished fifteenth, but was promoted to the 'R' form much to my own and everyone else's surprise. Maybe they discounted the low marks in Art and Woodwork because they were non-academic subjects, and Joe Plug's bilious bad temper was distributed so widely that his report became relatively meaningless.

Joe Plug taught in the science block, which seemed invariably to be enveloped in a cloud of noxious gases which could have been the result of legitimate scientific experiments, but which I always felt more likely to be the result of thirty boys' digestive systems responding to the school dinners.

Jewish boys didn't eat school dinners, because of the fear of contamination by non-kosher products. We all brought sandwiches to school, which we were allowed to eat in the unhygienic surroundings of the cloakrooms next to the boys' toilets. The sandwiches were accompanied by vacuum flasks, and mealtimes were punctuated by the sound of flasks coming into uncompromising contact with the tiled floor.

The consequent sound of shattered glass as the owner shook the flask always coincided with a mighty roar of *schaden-freude*. My mother, distrusting the vacuum flask, settled on a much cheaper plastic bottle, which she filled daily with orange cordial. It never broke, though it frequently leaked, but at least I was spared that roar of derision. Unfortunately, it made the orange cordial taste of plastic. I was astonished (and secretly envious) of the boys who were given salami or roast beef sandwiches on white bread. My mother ensured my sandwiches were carved from a wholemeal loaf and contained lumps of cheddar cheese and, to my constant dismay, watercress. I was the only one with a nutrition-conscious mother.

Jeffrey Edis, still growing exponentially, rarely remembered to bring his own lunch and instilled a reign of terror in which he would beat up the members of his own year and below unless they paid a tribute to him of offering a choice from their own sandwich box. It was like the Jewish equivalent of a church tithe. He very quickly learned to avoid me, as the prospect of wholemeal cheese and watercress sandwiches, however nutritious, would have instantly blown his reputation for being hard. You can't be a hard vegetarian. Not at twelve years old, you can't.

Bury is eight miles north of Manchester, four miles north of the middle-class Jewish ghetto of Prestwich where I was raised. The school's catchment area stretched from Bolton in the west to Rochdale in the east and Ramsbottom and Raw-tenstall in the north. The boys from these towns talked differently from what I had been used to at Park View. Their accents were pure Lancashire, like that of the present-day England cricket coach, David Lloyd. The Manchester accent is more like that of the Neville brothers, the United full-backs.

My new colleagues also had weird mealtimes. Instead of Breakfast, Lunch at 1pm and Dinner at 6.30, they had what they called Dinner at lunchtime, Tea, which was a kind of High Tea, at 5pm and Supper around 10pm. They could have been living in Australia. I learned later that it was the product of shiftwork at the local cotton mills. We didn't have cotton mills in Prestwich. We had kosher butchers.

These hard strangers dominated the school's sports teams. The glory of the Crofton Cup was long forgotten. I was on the two-year rundown to my barmitzvah, so Saturday mornings were now reserved for a compulsory attendance at synagogue. Anyway, I knew I wasn't good enough to be picked for the school Under-12 team. Jeff Cohen was appalled to find that his way was blocked by David Chaytor, who was not only a more spectacular goalkeeper, and as such caught the eye of the master in charge, but was also in the same house as we were so that in house matches Jeff and 'Chats' had to alternate games in goal, much like Shilton and Clemence in the England team of the 1980s. In May 1997, 'Chats' was elected the Labour MP for Bury North.

Jeff's chances were not helped by a controversial refereeing decision in the key trial game. He came out of the six-yard box to gather a long ball downfield which was easily bouncing into his arms when the opposing centreforward raced towards him and, unable to reach the ball legitimately, blatantly punched it past Jeff into the net. Mr Holt, the referee, was near the halfway line, didn't see anything amiss and awarded the goal, despite being pursued by Jeff. The grinning, cheating centre-forward was, inevitably, David Green.

David Green's provocative behaviour was apparent from the first day. He was adept at stirring up trouble and enjoyed nothing more than provoking the mild-mannered boys to exhibitions of atypical violence. He, Jeff and I were the only City supporters in our year and as such should have been the best of friends. I suppose we were, in a way – but David

Green's way was to make himself thoroughly disliked by his best friends.

In the early 1960s, the Co-Operative Insurance Society built the tallest skyscraper in Europe on the edge of Manchester city centre. On top of the building were the letters CIS, which David would always refer to as 'Cohen Is Silly' as we passed it on the way to Maine Road. It's not funny now, it wasn't funny then, but, goaded beyond endurance after hearing this remark every other Saturday afternoon for three seasons as the number 75 bus rounded Corporation Street, Jeff suddenly launched an almighty punch at David and a mighty scrap ensued. When we got off the bus and saw it disappear into the distance, we noticed the advertisement for a scrap-metal dealer on the back. It read: 'Cohen's For Scrap.'

Afterwards, they refused to talk to each other for six months. In the middle of this period of non-communication, they realised they had already booked to go on a school holiday together to Switzerland. The silence lasted all the way there on the sleeper train, up the Matterhorn, round Lake Geneva and back across the Channel. Neither wanted to be the first to break the deadlock.

I didn't go on the trip to Switzerland because by this time, genuine tragedy had struck my family. Uncle Laurence moved from Manchester to London about the time I started secondary school. It all left me feeling that my childhood had been abruptly terminated without consultation. I knew that my father didn't run his chain of raincoat shops any longer and that his 'business' was not thriving, but I had no knowledge of the extent of his troubles.

More significant to me was the disintegration of our domestic life. As my brother grew up and moved into an age of adolescence so advanced that he was even allowed to go out on Friday nights (albeit only to rehearsals for the annual school play), I became more and more unhappy at home. My father and mother were constantly arguing and I could see the effect it was having on my mother, with whom I still spent long hours. As children always do, I began to think that their unhappiness was something to do with me.

In June 1962 I reached my thirteenth birthday, the time of my barmitzvah. I understand the historical origins of the ceremony, but their significance appear to have been lost in the mists of time. I could never (and still can't) equate the religious nature of the coming of age with the conspicuous consumption it seemed to bring in its wake. All my friends were barmitzvahed within the same few months, and each set of parents seemed to want to outdo the rest in the richness of the display they put on.

They were changing the rules. I expected to wear my brother's hand-me-down clothes, to buy butter scooped from a tub into a piece of greaseproof paper because it was cheaper than the pre-packaged variety. I never felt unduly poor, not like the kids from the council estate on the other side of Park View who came to school with holes in their clothes, but all my life I felt I had lived in a time of austerity.

This wasn't only the austerity of the post-war governments, of rationing and make do and mend. It was also an austerity conditioned by the fragility of Jewish life. If ice-cream cones were on sale at threepence, sixpence and a shilling, we would have the threepenny ones. I don't think I resented this, particularly. That was how it was. When we went out with other families, a father who showed off unforgivably would toss half a crown to his son and tell him to buy a couple of ice creams. This was much frowned upon in my family. My mother would rummage in her handbag for sixpence or a shilling before issuing a similar order. Two shillings was a lot of money to be wasted on inessential fripperies like ice cream or chocolate. Now, suddenly when we got to thirteen years of age, there was money to burn for some families. I couldn't understand it.

Our family was one of a group of a dozen or so who formed a tightly knit circle in north Manchester. The parents, who had all known each other from their teenage years in the 1930s, had met in the Jewish Youth movement, Habonim, and remained loyally close until death eventually decimated their ranks. The men went off to fight Hitler and the women remained at home with their babies, knowing that if Hitler won it meant for them not occupation by the Nazis but death in an extermination camp. After Hitler there was the British Mandate in Palestine, the establishment of the State of Israel and the first Arab–Israeli War to keep them all united. Israel's early success, and growing prosperity in Britain, loosened the ties but they still expected their children to behave and think as they had. To them it was a matter of sheer survival. To me such thinking eventually came to seem restrictive and parochial.

I grew up on stories of pogroms and evictions, of the bondage in Egypt and the Holocaust in Central Europe. I was born a year after the first Arab–Israeli War, four years after the film of concentration camps reached Britain. I wasn't just a little kid growing up in a conservative and Conservative Britain of the 1950s. I was connected to a historical chain of disaster which exceeded what happened at Maine Road and Old Trafford on Saturday afternoons.

In every Jewish house there was a blue-and-white box decorated with the Star of David, the flag of the new State of Israel. Every spare penny went into that box. It was like an insurance policy, a hedge against a time when we would be forced to move on, as our grandparents had been forced to move on half a century before. Over my bed was a framed certificate proclaiming to the world that fifty trees had been planted in my name in Israel. I was inordinately proud of those trees. I never got to see them and nobody ever satisfactorily explained precisely where they were, but they were there somewhere and they were mine, a tiny bulwark of faith in the future of the Jewish people, who had been on the run since AD 70 when Solomon's Temple had been destroyed by the Romans.

I was raised in the Orthodox faith, which meant men and women sitting separately in synagogue, everyone walking from home to the service and cultivating a fine contempt for the Reform *shul* where men and women sat together and, horror of horrors, the service was conducted (at least partly) in English. Surely this was an abomination before the Lord. Religious services were supposed to be conducted in Hebrew, which I struggled to read and couldn't understand at all.

For the High Holy Days, which come crowded together in September and October, the synagogue was full to overflowing. On Yom Kippur, the Day of Atonement, a man would pass among the congregation squirting something out of what looked like a bicycle pump with a tin on the end. I was informed it was air freshener, but it reminded me strongly of whatever it was my mother used to spray insect poison on the plants.

I have long maintained a scepticism about my religion, without ever denying that I am a Jew. It stemmed from those early days, cooped up with men who behaved as if they had the secret of life but were unwilling to pass it on – not in English, anyway. Whatever you did was wrong. It was axiomatic. One of the great sins was to go into the synagogue, or leave the place, *at the wrong time in the service*. One day, caught short and desperate for immediate relief, I made this classic error.

The irritating part of it was that I had consulted Jeff, whose learning in these matters I considered superior to my own. We then waited until we felt it was safe to exit, which I did at record speed. I was pursued into the toilets by the warden, who was red-faced with anger. 'Don't ever, *ever* leave *shul* again in the middle of the Kaddusha!' he yelled at me. I wanted to remonstrate with him, to enquire why it was all right for him to pursue me but not all right for me in the first place, and if God had needed me inside that urgently, how come he instituted that call of nature in the first place? Instead, I turned red and started to cry.

Despite his superior learning, Jeff suffered equal humiliation. After his barmitzvah, Jeff was permitted to carry out the duties of the Cohens, the holiest tribe of all the Jews. At a particular point in the service, the Cohens would leave the congregation and go into the washroom, followed by the second tribe, the Levys. Ritually, the Levys wash the hands of the Cohens and the Cohens remove their shoes. The difficult bit for Jeff was the shoes. To his horror, as he kicked off his shoes without undoing the laces, in the practised way young boys do, he discovered he had a hole in his sock. Not a small hole or a thinning of the material through which bare flesh could just about be discerned, but an enormous hole revealing the entire length of his big toe.

As the horror presented itself to him, the order came for them all to return to the synagogue. The idea is that the Cohens line up in front of the Ark (where the sacred Scrolls of the Law are kept) with their backs to the congregation. They put a prayer shawl over their heads, holding it in front of their faces with their hands – the thumbs of the hands must be touching, with the fingers parted between the middle and third finger – very much like Mr Spock in *Star Trek*. The Cohens then turn to face the congregation, chanting the priestly blessing. Jeff, feeling that he was destroying five thousand years of unblemished rectitude, turned the wrong way in trying to tread on the end of his sock in order to obscure the hole from the horrified gaze of the congregants. Jeff's only hope was the belief is that if you gaze upon the priests you will go blind. It is at least a neat Jewish variation on the traditional reason for going blind in adolescence.

Jeff, like most of my friends, went to *cheder*, Hebrew

School, twice a week in the afternoons, after school. Michael Chadwick left school early nearly every afternoon to prepare for this momentous ritual. It probably contributed towards Mrs Newlands's dislike of him. Jeff was taken down to *cheder* for the first time by his father, who insisted that the boys stop playing football long enough to listen to his introduction. 'This is Jeffrey and he's only five but he's going to be the best footballer in the world.' Mr Cohen didn't believe in doing things by halves. The surly group of seven- and eight-year-olds stared with evident hostility at the newcomer. 'Come on,' exhorted Mr Cohen, 'kick the ball to him.' Reluctantly, the ball was rolled slowly in Jeff's direction. He wound himself up and launched an almighty kick at the ball, missed it completely, skidded on the gravel and fell flat on his bottom. It was an inauspicious debut.

I didn't fancy *cheder*, just as I didn't fancy the Jewish Scouts, the Jewish Lads Brigade or any other form of Jewish youth assembly. Instead I had private Hebrew lessons at home, which cost my mother ten shillings. This was an attempt to get me to read and speak Hebrew and, from the age of eleven onwards, to prepare for my barmitzvah. Interspersed with that was a study of Biblical history, which was the only part of the exercise I really enjoyed.

By the time the great day dawned, I was thoroughly fed up with the whole thing. The original purpose, as I understood it, was to mark the passage from boyhood to manhood. I was fine with the concept, although already I was unsure that I cared greatly about being accepted into a community of hypocrites, men who forbade their sons to play football on Saturday but went to work themselves, men who pursued little boys into the toilets to shout at them as if they had committed a criminal offence.

It was no longer a celebration of the rites of passage; it was, as I say, a display of parental spending-power. Who booked the most prestigious hall for the reception, the best caterer? The kids became equally avaricious. Who got the most presents, the biggest cheques? I didn't feel I was coming home to a community which cared about me, valued what I might contribute. I felt more at home in the Hornby Stand at Old Trafford watching Lancashire, or caught up in the fervour of the crowd at Maine Road as they yelled abuse at Les McDowall.

The Manchester comedian Al Read used a line in one of his monologues which spoke volumes about the behaviour induced by social ceremonies. 'There was enough said,' he intoned meaningfully, 'at our Enid's wedding.' My brother's barmitzvah in 1955 had been the occasion of the breakdown in relations between my father and his London-based family, some of whom, we believed, denigrated our provincial ways. My own barmitzvah seemed to widen the breach with Uncle Laurence.

He was never the same jokey figure after he moved to London. Divorced from the routines we had enjoyed at rugby and cricket matches in Manchester, the atmosphere he now created felt tense and awkward. I spent one Easter holiday at his new home in Hampstead when there were moments of the old magic, mostly when we walked up the road to Hampstead Heath, hammered three stumps into the ground and cousin Ronnie bowled as fast as he could while I tried to pull him through midwicket into the long undergrowth. This part of the Heath, I am informed by my local paper, is now the preserve of gay men cruising for sex.

Laurence had married a beautiful girl called Ada, whom he had met while on service in Palestine when it was still part of the British Mandate. My mother and her sister despised Ada for being unable to bake her own cakes, but kept their disapproval from their brother. Ada brought her parents to live with her and Laurence. They were refugees from Hungary who had fled to Palestine before Hitler could send them to a concentration camp. They were called Mimi and Papu, because they were Ada's mother and father. They weren't, however, my Mimi and Papu, and I resented being forced to call them so.

It seemed like Laurence was coercing me into a betrayal of my own parents, which, in view of what was shortly to follow, might well have been the case. Previously, I had copied his opinions because he was the only adult I knew who cared what children thought. Now I felt he only cared about children if they copied his opinions – a very different concept. For a man who publicly struggled against any manifestation of fascism or colonialism, from Henry Brooke, the unpopular Home Secretary, to the MCC (a short step), Laurence was paradoxically dictatorial at home. He seemed now to be more tolerant of the Nigerian rebel leader Chief Enaharo, on whose behalf he spent considerable time campaigning, than his own children. A split was coming.

The dominant memory of that Easter holiday in London is clamouring to be taken to White Hart Lane to watch Manchester City. Persistence clearly paid off, because Laurence eventually subcontracted the task to Ada's sister's boyfriend. This was the season before their glorious Double but as Easter approached, Tottenham were pushing Burnley hard for the title. The match against City was to be followed by a local derby against Chelsea. They badly needed to beat City who, for their part, also needed the points just as urgently to stay up, even though it wasn't quite the desperate times of the previous season's D-Day.

Playing in a bizarre change strip of yellow, City were soon reduced to their traditional performance of scrambling, last-ditch defence. Dave Ewing, sadly approaching the twilight of his career, coped well with the constant threat of the England international centre-forward Bobby Smith, and

Bert Trautmann was at his magnificent best. He had to be, because Denis Law was already a limping passenger on the right wing and Spurs completely dominated the midfield. Finally, the constant pressure took its toll and Cliff Sear, the gangling left-back with legs like Bambi's on ice, handled the ball in the area. The White Hart Lane crowd screamed as the referee pointed to the spot. Cliff Jones, the Welsh winger, stepped up to take the penalty. Trautmann, still in inspired form, dived, blocked it but couldn't hold onto the ball. Jones moved forward and smacked it into the empty net. He wheeled away in triumph, the crowd bayed its relief. The familiar cold hand of doom clutched at my stomach.

Then came one of those decisions that gave me more faith in the existence of God than forty days and forty nights sitting in a synagogue with the most religious men in the world. Instead of pointing to the centre-circle, the referee, the saintly Mr G.W.Pullin of Bristol, was pointing to the dressing-room. A stunned crowd eventually learned that the forty-five minutes had expired when the penalty was awarded. The half was extended sufficiently for the penalty-kick to be taken, but not for the rebound to be netted.

In the Seder Night service which is recited on the First Night of Passover, there is a passage which is usually translated as: 'With a mighty hand and an outstretched arm, the Lord Our God brought us forth from Egypt, out of the house of bondage.' Ignoring what was clearly not meant as a reference to S&M, I have always seen that particular refereeing decision as deserving of similar Biblical prose. Unlike Moses, who suffered for proclaiming that he was responsible for a particular miracle performed by God for which he was in fact only the human instrument, I am not going to fall into the same trap. I am very happy to acknowledge that Mr Pullin's mighty hand and outstretched arm was dictated by God. In view of the supernatural saves Bert Trautmann made to repel the frantic Tottenham attacks in the second half, I Know That My Redeemer Liveth.

After sixty-six minutes, Bill McAdams, City's Irish centre-forward, accepted a pass from Clive Colbridge and, completely against the run of play, shot past Bill Brown for the only goal of the game. It was Easter Saturday. The miracle of the Resurrection hung over White Hart Lane that afternoon, and it seemed only just that a small portion of God's grace should descend on City. After all, it came with an infrequency that might otherwise lead a religious man to atheism.

Although City eventually finished fifteenth that year and in the bottom half of the First Division in both 1960–61 and 1961–62, they had almost achieved the dizzying heights, for that team, of a position of mid-table respectability. United declined to fifteenth in the table in 1962 and the following year fought a long battle against relegation, which was only won on the last day of the season. United's travails were one of the few sources of comfort in these trying years. Lancashire were no help at all. They plummeted from second in the County Championship in 1960 to thirteenth in 1961. In 1962, they achieved the sort of *reductio ad absurdum* of which Manchester City would have been proud.

In 1954, Lancashire had appointed Cyril Washbrook to be their first professional captain. Washbrook retired after the 1959 season and the talented young amateur R.W.Barber, of Ruthin School and Cambridge University, was appointed in his place. Forbidden to stay in the same hotel as the rest of his team, Bob Barber cut an increasingly unhappy figure, failing to fulfil his own undoubted talents and watching his team of Geoff Pullar, Peter Marner, Ken Grieves, Brian Statham, Ken Higgs and Tommy Greenhough signally underachieve. The Lancashire committee, which had plucked him from the ranks and then made his task impossible by the limitations they had imposed on him, responded in the traditional way of bureaucracy. Barber was sacked as captain after the end of the disastrous 1961 season.

Instead of learning that times had changed and that amateur captains belonged to an age before Elvis Presley and commercial television – those twin evils of the modern age – the committee renewed its search for an amateur captain. They eventually arrived at J.F.Blackledge, a thirty-three-year-old whose deeds had failed to excite the Northern League in which he played for Chorley CC. Blackledge wasn't worth his place in the county side as batsman, bowler or captain, and a full-scale mutiny followed. Shortly after the end of the most disastrous year in Lancashire's history, Black-ledge was also relieved of the captaincy and Barber sought permission to move to Warwickshire, where he blossomed into a fine attacking opening batsman and useful leg-break bowler, winning 28 Test caps.

Meanwhile, I was struggling in the school cricket team. In 1961, my first summer, I batted at number three in the Under-12s. The following year we discovered there was no Under-13 team, but for some unknown reason our year and the one above were joined together and then divided by two to form an Under-14 first XI and an Under-14 second XI. To add to all the other miseries I was suffering from, I was selected for the second XI, not the firsts, despite the fact that I was the best slip-fielder around and I genuinely turned the ball on the rain-sodden turf we played on.

There was an incident in my first year which might have had some bearing on the decision. We played Xaverian College, a Catholic school in south Manchester, where the master in charge of cricket wore a long black cassock and an intimidating cross, instead of the traditional anonymous white coat. We were instructed firmly that on arrival in the middle we were to ask for a guard with 'Centre, please, Father' rather than the usual 'Centre (or middle-and-leg), please, sir.' Faced with this daunting vision at the other end of the wicket, I refused to submit to further tyranny by the Catholic Church. The Crusades, I had recently learned, were an excuse for European Christians to ride through the continent and Asia Minor like mediaeval football hooligans, slaughtering Jews along the way.

Here was my chance to stand up for my people. 'Centre, please,' I said firmly, eyes riveted on the cross. I was given centre. At least, I was given a guard of some description. The second ball was a full toss, swinging away down the leg side. I launched a David Gower-like airy flick at it, hoping to send it whistling over the boundary at deep fine-leg. It missed the bat and struck the pad. A raucous shout went up from the fielders on the boundary at deep extra-cover and third man. The black-garbed figure straightened and raised his index finger like a Crusader knight hacking down the helpless Jews in his path. Another pyrrhic victory to the Church of Rome.

When it was time for us to take the field, I thought it politic to ask to bowl from the end our master was umpiring, but that left Michael Alexander, who looked even more Jewish than I did, to bowl from the Vatican End. I can't remember the exact result, but I suspect Xaverian College maintained their unbeaten run against us. In 1987, during the time of the notorious Shakoor Rana–Mike Gatting incident, I felt a curious sense of *déjà vu*. Those bizarre umpiring decisions that always seemed to go against the visiting team, where could he have learned them? Was it possible that Xaverian College had been harbouring an Islamic militant in its midst?

Was it my Gatting-like truculence that caused me to be omitted from the Under-14 firsts? I fear we shall never know. The summer of 1962 continued to provide misery both on and off the field. My report for the school year ending in July was full of Bs and Cs, with the inevitable F for Physics. 'He has

89

not managed to make up for the work he has missed yet,' wrote Mr Andrews, the new Physics teacher who had taken over from Joe Plug. I had been absent twenty-six times over that term. My form master, who liked me, wrote, 'He must make a real effort to recover lost ground' and then, with one of those phrases which teachers write because they think parents will like them, he added, 'He is a very happy boy.' For a boy who was pretty much sunk in misery most of that year, I still find that an extraordinarily unperceptive comment.

Shortly after school finished, I travelled with my parents to Cornwall for the annual holiday. We had spent the summers of 1958 and 1959 in a hotel just outside St Ives. They had been very happy, Blytonesque vacations despite the awful journey from Manchester, nearly twelve hours, longer than it now takes to fly to Los Angeles. We would park in a field near the Clifton suspension bridge outside Bristol and eat our sandwiches, looking down on the River Avon. We reckoned this spot was halfway to our destination. Then years later, my college team and the women of Somerville College, Oxford, were locked at level points in a desperately closely fought *University Challenge* game. Bamber Gascoigne's final starter for ten was: 'Which river flows under the Clifton suspension bridge?' He was hardly to know our family's travel habits, and we sneaked into the quarter-finals on the basis of those lunch stops.

For the summer of 1962, we went to Newquay. The Cornwall magic was missing this time. My brother, who was now nearly twenty, was too old for family holidays. He had won a much coveted place at Gonville & Caius College, Cambridge, and was going to start there in October. He spent the summer with his Jewish youth club somewhere in Europe, leaving me to trail along after my arguing parents. It wasn't just the arguments that made it so miserable. It was the feeling that these weren't rows which could be made up and forgotten about. These were rows which were symptomatic of a far deeper malaise. I couldn't wait for the holiday to end. Anything was better than this, even watching Lancashire. Then I watched Lancashire under the captaincy of J.F.Blackledge and found that it wasn't really.

Ironically, as a treat, I was taken to the film that was playing at the only cinema in Newquay. It was the movie that had made headlines everywhere that summer, the film version of Leonard Bernstein's *West Side Story*, directed by Robert Wise. It was indeed a wonderful movie and I fell desperately in love with Natalie Wood as she mimed, 'I feel pretty.' To this day, Bernstein's music, brilliant as it is, evokes that summer of misery. I just wanted it to end. That was why I couldn't wait for the start of the new football season. City would come along and dissolve this cloud of doom which hung over me. Ha! As Liza Minelli sings, echoing the thoughts of all football supporters, 'Maybe this time . . .'

I was sitting on the beach in Newquay when I heard that familiar signature tune to *Sports Report*, which confirmed that soccer was back. City were the leading headline. We had lost the first game of the season to Wolverhampton Wanderers 8–1. For a moment, I thought it was some kind of a joke. This is the sort of score we get in a schools game when we are up against a team that can only find eight boys, the class cissy and a fat boy wearing glasses. The report from Molineux soon made it clear, however, that this was no mistake. Eight goals had been thumped past the hapless Trautmann. City's single reply was, appropriately, an own goal.

There were two consequences. City immediately signed centre-forward Alex Harley from the now defunct Scottish club Third Lanark for a paltry £17,500. It was one of McDowall's smarter moves in the transfer market. On 5 September, Harley scored twice as City won for the first time that season. The other consequence was that the defence got worse. On 8 September, City were beaten 6–1 at home by

West Ham United and Bert Trautmann was sent off. Jeff Cohen was in shock. After eight games, City had gained four points and conceded twenty-seven goals.

The first derby match of the season found City at the foot of the table. United had just signed Denis Law for £115,000 from Torino. We knew how brilliant Denis was, and it was no surprise to see him score twice against us. What was more of a surprise was that Peter Dobing had given us the lead from a penalty and Joe Hayes doubled it before Denis squared things for the Reds. We stood there in the Paddock as United threatened to overwhelm us. Surely we couldn't hold out for a point. We couldn't. We didn't. With the penultimate kick of the match, the real Bobby Kennedy belted the ball out of defence. Alex Harley and his marker, centre-half Bill Foulkes, chased it as it bounced towards the United penalty area. David Gaskell came out to collect it but Harley got there first and smashed it past him into the net. The referee blew for full-time before United could restart the game.

Victory over United was always a harbinger of things to come. I truly believed my year of disasters was now officially over. City were going to climb the table; Lancashire had sacked Blackledge and next season promised 'Brighter Cricket' and the new one-day knockout cup, sponsored by Gillette. Two days after that unbelievable derby victory at Old Trafford, my mother banged her head on the skirting board while doing her daily keep-fit exercises. She was taken as a precaution to Crumpsall Hospital for a check-up. A week later she was dead.

Chapter Five

Even at a distance of thirty-five years, the memory of my mother's death retains its powers of devastation. A few years ago I took my children to visit her grave. Like all Jewish cemeteries, the one outside Oldham is notable for its lack of ostentation. Stones, not flowers, are placed on the grave to indicate a visit. I had no means of isolating my mother's grave from the hundreds of others surrounding it, except by walking up and down the rows until I found a headstone marked 1962. Even this wasn't foolproof, and the children joined in the game as we wandered around the deserted cemetery on a day overcast by lowering rain clouds in a slate-grey sky. Dickie Bird would have been fussing over his light meter and shepherding everyone into the pavilion long ago. Then we found it.

I had been fine till that moment. I was keen to show the children the headstone of the grandmother they never knew, but it wasn't a particularly heavy task for any of us. The moment I found the grave and read the words carved onto the marble slab, it all changed. I was transported to that black night in September 1962 and the tears erupted as if a tap had been turned on. The children clutched my hand to theirs and the moment eventually passed, but it was terrifying to experience that sense of utter desolation again, and sobering to realise that the passage of more than a quarter of a century had failed to diminish the power of her death.

It was all so innocuous. One Monday night, she kissed me goodnight and turned out the light. I left the house at five to eight in the morning, so I never expected to see her until I got home from school. That day, my brother, who had left school the previous summer, found me during afternoon break. He told me the story of the accident and that my mother would be kept in hospital overnight for observation. I was to spend the night with my aunt and her two daughters, who lived half a mile away.

I wasn't unduly alarmed since my brother made it sound so routine, although I wasn't that crazy about staying the night with my aunt, whom I found a very cold woman who interspersed her indifference with disconcerting moments of over-exuberant emotionalism. The following day, I was told that 'the best surgeon in England' was going to be operating on my mother on Friday. A small doubt entered my mind, but was dismissed in the face of such certainty. What was the operation for? And if it was an operation to the head, wasn't that rather dangerous? It was many years later that I learned that the post mortem revealed she had a congenital weakness in the blood vessel which burst in her head. On Friday night after school, I was told the operation had been a triumphant success. I clamoured to see her, but was told I would have to wait for the hospital to give its approval, which might be another couple of days.

I spent the weekend with my cousins but was counting the hours before I could return home, with my mother in fully restored health. The following school week began with no further news but I remained hopeful, even when Monday night came and went with no more indication of when I could see her. On the Tuesday, I came home from school and I noticed that the cars of both of my parents' best friends were outside my aunt's house.

I thought it was odd and slightly worrying. I couldn't at that moment conceive of a situation that would necessitate the presence of both of them during a working day. Certainly not at my aunt's house, as they didn't know her well. I walked round the side of the house to the back door (children were not allowed in by the front door). As I came into the kitchen I saw my father, with his glasses off, coming towards me, crying. Beyond him were his friends, with bleak faces, and my brother, also crying. My aunt took my briefcase from me. In Hollywood films, characters always say at these moments, 'Is she . . .?' I recall no words at all, but I recall those images in every detail.

The next week is a blur. I was terrified I would be made to go and watch my mother being buried in a hole in the ground. My brother ensured I was spared that particular nightmare. A year later when it was time for the unveiling of the headstone, a ceremony in Jewish religious practice signifying the end of the official period of mourning, I claimed a similar indulgence. This time it was refused. A fleet of cars drove the five miles to the cemetery. I kept my eyes firmly shut, partly to avoid looking at anyone and anything, and partly to stem the avalanche of tears which still cascaded down my cheeks from eyes clenched tightly shut. When the Rabbi mentioned my mother by name, a low sob escaped me. He didn't know her. What right had he to talk about her?

The night of her death, I was sent to bed by my aunt with a toilet roll. Kleenex was considered a luxury and a toilet roll was a more practical object to be used during the night. My aunt was right. When she came in the following morning, the toilet roll was reduced to its cardboard base. I had cried my way through the entire roll.

In the Jewish religion, for seven days after the burial, the house of the loved one holds a service where there is much wailing and rending of garments. This is called sitting *shiva*. I learned later that Jeff Cohen was told he was going to the *shiva* house to pay his respects whether he wanted to or not. He certainly didn't want to. That same day, he had been to Frost's the barbers and, as a City supporter, he had been given not just the traditional bad haircut but an Oscar-winning horrendous one, leaving tufts of hair standing upright like on a cartoon character. His parents insisted, he resisted and the disagreement developed into a row and consequent tears. Dragged unwillingly into the car, Jeff now faced the prospect of greeting me, not knowing what to say, mortified by Frost's horrible haircut and thinking that his tears would be regarded as a weird demonstration of sorrow at the death of my mother, whom he had barely known. In the event, of course, I wasn't even there, it having been deemed wiser to keep me at my aunt's for the week although because my mother died just before the start of the Jewish New Year the *shiva* house lasted only two nights. Jeff's demonstration of solidarity, though much appreciated in later life, was entirely pointless, prompting still further tears.

In theory Jews deal with death very well. The body is buried quickly, a consequence of mortality in the Middle East where letting bodies decompose in the heat was a clear sanitary risk. Sitting *shiva* is supposed to be a way of letting all the rage and grief out of the system in a way that is officially sanctioned. Thereafter, prayers for the dead are said every Sabbath until the headstone is unveiled and the period of mourning is officially over. Didn't work for me.

I was allowed to remain off school for three days. The following Monday I was back. Although everybody knew what had happened, nobody mentioned a word. I apologised to the Physics teacher for not doing the weekend's homework. He looked deeply embarrassed and said I could catch up the work later. It was as if a policy decision had been announced in my absence never to refer to Shindler's tragedy. It was perhaps a way of allowing me to cope in private. There is no doubt that an arm round the shoulder from someone, anyone, and a word of comfort would have caused me to collapse again – but I desperately wanted to hear that word, and it never came.

About a month later, I was walking through the centre of Manchester when I saw one of my mother's close friends coming towards me. I gathered my strength, forced my mouth into a smile and saw the look of relief as it flashed over her face in response. We passed a polite word or two, as meaningless as two characters in a Victorian novel of manners, and went our separate ways. The pain was buried underground. It took years to emerge.

Uncle Laurence came from London for the funeral. I was pleased to see him again and I thought he understood the depth of my grief. He bought me the recently published *The Boundary Book*, a miscellany of stories and articles about cricket. It was exactly what I wanted at the time and it sits on my shelf still. I thought that the tragedy and this gift was the start of a rapprochement. I was sadly mistaken. I learned shortly afterwards that Laurence had consistently urged my father to send me to boarding school, presumably Carmel College, which was the only recognised Jewish public school.

To my unspeakable relief my brother Geoff again stood up for me, telling Laurence that I had enough to cope with at the moment without being sent away from Manchester. Laurence was appalled at Geoff's effrontery and let him know in no uncertain terms that he didn't propose to take any notice of someone he thought was still a kid himself. In the event, my brother's courageous stand was backed by my father and Laurence retreated, though, in view of later events, he must have done so vowing the revenge which he exacted in the future. The thought of being sent away from Manchester at the time of my greatest distress was too horrible to contemplate.

How could Laurence have advocated it except out of expediency? Something in me died the day I found out.

My mother died on 25 September 1962. After the funeral my brother unselfishly offered to transfer to Manchester University in order to stay at home and look after me. The offer, I'm sure to his relief, was rejected but I remain deeply touched by it. Instead, like a World War One hero, we said goodbye to him as he left for the railway station. Three weeks later it was the school half term and my father and I drove across country to Cambridge, where we found Geoff had been allocated a room at the top of C staircase in St Michael's Court. This was my first experience of a lifestyle which had previously been restricted to the pages of *Tom Brown's School-days*, Billy Bunter books and other escapades set in the world of the public school. Life there seemed full of pranks in the dorm and Latin conjugations, tuck shops and cricket matches played on long hot summer afternoons. It was, however, only something to be admired from afar, for the prospect of actually going to boarding school filled me with alarm. Cambridge was different. I wanted to go to Cambridge the minute I set eyes on the place.

The traditions of public school, attractive as they were in the pages of novels, held no charms for me in view of my inability to settle easily into those of Bury Grammar School. The traditions of Cambridge University, however little I absorbed of them from my brother, I found instantly magnetic. I never discussed it with anyone because I knew it would arouse incredulity among the teachers, who mistook my shyness for ineptitude. But the ambition to go to Cambridge bubbled away fiercely for the next five years.

The journey home was one of the most agonising I have ever made. It was an October evening and the autumn sunshine, which had illuminated the colleges and their sports fields, had now disappeared. I can still experience a trace of what I felt that day as I drive home from the last match of the cricket season, which I play at the end of September in Eltisley, a small village between Cambridge and St Neots. The sight and smell of burning stubble in the flat Fenland fields soon evokes those feelings of desolation and despair. Although logic and experience dictates that spring will eventually arrive and the world will burst into life again, it can't assuage the depth of melancholy brought on by those early autumnal evening mists. With my mother dead, my brother installed in a new world and my father still struggling to earn a living, I felt on that long cross-country journey back to Manchester that I was incarcerated for life in a prison of my own pain.

My mother had been a post-war housewife. She had left school at fifteen to help her parents and had neither expected nor wanted a career. As far as I am aware, particularly given the mores of the age in which she lived, being a good mother was all she aspired to. Although I adored her, I recognised that she had her bigoted moments. One of the few non-Jewish boys I ever invited back for tea was Dave Hutton, our Under-12 wicketkeeper, who started out at number four in the batting order and finished the season at number eleven. When I invited him to the house a second time, he looked a little anxious. 'Will your mother be there?' he asked. I was puzzled. Of course she would be there. She was always there. You needed a fork-lift truck to get her out of the place. Dave never returned for a second visit.

We went to watch Lancashire at Old Trafford instead. Walking round the ground, I met Brian Statham, our heroic fast bowler. I pleaded for his autograph, assuring him that 'my uncle, Laurence Weidberg, sends his regards.' Laurence knew the players, which impressed me mightily. Statham signed with a smile. I fled back to Dave Hutton, told him of my encounter and together we raced back to the spot where Statham had last been seen. There he was, still in conversation. We hovered. We swooped. Another autograph safely collected. Later that day, I met Noddy Pullar but only had with me my scorebook. I got him to sign the back of the stiff cover, but it was like carving into marble with a penknife. I decided to ink in where Pullar had left his outline. Dave Hutton instantly declared the autograph invalid. I contested the ruling as bitterly as Middlesbrough fought for the restoration of their three points deducted by the Premier League. The final result was identical.

There remained the awkward problem of who was to look after me after school. At the age of thirteen, I was not permitted to become a latchkey child. It was an accepted tradition that the Jewish community was close enough to support each other through crises like these. Without any consultation with me, a routine eventually emerged. I was to go to one house on Mondays and Tuesdays, another one on Wednesdays and Thursdays, to my grandfather's after school on Friday and to the synagogue on Saturday mornings, followed by lunch at yet another house.

Sundays were spent on homework and watching my father struggling with the washing machine and the oven, pretending to be my mother. He did his best but it wasn't the same. My mother's natural domain was the kitchen and she ruled her kingdom with an iron hand. Pots and pans and other inhabitants obeyed her every wish. My father strove manfully to cope with the insurrection of the inanimate objects brought on by years of my mother's dictatorship over them.

Over lunch, there was a brief palliative for the pain I was feeling when I insisted we listened to *The Navy Lark/Round the Horne/The Clitheroe Kid*/Al Read/Ken Dodd. I grew addicted to those radio comedies not necessarily because they made me laugh (*The Clitheroe Kid*, in particular, caused me to squirm in embarrassment) but because I felt an affinity with the art of making people laugh. These must have been the first stirrings of a desire to forge a career in show business. The comedies were succeeded by *The Billy Cotton Band Show* and then the Cliff Adams Singers in *Sing Something Simple*. The first note of this latter programme would plunge me into despair. It was a symbol that Sunday night was almost upon me and that it would be succeeded inevitably by Monday morning and the prospect of still further misery at school.

The only time during the whole week when I came alive was for a few hours on Saturday afternoons. After the post-synagogue lunch, once the watch hands had crept round with agonising slowness to twenty to two, I was allowed to leave the house of the kind people who had taken me in. I would race up Scholes Lane to Grand Lodge, where the four of us, Jeff Cohen, Michael Chadwick and David Green and I, would wait for the number 75 bus to take us to Maine Road.

Maine Road – and, on alternate Saturdays, Old Trafford – became my home. I was at one with the crowd, sharing a common experience, a common purpose. What had been a passionate interest in my team developed in that season of 1962–63 into a fanatical obsession. I had seen the occasional game before, but now, in the absence of my mother, Manchester City filled the vacuum in my life. City gave me a reason to carry on living. The whole ritual of going to the game became important. After the escape from the Sabbath table and the bus journey, there was even the welcome sight of an old man in a bowler hat parading up and down the forecourt outside the Main Stand, holding up the sign: 'THE END OF THE WORLD IS NIGH.' After yet another wretched home defeat, the end of the world no longer felt merely imminent.

It cost three shillings to sit in the Platt Lane Stand, now a miserable gimcrack testament to the cheapskate nature of the Swales era. If you were over fourteen years of age, the price dramatically escalated to five shillings. The four of us remained under fourteen until we reached a collective age of seventy-two. Into the ground we went, pushing aside the rusty turnstile, buying the match programme for another sixpence, climbing the iron staircase and looking through the holes in its floor as we got higher and higher to emerge finally at the back of the stand, rather breathless but with that seductive combination of pristine green grass carpet and the rapidly filling, imposing and enclosing dark terraces laid out in front of us.

As we neared the top of the staircase, the pace quickened. Even if it wasn't yet twenty to three and the kick-off was over twenty minutes away, we ran to the top, desperately afraid that we might miss something, anything, of significance. We could hear the murmur of the crowd's expectancy increasing as we got nearer to the ground. They must be reacting to something important. In the bowels of the Main Stand, our heroes were loosening up, listening to the last-minute words of tactical brilliance from Les McDowall which would lead to the inevitable triumph.

The triumphs were few and far between that year. We remained unbeaten from December to March, but only because we played just three matches in three months. It was the winter of the Great Freeze. The FA Cup third round tie against Walsall was postponed ten times and the Cup final itself was not played until the last Saturday in May because of the backlog of fixtures. In the days before undersoil heating, no pitch stood a chance against the ravages of the icy weather. Just when I seemed to have found a means of getting through the week, the Hand of God stretched out and presented it to the Pools Panel instead. The Panel was chaired by the war hero Douglas Bader, who had played rugby before the war but knew nothing about football – and was therefore considered the perfect dispassionate observer.

United were drawn at home to Huddersfield in the third round and went to prepare for it, as was traditional, to the Norbreck Hydro, a grand hotel north of Blackpool. They were joined there in the first week of January 1963 by my father, my brother and myself. Although it was United, not City, I cannot believe that proximity to Alex Harley and Bert Trautmann could have given me much more pleasure than that which I obtained by being able to stare at the United players at consistently close quarters.

It was soon apparent which players welcomed the attention. Bill Foulkes and Bobby Charlton were particularly surly, while Denis Law was as friendly and extrovert as his exciting play had always suggested. The player whose company I most enjoyed was Tony Dunne, who had only recently been elevated to the first team and who tended to be the only other person besides myself in permanent occupation of the television lounge. Over all the players, the influence of Busby was palpable. When the Boss came into the dining-room, the footballers' table fell silent. When the match was postponed on the Friday lunchtime, Busby stopped by our table and told my brother, in that soft Scottish burr, 'The game's off, son.' It was the 'son' that made it significant. It sounded as if he had been talking to one of the players. My brother was the same age as Tony Dunne.

United went on that year to the FA Cup final. After ten postponements, City finally and fortunately defeated Third Division Walsall 1–0 and then went on to beat Bury by the same score a week later. Predictably, Alex Harley scored the only goal in both matches. Four days after the Bury match, City played their third Cup match in twelve days, losing at home 2–1 to Norwich City. This was the game in which the wing-back 2–5–3 plan was finally abandoned. McDowall's blueprint had lasted for six matches. When it was first revealed a few weeks before, in a deathly boring

1–1 draw at Leyton Orient, the *Daily Express* was moved to comment:

> The opposition forward-line is enticed into City's muscular massed defence and then barged, tackled, body-checked or enmeshed until they lose interest or their tempers.
>
> Now comes the deliberately diabolically cunning bit. When the opposition are crammed into City's half, a big kick is fired upfield so that the three forwards can rush away and score against an outnumbered defence.
>
> McDowall launched his Revie Plan in 1954 and it was vivid and exciting. But his 1963 plan is dull and destructive, the sort of scheme that might be devised, by a manager who feels he is facing relegation with a poor set of players.

Fateful words. Owing to the fact that most of January and February had been entirely wiped out by the Arctic weather, the worst experienced in Britain since the winter of 1946–47, all clubs were forced to play two, or even three matches a week. There was no moaning about this unsatisfactory state of affairs, even from Manchester United. In 1958, with most of their senior squad killed at Munich and a traumatised reserve team, buttressed by the goodwill of the rest of the world United managed to finish the season without demanding an extension. How times have changed.

Locked together in spectacular incompetence, City and United spiralled down the league table. Four days after being knocked out of the Cup, City went to Goodison Park, where they took the lead against the champions-to-be, Everton, only to lose 2–1. They returned to Maine Road comforted by the quality of their much-admired general display and the discovery of a brilliant new goalkeeper, Harry Dowd, who had replaced the injured Trautmann. At home, they were pulverised 5–2 by Burnley. Dowd had a nightmare and was immediately dropped. At the end of April, City lost 5–1 at home to West Bromwich Albion and I joined the disgruntled hordes outside the main entrance to watch bricks being hurled at the windows of the administration offices. 'Sack Mac,' shouted the crowd. I joined in with gusto.

There were now six matches left, to be played in the space of eighteen days. Defeats by Blackburn, Blackpool and Aston Villa left us favourites for the drop, since our remaining games were at home to Spurs and United and away to West Ham, who had belted us 6–1 at the start of the season. The Spurs side of Greaves and Blanchflower were cruising towards the final of the European Cup-Winners' Cup, where they were to become the first British winners in Europe. They came to Maine Road and were played off the pitch. It was only 1–0, but it should have been many more. Alex Harley scored the only goal. Typical City. Inconsistent even in their ability to disappoint.

The stage was now set for the most crucial derby match of all time. United had just lost to fellow strugglers Birmingham City and were now only one point ahead of City with a game in hand. If City won this match, United would drop below them. The gates were locked with 52,424 inside and thousands more denied admission. The four of us were stuffed at the back of the Platt Lane Stand from six o'clock on a warm evening in the middle of May, as the crowd squeezed into every available space in Maine Road.

With the signing of Pat Crerand, bought from Celtic for £50,000 in February, United's line-up, including a forward-line which read Quixall, Giles, Herd, Law and Charlton, now looked formidable. They trotted out with their traditional air of superiority. They had taken only eight points from the previous fifteen games, but their form in the Cup had been good and they were considered 'too good to go down'. It would be a pleasure to disprove the adage and give them a helpful shove in the direction of Division Two.

City were by far the superior side that night and should have won comfortably, a fact endorsed even by the press, which has always been biased in United's favour. Over the years, City supporters have uncomplainingly accepted that the press is run by and for the Red half of Manchester, much as the Labour Party had to accept during the Thatcher years that the national press, with two broadsheet and one tabloid exceptions, were unofficial Tory spokesmen. Not even the Red press could complain when City took an early lead. Bobby Charlton lost the ball, which was whipped out wide to Joe Hayes and transferred inside to Peter Dobing. He slipped a perfect through-ball into the path of the predatory Alex Harley, who shot unerringly past Gaskell. City were ahead after less than ten minutes and it was nothing less than their play had warranted.

In the Platt Lane Stand, we had acclaimed the goal, exulted in the superiority of our play and been worried sick every time United carried the ball over the halfway line. In the first half, this happened infrequently as United, thoroughly out of sorts, only kept the score down to one by virtue of three good saves from Gaskell and some timely interceptions by Nobby Stiles. United's other hero was the referee, who disallowed a perfectly legitimate second goal by Harley which might have changed the destiny of a nation. Instead, it was a free-kick to United for offside.

Tempers shortened and just before half-time, Crerand tangled with Wagstaffe in a particularly ugly incident. Both were booked and could count themselves fortunate to stay on the pitch. For all his skill, Crerand was short of pace and Waggy's dazzling bursts down the left wing were threatening to settle the game in City's favour. It was later alleged that Wagstaffe had also punched Crerand, which the Scottish wing-half hadn't greatly enjoyed. He planned an appropriate revenge. As the teams left the field in the interval, Crerand thumped the unsuspecting Wagstaffe, who was laid out on the floor of the tunnel.

'Did you see that, ref?' called an incensed City player.

'No,' said the referee bravely and scuttled away into the security of his dressing-room.

One man who had seen it was Busby. The United manager stormed into the dressing-room and rounded on Crerand. 'Did you just hit David Wagstaffe?' he demanded. Crerand gulped, and answered as only a United player brought up in the honourable traditions of Busby's Manchester United would, in such a situation. 'No,' he said. Busby was speechless, and couldn't, apparently, think of a riposte to this denial. Anyway, he soon decided he had other pressing matters to which his attention had to be directed, but so angry were the City players that they reported the attack on Waggy to the FA, although they didn't point the finger directly at Crerand. As with John Major's response to the hundreds of pages of testimony in the Scott Report, it was officially decided that there wasn't enough evidence to prosecute, although after the reports in all the papers, everyone knew what Crerand had done – as he himself will cheerfully admit today.

The second half continued as the first, with the Blues well on top. Alex Harley went desperately close with a header and could easily have had a hat-trick on the night. At the back of the Platt Lane Stand, the four of us didn't talk about the possibility of something going wrong, for fear of inducing calamity. In the event, it happened anyway. With five minutes to go, the collective anxiety felt by the City supporters clearly transmitted itself to the players and Wagstaffe sent a stupid, stupid, stupid thirty-yard back-pass in the general direction of Harry Dowd.

Denis Law, thankfully anonymous all evening, seized on the loose ball. Dowd came racing out of his goal to close him down. Law turned away from goal towards the corner flag.

Dowd dived to the ground and tried to knock the ball away for a corner. Law fell over. The linesman signalled a corner, but the referee pointed to the spot. Dowd frantically maintained he had grabbed the ball. Law just as fervently claimed then, and still claims, that Dowd grabbed his ankle. That old familiar sinking feeling clutched our stomachs. Quixall stuck the penalty away with most of his team-mates not daring to watch – whether out of anxiety or embarrassment it wasn't clear.

It was a scandal, but it was fact. City, their hearts broken, went to Upton Park knowing that even if they won, it wouldn't be enough if United took a point off the already-relegated Leyton Orient. United duly beat Orient and City decided to cave in to West Ham, losing to them for the second time that season by the conclusive margin of six goals to one. United went on to win the FA Cup and inaugurate the golden years of Busby's third great United team. City went into the Second Division, where they stayed for three years. When Danny Baker calls on fans to picket the homes of bad referees, he is touching a very sensitive spot in all true supporters.

Three days after United returned in triumph to Manchester to parade the FA Cup, Les McDowall left Manchester City to concentrate on his business activities. It was never clarified what these activities might have been, but it did leave City supporters to wonder whether he had already been concentrating on them a little too much, when he might have been more profitably engaged upon the affairs of the team he was allegedly managing.

The papers were filled with rumours that Ken Barnes, player-manager at Wrexham, and more interestingly Don Revie, who had just taken over at Leeds United, might be returning to take charge at Maine Road. Unsurprisingly, the job actually went to George Poyser, McDowall's chief scout and assistant who smoked his pipe so much it had worn all his teeth away. Poyser was principally known for the hours he spent playing snooker and eating egg butties. Just as Busby was a players' manager, Poyser was a directors' manager. Under instructions from the boardroom, Poyser stood firm against the demands of the three 'pay rebels' – Matt Gray, Peter Dobing and Alex Harley. Each of them thought they were worth more than the £32-a-week basic wage they were being offered. Gray, a useful inside-forward who had followed his friend Harley from Third Lanark for £30,000 during the course of the season, eventually gave in and signed the new contract. Dobing and Harley held out.

The elegant Dobing, bought from Blackburn for £37,500, went to Stoke for £42,000, where he joined Stanley Matthews, Dennis Viollet and Jimmy McIlroy in a side which graced the First Division. Harley went to Birmingham City for £42,500, which represented a profit of £25,000 in one year. The transfer could be justified also on the grounds that he never repeated the phenomenal scoring feats of his only season with City.

We went to watch him when Birmingham City played at Old Trafford and took enormous pleasure in seeing him score the winner in Birmingham's 2–1 victory. Harley was like a shooting star. He appeared briefly in the sky over Moss Side, illuminating everything under him, but burnt himself up rapidly. There was clearly a character flaw there somewhere, because within a year he had left Birmingham and soon dropped out of football altogether to become a croupier. A few years later, I read that he died of a heart attack. Over the years, in conversation between David Green and myself, 'Alex Harley' has become a synonym for both 'goalscorer' and 'tragic end' – a forgotten hero to all but a few who remember that dramatic season of 1962–63.

There was one bright spot in that benighted spring. Swinton Rugby League Club, still a highly unfashionable club and the recipient of my early passion, won the Rugby League. They clinched the Championship on the day United beat

Leicester City at Wembley, and they did so in style after seventeen victories in a row. Swinton had an irresistible three-quarter line of Speed, Fleet, Buckley and Stopford. It was a headline writer's delight. More to the point, it was an enormous pleasure to watch Swinton's heroic captain, Albert Blan, lift a trophy that seemed to belong exclusively to the more fashionable clubs of Widnes, Wigan and St Helens.

I suspect I was drawn to Swinton not only because of Uncle Laurence and those early years, but also because they *were* so unfashionable. Stopford was a terrific try-scoring winger, but he lacked the charisma of Billy Boston of Wigan or Tom van Vollenhoven of St Helens. The unspectacular Ken Gowers played at either full-back or scrum-half and was a highly reliable goal-kicker in either position. Above all, there was the old warrior, loose-forward and captain Albert Blan, whose very name sounds like it might have been inscribed on a war memorial dedicated to those who lost their lives on the Somme.

However comforting Swinton's victory, it couldn't compensate for City's trauma or for what was clearly going to be a long, hard summer for Lancashire. On Whit Bank Holiday Monday, I persuaded my father to drive me over the Pennines to Bramall Lane, Sheffield, where I sat in a crowd of more than 15,000 on the hard concrete terraces of Sheffield United to watch Yorkshire pile up a first-innings lead of 233 over Lancashire, thanks to a stand of 249 between Brian Stott, who made 143, and a bespectacled newcomer whom I had never seen before. His name was Geoffrey Boycott, and it didn't take a cricket analyst of genius to recognise that the century he ground out that scorching June day was going to be the first of many.

The only light relief came from Brian Close, who had been sitting with his pads on in the pavilion as the stand rolled relentlessly on. Close came in after Stott had been caught at slip off the occasional leg-spinner Brian Booth. The Yorkshire captain swished at the first ball from Booth and missed, danced down the wicket to the next one, missed, and continued his trot back to the pavilion not bothering to turn to see if Geoff Clayton had gathered the ball cleanly and removed the bails. He had. Close eventually declared at 384 for 6 leaving Lancashire half an hour's batting, in the course of which they lost two wickets. The following day, they never looked like improving on their first-innings total of 151. Don Wilson took five for 57 and Lancashire lost by an innings and plenty before lunch on the third day, their last two wickets falling to stupid run-outs.

Sitting high up on the terraces, I could see the chimneys of the last few dark satanic mills and their smoke as it curled wistfully into the still air. The reason it became memorable was that Boycott's century coincided with the day Pope John XXIII died, and white smoke was shortly to arise from the Vatican to proclaim the advent of Pope Paul VI. It became even more memorable when I realised that, in addition to an agonisingly cramped bottom, I had inadvertently acquired two very sunburnt arms. Somehow the combination of physical discomfort, Yorkshire triumphing routinely in the Roses match and the death of the Pope were peculiarly apposite to that first long innings by Geoffrey Boycott.

That half-term holiday of 1963 was crowded with significant events. Thursday 6 June, which all the papers referred to as D-Day, evoking yet more painful memories, saw the announcement of the resignation of the War Minister, John Profumo. Like other adolescent boys, I was unaware at the time how significant this was to be for the development of my sex life. More important to me was that we were still out of school for the first three days of the first Test between England and the West Indies, which was to be played at Old Trafford.

Without the influence of Uncle Laurence, I was reduced to sitting on the grass behind the boundary rope underneath the Clock Stand. It was from there that we saw Brian

111

Statham, our great Lancastrian hero, drop a straightforward catch from the West Indies opener Joey Carew off the bowling of Fred Trueman. Trueman made amends by getting Carew caught behind shortly afterwards, but the other opener, Conrad Hunte, went on to reach 182 before he was out after lunch on the second day. His dismissal brought in the skipper Frank Worrell, who, despite being missed twice by Brian Close, scored 74 of the silkiest, most memorable runs ever to grace Old Trafford. Regardless of the butchery of my hero's bowling, I was glad I was there to see Worrell late-cut Statham to the third-man fence off successive balls. His innings consisted of 15 fours and 14 singles.

Worrell eventually declared at 501 for 6, and then came an equally memorable sight. The Surrey pair John Edrich and Mickey Stewart came out to face Wes Hall and Charlie Griffith, who had clearly been straining at the leash for an hour or so. When Wes Hall marked out his run, I thought he was joking – he seemed to walk back to within a couple of yards of the sightscreen. He tossed down the metal disc and limbered up as the imperturbable Edrich took guard.

Just as Wes Hall seemed seven feet tall, so John Edrich looked minuscule in comparison. I feared for his life. Hall seemed to push off from the sightscreen as he came pounding up to the wicket, a gold crucifix flapping against his bare chest. Before the end of that first over, Hall had launched himself into his follow-through with such force that he swung himself off his feet and finished up on his hands and knees, three yards from the gum-chewing Edrich. England lost that match by ten wickets before tea on the fourth day. West Indies' second innings lasted for just the one ball it needed for Conrad Hunte to score the single run they required for victory. They also won the series 3–1, with the Lord's Test famously drawn in dramatic fashion.

By the time that Test series was over, I had received a

sexual education from the pages of the *Daily Telegraph* which far exceeded in exotic detail anything that could be gleaned from the pages of the books on sale in the seedier bookshops of Manchester. I was traditionally a *Manchester Guardian* reader, but I soon realised that the *Daily Telegraph*, in its desire to report salacious matters comprehensively, offered the kind of accounts that fourteen-year-old boys with raging hormones fully appreciated.

Sexual instruction had traditionally been the province of boys slightly older, or certainly more experienced than myself, who would offer mystifying facts on the 4.20pm train from Bury to Manchester. For some reason, no smutty conversations took place on the morning train, which induced a scholarly silence while those of us who had done the homework offered it up to those of us who hadn't. Similarly, if we got out of school early and raced for the 4pm train, the exhaustion engendered by the ten-minute sprint rendered us incapable of doing anything other than getting our breath back before we reached our own stations. If we had to stay behind for school play rehearsals or sports practice, the train journey was made in company with adult workers, in whose company we would never have dared to discuss the private thoughts which tormented us all through the night.

The revelations of the Profumo Affair, combined with the evidence given at the trial of Dr Stephen Ward for living off the immoral earnings of Christine Keeler and Mandy Rice Davies, excited the prurient interest of a nation.

> Sexual intercourse began in 1963
>   Between the Lady Chatterley ban and the Beatles'
> first LP

wrote Philip Larkin, whose diaries and later biography indicate that he was as affected as the fourteen-year-old

113

schoolboys whose experience led them to echo such thoughts quite genuinely.

When the details of the Profumo Affair and the Ward trial reached the public, I shared the mounting frenzy as each new revelation appeared – the man in the mask, the naked butler with the notice 'If my services don't please you, whip me,' the two-way mirror in Ward's apartment, the Mayfair orgies, the casual promiscuities of London nightlife, nude swimming parties during weekends at Cliveden – all were devoured with relish. Rumour fed on rumour. I particularly enjoyed the one about the cabinet minister who had been discovered by police beneath a bush in Richmond Park, where he and a prostitute had been engaging in an act later immortalised by Hugh Grant on Sunset Boulevard. I always wondered where the deer were at the time.

For a previous generation, the sexual icon had been Betty Grable and her fabulous legs or Rita Hayworth in that black strapless dress in *Gilda* singing, 'Put The Blame On Mame, Boys', even Marilyn Monroe's famous calendar pin-up. For me, it was that black-and-white photograph of a coyly provocative, naked Christine Keeler sitting astride a chair with her breasts squashed against its back. No wonder it became the key image of the movie *Scandal*, which showed the actress who played her, Joanne Whalley, in the same position. I shall always remain grateful that the discredited Tory government of the early 1960s remained in office long enough to generate the raw material that sustained me through puberty. I feel comfortably certain that I was not alone in my response.

Chapter Six

The adolescent who returned to school in September 1963 was significantly altered from the shy, traumatised young boy of September 1962. The transition had been effected partly by the sexual awakening brought on by the Profumo Affair, partly by the recognition that there was life after the disaster of relegation, but also by the summer holiday of 1963.

I shall always be grateful to my brother and his two friends from his days at Bury Grammar School: Roger, who had just finished his first year at Brasenose College, Oxford; and Negley, who was studying at the London School of Economics. They had planned the trip of a lifetime, driving across Europe as far as Yugoslavia, taking in Bruges, Brussels, the Black Forest, Munich, Salzburg, Vienna, Florence, Lake Como, the St Gotthard Pass and Paris. It may well have been that the price for borrowing my father's car was the imposition of the younger brother, but they all behaved with a kindness I have never forgotten. They treated me as an equal, not easy when they were nearly twenty-one and I was fourteen, and the relatively grown-up conversation at mealtimes was something I learned to appreciate.

This was my equivalent of the eighteenth century's Grand Tour. Europe, its history and culture, came alive for me in a way that was to be very influential. To read about the First World War in books is one thing. To see the rows of white crosses stretching into the distance is quite another. To drive through Alsace-Lorraine was to appreciate what it must have been like to have been living in France and to have experienced German invasion in 1870, 1914 and 1940.

In Florence, the boy who couldn't draw saw the masterpieces of the Uffizi Museum and realised that Art consisted of more than forty minutes of boredom once a week. In Salzburg, I found a city which was still associated with Mozart rather than Julie Andrews. (*The Sound of Music* was shot there the following year.) The house of Mozart's birth had not yet been submerged beneath the crowds trying to get into the McDonald's next door.

We arrived in the middle of the Salzburg Festival but managed to acquire tickets to hear a string quartet playing Haydn's opus 76 no. 3. The concert took place in a small chamber in the Schloss Mirabell lit only by candlelight. It was a great surprise to hear the slow movement whose theme was the melody for 'Deutschland Über Alles'. I was delighted to see that my brother even got hold of a precious ticket to hear Karajan conduct *The Marriage of Figaro*. I swore I'd go back one day when I had the money to enjoy the Festival fully. I'm still waiting.

That holiday converted me to Europhilia. It was only six months after De Gaulle had vetoed Macmillan's application to take Great Britain into the Common Market, and people were more offended by the rudeness of the man whom we had helped during his leadership of the Free French than they were frustrated at their continuing economic and political isolation. We still had the Commonwealth, New Zealand lamb, Australian peaches and Anchor butter. We didn't need Europe. I felt instinctively then that such thinking was outmoded. I find it extraordinary that the same debate still rages today and shows no sign of abating. The only time Europhobia should be actively encouraged is during the football season, but even then I have in my time been seen to support the cause of various European teams. Sporting Lisbon in 1964, Partizan Belgrade in 1966, AC Milan in 1969, Galatasaray in 1994, Barcelona in 1995, Borussia Dortmund in 1997 – you get the drift.

What I missed on my tour of Europe in 1963, and on all subsequent ventures abroad, were the English newspapers. By the time we had arrived in the Black Forest, we had seen the headline 'WARD IST TOT', but neither *Das Bild* nor *Die Frankfurter Allgemeine Zeitung* was the right newspaper to buy if you wanted all the sordid details of Stephen Ward's suicide the day before the jury technically found him guilty of living off immoral earnings.

A few days later, another significant chapter in British social history was opened when £2,600,000 was stolen from the Glasgow to London Royal Mail train. (The Great Train Robbery was later to have an enormous impact on my life, in the sense that it provided the raw material for my first feature film, *Buster*.) We paid for a meal in an Italian trattoria with a million-lire note. The waiter held it up to the light playfully. 'Great Train Robbery?' he asked smilingly. It wasn't just the pop music that was making Britain the focus of so much external interest.

We lived off a pound a day. The camp sites where we pitched our tent cost a few shillings, breakfast was a bowl of cereal and a glass of orange juice, and lunch was a piece of cheese, a freshly baked roll and a piece of fruit. The only time we sat down to eat was in the evenings, when it was still possible to eat a decent meal for the local equivalent of fifty to sixty pence.

In Vienna, I discovered not only the delights of the Wiener Schnitzel but the echoes of a previous life. As the pages of this book have presumably made clear, I am grounded in the realities of supporting Manchester City in the winter and

Lancashire in the summer, which I have always felt forms a barrier against any kind of indulgence in the paranormal. I must confess, however, that in the back streets of Vienna in the old Jewish quarter, I felt a spooky sensation of *déjà vu* – as if I were about to meet the ghosts of my ancestors who had struggled against the pogroms of the Habsburg Empire. This was particularly odd as my ancestors came from Bialystock in Poland and Galicia on the Russian border.

Perhaps even odder was a fascination with Germany which had nothing whatsoever to do with the understandable knee-jerk 'wicked Nazis/Holocaust' routine in which I had been inducted for many years. I had already started to learn German in school, and was intrigued to discover a link between this new language and the few words of Yiddish spoken around the house by my parents and assorted relatives and friends. I showed an aptitude for German which came as something of a surprise, since I had found French and Latin a hard slog. I coped with the latter two subjects, but I couldn't claim the disconcerting kinship I discovered with German.

Travelling through Germany was strange, because I sensed the schizophrenia in the country. West Germany was a new country; the coinage, the Deutsch Mark was new, cities like Mannheim were newly rebuilt after the damage inflicted by Bomber Command. The West Germans were understandably keen to promote their economic miracle, but a few miles outside Munich lay the neatly tended grounds of the concentration camp at Dachau. I didn't need reminding what had taken place there less than twenty years before. Twenty years . . . The waitress in the café, the man behind the counter in the Lebensmittel (easily confused with Lebensraum), the driver of the car in front, the bus behind. They were in their forties now, so twenty years ago . . .

Maybe they were part of the internal resistance to Hitler, the ones who hated him, the ones who reluctantly had to go along with what was happening. They certainly couldn't have been part of the thousands who worshipped him in Nuremberg, the millions who voted for him in the 1932 election which gave the Nazis a firm grasp on power in the last days of the Weimar Republic. They couldn't possibly be the cultural inheritors of Bach and Goethe who carried out his genocidal policies.

Some of my friends were forbidden by their parents to enter Germany even as tourists. Bury Grammar School was twinned with a school in Cologne. Every other year, they came to play us at football and the call went up for parents to offer accommodation. In my final year studying German for 'A' Level, and principally as a means of improving my chances in the German Oral exam, I volunteered to act as host for one of the lads. I was rounded on by my Jewish friends for making concessions to the Nazis, for betraying those ghosts of the martyred dead. David Green proclaimed himself the most outraged of all, although when I was the prefect in charge of Jewish prayers, he had to be driven in there with threats.

It took me a long time to come to terms with the appeal of Mitteleuropa. There were moments in Germany and Austria when I genuinely felt close to something that had been buried in the past. I couldn't tell if it was a person, a place or a movement. It was in the mountains of the Bavarian Alps as the dying rays of the sun illuminated their glorious peaks, and it was in the cafés of Vienna as I drank their coffee and devoured their cakes. It was in the sadness behind the superficial gaiety of the music of Lehar, it was in the solitude of the Domplatz in Salzburg, knowing that this was where Max Reinhardt had presented his famous productions of *Jedermann*. No wonder Lubitsch remade *The Merry Widow* at MGM in 1934, that Max Reinhardt, exiled from his native land, could never settle in Hollywood although the studios acclaimed his Hollywood Bowl production of *A Midsummer*

Night's Dream. They must have felt it too, that nostalgia for a lost Middle European culture of music and theatre and politics, all discussed with passion over coffee with cream and a large slice of Sachertorte.

Maybe it was the sense of dislocation, the feeling that I was out of step with the times, that made me want to explore the emotion a little more deeply. I am not being entirely fanciful when I suggest this was all part of supporting Manchester City, a team whose failures were many and whose triumphs were brief but glorious. I didn't enjoy losing, but I did rather enjoy the feeling of exclusivity. Boy, you had to go through a lot of misery before you could join *my* band of brothers.

Doesn't that sound like a particularly Jewish piece of reasoning? We Jews are (historically, at least) the most despised race in the world. We have been the subject of attempts to annihilate us since the days of the Hittites and the Amalekites. We are threatened now by the inevitable consequences of assimilation. But does the Chief Rabbi make it easy for anyone to join us and help to swell our depleted ranks? You must be joking. We don't want anyone, thank you very much. We would prefer to sit here and feel resentful, superior only in the knowledge that nobody has ever suffered like us and produced such wonderful Nobel prize winners, musicians, playwrights, comedians, movie moguls – you name it, we've got one of ours there somewhere. Chances are, though, it's someone who grew up Jewish and fought against the stifling Orthodoxy of his parents. I could develop this thesis, but it should be done in New York over a gigantic pastrami sandwich on rye bread in the Carnegie Delicatessen on Seventh Avenue, or, more relevantly for this chapter, over coffee and cake in the Café Central in Vienna. That is my idea of a Jewish life.

That grand tour Sixties-style gave me a cultural injection

of new interests – the music of Vienna from Mozart to Strauss, the art of the Renaissance, the architecture of the great houses and palaces of Europe. Music, Art, History and Politics were no longer dull subjects at school involving written essays repackaging the notes already given to us, but living, vibrant areas of passion.

The problem was that this growth of knowledge, and the enthusiasm to explore it still further, didn't go down very well at school. A fourteen-year-old schoolboy's interests were mostly circumscribed by hairstyles, the *New Musical Express*, smoking under the railway bridge, and which girls did and which girls didn't – or more accurately, which girls were rumoured to do it and which girls were rumoured to have refused, and where to go on Saturday nights to test the truth of the rumours. Unfortunately, I couldn't get particularly worked up about any of these, as a consequence of which I felt still further isolated within my own peer group. It was only cricket and football which maintained any connection at all.

In school, enthusiasm for cricket began in the middle of April and terminated abruptly with the end of the summer term. Lancashire's poor form throughout my time at Bury Grammar School made it increasingly difficult to find other boys to go with me to Old Trafford. In the summer of 1963, there were two crumbs of comfort. Lancashire played Leicestershire in the preliminary round of the new knockout cup competition sponsored by Gillette. They won quite easily and subsequently triumphed over Essex. By the time we left for Europe, Lancashire had battled their way through to the semi-finals of this first limited-overs contest.

Geoff Pullar, our Test opener who hadn't played since he returned home early from the 1962–63 Ashes tour for an operation on his knee, was ready to return in the middle of July, which gave us a welcome boost. Nobody fancied facing

Statham and Higgs with the new ball and with the gradual emergence of Peter Lever as the third seamer, we looked like having a useful attack. With Pullar as sheet anchor and Bond, Grieves and Marner to get runs in the middle order, we had the makings of a useful one-day side. Worcestershire, whom we were drawn to play in the semi-final, relied too much on the old warhorses Jack Flavell and Len Coldwell. If we could see those two off, we only had to worry about Basil D'Oliveira and the two spinners, Slade and Gifford. A first Lord's final looked on the cards.

We bought the three-day-old copy of the *Daily Express* when we got to Munich. So high had been the hopes that it was hard at first to absorb the scale of the disaster. Flavell and Coldwell had bowled Lancashire out for 59, compiled in 31 agonising overs. In reply, Worcestershire had scored 60 for 1 in 10 overs. It took them precisely 35 minutes. Standing reading this in the middle of Bavaria in no way lessened the pain. It was small comfort that Worcestershire lost to Sussex in the final.

The other hope for the future was provided by the appointment of Ken Grieves as captain. Having consigned J.F.Blackledge to the dustbin of history, Lancashire turned in their hour of need to their old Australian stalwart, who, in addition to scoring thousands of runs over the years for his adopted county, also played in goal for Bolton Wanderers. It soon became apparent that the Lancashire committee had not changed its spots. Facing the prospect of a turning wicket, leg-break bowler Tommy Greenhough was dropped, against the captain's wishes. Grieves complained, but the best the committee could do was to advertise the fact that Lancashire were going to ask other counties to lend them some players because the ones under Grieves's command were so bad. They were indeed a pretty poor lot, but the morale in the dressing-room could hardly have been improved by that announcement.

It was the era of the constant call for 'Brighter Cricket'. Since the early 1950s, attendances at county matches had been declining dramatically, along with over rates and general interest. The advent of the Gillette Cup, followed within nine years by the John Player Sunday League and the Benson and Hedges Cup, was designed to arrest the slide. Quite how successful these competitions were can be seen from the fate which befell a certain Andrew P. Cassells who, according to the *Manchester Evening News*, admitted to being found drunk and incapable in City Road, Old Trafford, when he appeared before the Manchester County Magistrates Court. He told the court that he had been to watch Lancashire at Old Trafford and that the cricket was so awful it had driven him to drink to deaden the pain. He was fined two pounds.

We were still on the Continent when the 1963–64 football season began. The sale of Peter Dobing to Stoke and Alex Harley to Birmingham City took place in the last week of the close season, which necessitated a panic buy. Luckily, Derek Kevan, the former West Bromwich Albion striker, had not settled at Chelsea and Tommy Docherty was keen to offload him. Kevan joined City in time to take part in their first match in the Second Division, at home to Portsmouth. It was lost 2–0. Clearly not a great deal had changed since relegation, except that we had sold our two best players. Three days later, we managed a 2–2 draw at Cardiff. It felt like a minor triumph.

United meanwhile, with substantially the same squad as the one which had stared relegation in the face a few months earlier, set off on a season of relative success. They pushed Liverpool all the way to the First Division Championship and, surprisingly in the circumstances, lost 3–1 to West Ham United, the eventual winners, in the FA Cup semi-final. In Europe for the first time since the year of the Munich tragedy, they progressed steadily to the last eight where they were drawn to meet Sporting Lisbon. They played the first leg at Old Trafford and won comfortably, 4–1. In those days, a two-goal lead was generally considered foolproof for a second leg away from home. United had a three-goal cushion.

To my indescribable joy, United went to Lisbon and lost by five goals to nil. I heard the crackly commentary on my transistor radio under the covers after lights-out. It was warmer than a hot-water bottle, less messy than a wet dream and ultimately considerably more rewarding. It was the first time I can really remember crowing about a United defeat. And what a defeat! Denis Law hit the post in the first minute, which would have put United 5–1 up on aggregate and psychologically out of sight. Instead, Sporting Lisbon gradually clawed their way back into the game and as the goals started to go in, United just collapsed. I had experienced enough humiliations in my time to know one when I saw one. This was one. Busby obviously felt the same way, because not long afterwards he transferred Maurice Setters to Stoke for £30,000 and Phil Chisnall to Liverpool for £25,000. Busby mistrusted Setters's influence in the dressing-room and concluded, sadly, that the skilful inside-forward Chisnall didn't have the bottle for the big occasion. As usual, he was right in both instances.

Busby could afford to release two doubts because he had ready-made replacements. In the close season, he had bought the fast, direct winger John Connelly from Burnley for £56,000, and he knew that Nobby Stiles was now ready to take Setters's place at left-half. Quixall and Giles, who had both played in the Cup final at Wembley in May, were left out of the opening game of the 1963–64 season and they, too, soon left the club, although Giles's subsequent success at Leeds came back to haunt Busby. It was one of his few errors of judgment in the transfer market. Bobby Charlton moved inside to join Denis Law and David Herd, leaving a place spare for one of the youth team to play on the opposite wing to Connelly. His name was George Best.

I was incredibly lucky to be growing up in Manchester in the Sixties. On one side of the town were the remarkable skills of Best, Law and Charlton; on the other, the glory that was Vic Gomersall and Dave Bacuzzi. City held my heart, but Old Trafford was worth visiting on the Saturdays when City were away. Of course, I went there hoping for United to lose, waiting for the City result on the half-time scoreboard. I was frequently disappointed.

The four of us were at Old Trafford on 14 September 1963 to see the seventeen-year-old George Best make his debut against West Bromwich Albion. We were standing down by the touchline, barely yards from the pitch. Best played at outside-right and was marked by the experienced Graham Williams, a tough Welsh full-back who must have seen the frail schoolboy as easy pickings. Every time Best received the ball, Williams came hurtling in to take ball and boy over the touchline and, with a bit of luck, into the wall. Williams barely laid a stud on Best that day as he skipped over the increasingly frenzied tackles. Best made his marker look foolish time after time but United could only manage a 2–2 draw, much to our barely stifled delight. Surprisingly to us, unversed as we were in the devious way of football managers, Best went back to the 'A' team after that match until the New Year, when Busby felt he was ready for a more prolonged exposure to First Division football.

Best returned to first-team action because United were threatening to repeat the disasters of the previous year. On the Saturday before Christmas 1963, United lost spinelessly at Everton by four goals to nil. They travelled to play Burnley at Turf Moor on Boxing Day, determined to do better. They did – they scored a goal. Fortunately, Burnley scored six of them. We never celebrated Christmas in the days of my youth. We

125

watched television and went for long walks until the rest of the country rejoined us. I never received a Christmas present until I got married. This is a statement of fact and not a cry for sympathy. Indeed, whatever I had been given, nothing that could be purchased could ever compete with two catastrophic defeats for United. And O, Father Christmas, if you love me at all, Bring me a big red india-rubber ball – and ten goals smashed past United in successive matches.

Unfortunately, the defeats caused Busby to send for Best. United won the return game against Burnley 5–1. Best scored one and ran the experienced Burnley full-back John Angus off his feet. He was now in the first team permanently and he played a significant part in United's triple assault on the Championship, the European Cup-Winners' Cup and the FA Cup. It looked highly unlikely they would retain the latter when, three days after the convincing 4–1 home-leg win over Sporting Lisbon, they were 3–1 down five minutes from the end of the sixth round tie at home to Sunderland. We had really enjoyed ourselves as a tiny but skilful Sunderland forward-line ran rings round the cumbersome United defence. Johnny Crossan, shortly to be a hero on the other side of town, scored one dazzling goal and converted a penalty. We hugged ourselves with delight. This was exactly why we came to Old Trafford.

It was too good to last. Charlton pulled one back and Best scrambled the equaliser in the last minute. It was a breathlessly exciting game and the crowd went predictably wild. The official attendance was 63,770, but David Green was one of many who charged down a gate at the open end and pushed in for free. Such was the emotion that many of the literal gate-crashers sent their entrance money to United on the Monday. David Green wasn't one of them.

Sunderland dominated the replay at Roker Park on the Wednesday, but again Charlton pulled out an undeserved equaliser. On the following Monday at the Huddersfield Town ground, after a League win over West Ham on the Saturday, United finally polished off Sunderland 5–1. They played the semi-final against West Ham at Hillsborough knowing that if that match, too, went to a replay, United would be facing four matches in six days. Busby's modest response was, 'We just hope it won't happen.' He completely forgot to mention taking the Football League to court if they didn't rearrange the rest of the season to make United's life easier. Four days after the semi-final defeat came the midweek humiliation in Lisbon. Still no word from Busby about how unsympathetic the English authorities were to Manchester United's selfless European toil.

Three weeks later, Best was picked to make his international debut for Northern Ireland, which meant that he was certainly playing six matches in four days because, worryingly for us, in addition to his international and first-team duties, George Best was the star of an outstanding United youth team. It was worrying because, for the first time, City, too, had a team capable of winning the FA Youth Cup, with players like Neil Young and Glyn Pardoe already having made their first-team debuts.

City and United were drawn against each other in the semi-final, with the winner favourites to lift the cup. We went to Old Trafford with high hopes. For a start, we wouldn't have to cope with the usual Old Trafford packed to the rafters with baying Reds. That was our first frustration. A crowd of 29,706 turned up to watch a match which had captured the imagination of the city and from the kick-off, Best and the two United wingers, Willie Anderson and John Aston, tore the City defence to shreds.

What was most noticeable was that they slavishly followed the Manchester United philosophy that the most dangerous ball in football is the one pulled back from the dead-ball line.

Defenders are facing the wrong way and the ball tends to find forwards racing towards the goal. It still seems to me the most deadly way to cross the ball but because of the greater mobility of modern full-backs and wing-backs, it has become a rare sight these days. Wing-backs seem to specialise in crossing from level with the penalty area, which in theory should make it easy for competent defenders.

In that Youth Cup semi-final, Anderson, Best and Aston got to the bye-line with frightening regularity to send lethal centres whistling across the face of the City goal. The opening goal came in United's first attack. Future City hero Mike Doyle, playing out of position at right-back, was left for dead by Aston, whose fiercely driven centre was volleyed past Alan Ogley by United's centre-forward Albert Kinsey. City responded in kind, well prompted by John Clay who hovered promisingly on the fringe of the first team during the Championship year but never quite fulfilled his potential. City's finishing, however, was poor and United's was clinical.

Glyn Pardoe, City's inside-right and youngest ever first-team debutant, pulled a goal back, but the final score was a depressing 4–1 to United. The return leg was an even more depressing 4–3 defeat in front of a crowd of over 20,000 at Maine Road. We had to wait a further twenty-two years before we had a youth team capable of beating United and winning the FA Youth Cup. Of those two highly promising sides in 1964, only Doyle, Pardoe and David Connor really made the grade for City and Rimmer, Best, Sadler and Aston for United. The fall-out rate among talented teenagers is extraordinarily high.

Between those two legs came a game of great emotional resonance. On Wednesday 15 April 1964, an almost full house turned out to acclaim Bert Trautmann in his testimonial match. I had seen his last home appearance a few weeks earlier on Good Friday, when City stuffed Norwich City 5–0. Bert had been largely a spectator as Derek Kevan scored a hat-trick and the City forward-line ran riot. Norwich's outside-left that day, I was glad to see, was a bald player called Bill Punton. In those days, many teams had bald players – genuine baldies, not like the shaven heads of Dion Dublin and Gianluca Vialli. Once upon a time, men like Jimmy Melia and Terry Hennessey could hold their heads up high, knowing their lack of hair was regarded as characterful. The idea of men shaving their heads to look hard would have been regarded as bizarre.

The 5–0 victory over Norwich was not Trautmann's last appearance for City. Just to make sure he didn't leave with a false impression, City contrived to lose 2–0 at Preston North End the following day. By Easter Monday, when City returned to Norwich to complete a rare double by winning 2–1, Trautmann had given way permanently to Alan Ogley and Harry Dowd. Neither of these two replacements figured greatly in the mind as the Maine Road crowd poured out its tribute to the man who single-handedly had kept City up year after year. Since they only went down by two points in 1963, it would not be unfeasible to propose that had Trautmann been a little younger, he could have performed another miracle and kept us up again.

The official figure of 47,951 was rumoured to have been doctored, and it certainly seemed to us that the real attendance that balmy April night was closer to 60,000. They packed the ground to watch an All-Manchester XI including Denis Law, nostalgically back in a blue shirt, and Bobby Charlton, oddly clad in the same coloured shirt, take on an International XI which included Stanley Matthews, Jimmy Armfield and old City favourite Bobby Johnstone. David Wagstaffe put the Manchester side ahead but, just to make Trautmann feel thoroughly nostalgic, Maurice Setters then smashed a high back-pass past him for the last of the many own-goals Bert had conceded over the years. A few minutes before the end of the totally irrelevant football which the Manchester side was winning 5–4, two little boys got onto the pitch, ran up to Bert and tried to hug him. It was a spontaneous gesture of emotion on a night when the sentiment overflowed from the terraces and washed onto the pitch.

As the little boys were ushered away, they were replaced by some larger boys, then some tearful men, who all wanted Trautmann to know how much he was loved in the city, a vast proportion of which had wanted to kill the ex-prisoner of war when he first signed for City in 1949. Finally, the wall of policemen was swept away as thousands poured out of the terraces onto the pitch to engulf the hero of the night. The police cleared a path to the safety of the Main Stand where Trautmann, demonstrably moved, made an emotional farewell.

Jeff was one of those who managed to get onto the pitch. He made a bee-line for the goalposts between which his hero had been standing only moments before. The groundsman, who had viewed this cascade of humanity with great alarm, sprinted towards the goalmouth to protect his professional reputation. When he got there, he was less than impressed at the sight of Jeffrey Cohen swinging triumphantly from the crossbar. Armed only with a bunch of keys, the groundsman swung the chain on which they were held and clattered Jeff on the side of the head. He limped, humiliated, from the scene, recovering briefly to demonstrate the marks of the bruise to our respectful gaze.

Perhaps the most interesting fact of an emotional night was that United and City supporters had stood together to pay their tribute to one of the immortals of Manchester football. It was less than a year since that horrific night when

Denis Law had acquired the dubious penalty which cost City their place in Division One. The mutual loathing was abandoned for one night as fans of both clubs stood to acclaim a man whose greatness of spirit and ability transcended the petty hatreds. A similar situation today would be rare. Did any City fans (or any fans at all, save those of Manchester United) acclaim the arrogant Cantona on his sudden retirement? Outside of Paul Lake, have City now even got anyone on their books whom United players and supporters would cross the main road, let alone Maine Road, to support?

Personally, I regret this new bile. Maybe the distance of time lends enchantment, but it seems to me that the hatred in football has grown exponentially. Denis Law played with a provocative arrogance, but other fans felt it was a bit of an act and, outside of his fiery temper, Law was a justifiably acclaimed artist. Cantona's arrogance was disliked because it was for real, and it widened the breach between United supporters and the rest of the world, which is why the infamous kung-fu episode aroused so much fury. United supporters felt that Cantona was initially sentenced to serve a prison sentence and punished so heavily by the FA because he was a much-maligned United hero. Other supporters felt just as strongly that if Joe Bloggs of Doncaster Rovers had launched himself into the crowd in that extraordinary manner, he would never have been permitted to kick a ball in England again. Cantona had been spared the proper punishment simply because he played for Manchester United, a club whose public pronouncements suggest they are somehow above the law.

Busby and Shankly were friends and rivals, as were Busby and Mercer. Despite the occasional platitude, it certainly appears as if Ferguson and Dalglish, for example, genuinely dislike each other, and the invective United supporters direct at Liverpool is matched only by the hatred that

131

is reciprocated. To judge from his hysterical 'He went down in my estimation after that' speech at the end of the 1995–96 season, Kevin Keegan isn't a big fan of Alex Ferguson either. The greatest indictment of Manchester City's current sloth is that United now feel about City as Bogart felt about Peter Lorre in *Casablanca*. 'You hate me don't you, Rick?' wheedles the creepy Ugarte. Bogart thinks for a moment.

'If I thought about you at all, I probably would,' he concludes.

While United finished that 1964 season second to Shankly's resurgent Liverpool, City made only a small impact on the Second Division as they concluded the campaign four places behind the two promotion spots. Derek Kevan, who was honoured to have played in the Trautmann Testimonial, proved an excellent buy, scoring thirty goals. He was joined in the attack by Jimmy Murray from Wolverhampton Wanderers and, supplied from the wings by Neil Young and David Wagstaffe, they formed a notably successful strike-force. Over Christmas they hit peak form, and the four of us were in the Platt Lane Stand to watch as City, having beaten Rotherham at home 6–1 on the Saturday before Christmas, celebrated Boxing Day 1963 by walloping Scunthorpe 8–1. Two days later they travelled across the Pennines for the return match, which they won 4–2.

Unfortunately, goals continued to flow unceasingly in the opposite direction. One goal in February 1964 at Maine Road caused particular anguish. The match was a new and unwanted local derby against Bury. Inevitably, the three Bury Grammar School City fans had had two weeks of ear-bashing from the local residents in the course of the build-up, but the buzzing of our new forward-line, and the deeply held belief that Bury didn't pose much of a threat even to this former giant fallen on hard times, were sufficient to keep us optimistic.

The optimism lasted about twenty-five minutes, at which point the seventeen-year-old Bury inside-forward making his debut that day, who had already turned our defence inside out, scored at the far post while the City defence remained stationary, appealing in vain for offside. The scorer's name was Colin Bell. In the second half, just to exacerbate matters, Harry Dowd damaged his shoulder after fifty-three minutes in preventing the second and possibly clinching Bury goal.

The Football League had not yet been convinced of the desirability of substitutes, so Dowd went into the forward-line and Matt Gray took his place in goal. With seven minutes left, and the prospect of disgrace in school on Monday morning staring us in the face, Wagstaffe centred, Kevan hammered the ball against the crossbar and Harry Dowd raced in to blast home the rebound, before falling in excruciating agony on his injured shoulder.

The football season finished with City in sixth place in Division Two but fifteen points behind Sunderland, who were promoted with Leeds. With United winning nothing significant that year, both football and cricket paled into temporary insignificance compared with the imminent arrival of 'O' Levels. I was taking eight subjects, although Maths and Physics were predictably proving the most likely areas where I would come a cropper. The problem was that I desperately needed the Maths, because one couldn't be admitted to Cambridge without English, Maths and Latin. Latin I felt I would scrape through, since the pass mark was set at 45 percent. On my very first exam in Latin, I had scored 92 percent. Thereafter it was like a cartoon graph with the line heading inexorably down towards zero. With one term to go, I had hit 50 percent and was still in free-fall. Fortunately I managed to achieve a Grade 6, which was given to marks between 45 percent and 50 percent. Two more terms and I would have been in single figures.

The Maths paper was divided into two parts. Section A, which included arithmetic, geometry and algebra, was worth 52 marks out of a hundred. Section B was divided into four difficult problems worth 12 marks each. Long and bitter experience had told me that I had no hope of even a single mark in this section. Therefore I turned my full attention to Section A, with the avowed intention of getting at least 45 out of the 52 available marks. I was greatly relieved to pass with another Grade 6.

In fact, though I finished with seven 'O' Levels, three of them (Latin, Maths and English Language) were at the rock bottom level of Grade 6. German, History and English Literature crawled up to the dizzy heights of Grade 4 (55 percent to 60 percent) and French was my best effort with a dazzling Grade 3. Fortunately, in those less competitive days, universities and employers only wanted to know the quantity of the 'O's achieved and showed little interest in their quality. The change to GCSEs has brought with it a far more intense pressure for grade 'A's than I believe is healthy.

I looked forward to the sixth form and concentrating solely on History, English and German. To free myself from the tyranny of logarithms and cosines, of Latin subjunctives and the laws of kinetic energy, was to feel as the Israelites must have felt as they stood on the other side of the Red Sea and saw the waters enclosing the chariots of the pursuing Egyptians.

In the summer of 1964, the Australians arrived to contest the Ashes against Ted Dexter's side. With no Benaud in the party, I felt confident we could wrest the Ashes back. True, City were still in Division Two, but the success of Derek Kevan, who had smashed Alex Harley's goalscoring record in his first season, together with his productive partnership with

Jimmy Murray meant we were bound to get up next year. Meanwhile, the advent of a new fresh, relatively young Labour government was only weeks away. My brother and I set off for our first sight of the land of Israel with a song in our hearts – in his case, 'When the Reds Go Marching in'; in mine, 'We'll meet again, don't know where, don't know when'.

Chapter Seven

The first sight of the Promised Land is usually a memorable and emotional moment. The East Berliners risking their lives crossing the Berlin Wall to find freedom in the West must have felt such a moment. The huddled masses yearning to breathe free sailing into New York harbour, their eyes switching in fascination from the Statue of Liberty to the city skyline, undoubtedly did. The ship which took my brother Geoff and me from Venice to Haifa docked at 5.30am – and instead of lining the rail, staring into the distance to make out the first outline of the Land of Milk and Honey like the helpless refugees on the deck of the *Exodus*, rather more prosaically we got up, had breakfast and walked down the gangplank into the customs shed.

In 1964, Israel was still the good guy of popular mythology. The image of the 'terrorist' outrages of the Irgun and the Stern Gang had been erased by the heroic War of Independence, when the fledgling country fought off the invasion by all the Arab countries of the Middle East. The rapidly rising reputation of the Israeli Army was justified by the speed with which it raced across the Sinai desert to take the Suez Canal in 1956. The army was populated by handsome young men and beautiful dark-haired 'sabras', named after the local fruit, prickly on the outside and sweet on the inside. They were supported by elderly reservists, all of them dedicated to a simple and praiseworthy patriotism. The Israelis made the desert bloom and the Holy Land available to the tourist industry. You couldn't buy this sort of publicity.

My brother and I arrived from Great Britain, a land where the recently ended conscription for young men of eighteen had been little more than the raw material for *Carry On Sergeant* and *Private's Progress*. It was a country whose political leaders had responded to the idea of change in October 1963 by replacing the Old Etonian Harold Macmillan as prime minister with the slightly younger Old Etonian, the Fourteenth Earl of Home. Home, who disclaimed his peerage to 'emerge' as Sir Alec Douglas Home, leader of the Conservative and Unionist Party, declared that he could only cope with the country's economics with the help of matchsticks.

Home also remarkably appeared to speak without moving his lips from the thin smile in which they seemed permanently creased. I always wondered if this was the result of the twin Etonian traditions of fagging and flogging. Home was, however, a gent and always raised his bowler hat with that style of *noblesse oblige* which has normally marked the true aristocrat. Israel's political leaders didn't even wear a tie, and in Golda Meir they had a woman whom Ben Gurion called 'the strongest man in my cabinet'. Margaret Thatcher at the time was only the backbench Member of Parliament for Finchley.

The sights and sounds of Israel were captivating. On the streets of the major cities, Haifa, Jerusalem, Tel Aviv, people could be seen eating in public. It might have been common in America, but in Britain in 1964 it wasn't done. The era of the takeaway hadn't arrived. In Israel, all the women were pregnant. Growing up in Manchester, I don't remember having seen a pregnant woman before. In Israel, you could see the birth rate increasing in front of you.

The least admirable aspect was the overwhelming rudeness. This was a country in a rush, all right. Drivers regarded the installation of traffic lights as an unnecessary infringement of their personal liberties, and tended to ignore them unless the vehicle approaching the green light was significantly heavier. To judge from the way the traffic behaved, the manufacturers must have concluded that they could shave their price by omitting the brakes and replacing them with an extra-powerful horn.

Israelis who had expelled the British in 1947 and the Arab armies a year later figured that they no longer needed such quaint Old World courtesies as the queue. The time to be acutely aware of this was after lunch on Friday. The entire public transport system came to a halt in time for the arrival of the Sabbath at sunset, so the last bus until Sunday left around three o'clock in the afternoon.

Trying to get onto the last bus from Tiberias to Kiryat Shmoneh on a Friday was like trying to get out of Paris before the Nazis arrived. Geoff pushed me ahead of him but then was thrown off himself. Since I had no idea where we were heading for, this induced a certain amount of panic. Fortunately, Geoff had seen enough rugby league matches to barge his way back like a second-row forward, past six old women in black dresses and onto the bus as the driver kicked the door shut in the faces of the frantic, gesticulating, screaming passengers, all of whom, it appeared, were in possession of valid tickets. It was a horrendous journey, as we were wedged in like cattle. A thought occurred to me and was instantly dismissed. There were people on the bus with tattooed numbers on their arms.

We eventually arrived at Kfar Blum, a remote kibbutz in the north of Galilee, founded by friends of my parents who had left Britain in the 1930s in the wake of the Depression and Oswald Mosley's Black Shirts. It was a strange but

139

fascinating world of practical socialism. You couldn't help but be impressed by the irrigation and other farming techniques, which had made a vital contribution to the fragile national economy. You couldn't fail to be aware, too, that the distant rumble you could hear was not thunder but gunfire. The Syrian border was less than ten miles away, and before the Six Days War of 1967, the Syrians controlled the Golan Heights.

Fortunately, we had the company of the BBC World Service, on whose cherished wavelength we heard about The Test That Died Of Shame. This was a reference to the fourth Test between England and Australia at Old Trafford, which we had been sorry to miss but which, to our relief, turned out to be the dullest high-scoring draw of all time. Being still in possession of the Ashes, the Australian skipper Bobby Simpson decided that it was up to England to get them back. When he won the toss, he decided to bat – and continued to do so for over twelve hours. When he was eventually out for 311, Australia were already safe.

They finally declared at 656 for 8 and England began their reply with gritted teeth. Edrich was out for 6 and Boycott for 58, but Dexter made 174 and Ken Barrington went on to 256, his highest Test score. England were eventually bowled out for 611 late in the afternoon of the fifth day, but the audience had left the theatre a long time before. Four Tests were drawn in that boring series, the only victory going to the Aussies at Headingley where Peter Burge's 160 proved to be the decisive innings. After the drama and excitement of the West Indies in 1963, indeed even in comparison with Benaud's tour of 1961, the Fight for the Ashes in 1964 proved a sore disappointment.

More relevant to us was the result of the Lancashire versus Warwickshire Gillette Cup semi-final, which took place the day after the Old Trafford Test finished. The memory of the spineless collapse against Worcestershire in

1963 was still fresh in the memory. Surely lightning couldn't strike twice in the same place, although we noted with some anxiety that Warwickshire had won the three-day Championship match played at Coventry a few days earlier by the comfortable margin of five wickets.

Bob Barber made a sparkling 76 as Warwickshire ran up the formidable total of 294 off their 60 overs. In reply, the Lancashire opening batsmen, D.M.Green and D.R.Worsley, two graduates from Oxford University, set off like a train. Sixty rattled up in the first ten overs, and M.J.K.Smith, the Warwickshire captain, replaced his opening strike bowlers with Tom Cartwright and Billy Ibadulla, whom he instructed to bowl short of a length to a deeply defensive field including no fewer than six men on the boundary.

Off the next ten overs Lancashire managed only 24, and after thirty overs the score had reached only 110. By now, frustration had gripped both the batsmen and the large 21,000 crowd, and inevitably the wickets started to fall. Nevertheless, when the wicketkeeper Geoff Clayton strode to the middle with twenty overs remaining, Lancashire needed 134 with five wickets left. In today's one-day cricket climate, that might be considered a sporting bet – but Clayton clearly was not of that opinion. It seems that, with the approval of the captain Ken Grieves, Lancashire had decided not to give Warwickshire the satisfaction of bowling them out, so Clayton made a paltry 19 in forty-five minutes.

The blame was laid entirely on M.J.K.Smith's negative field-placing and bowling tactics. At a distance of 2,000 miles, I couldn't quite follow the logic. Surely that just meant there were singles to be had all round the ground and six runs an over could be achieved quite simply. As the boos started to reverberate round Old Trafford, one man ran onto the pitch to remonstrate with the Lancashire wicketkeeper, but without noticeable effect. After 60 overs, Lancashire had reached 209 for 7 and had lost by 85 runs. To rub salt into the wounds, M.J.K.Smith was given the Man of the Match award.

Afterwards, Ken Grieves defended Clayton and his own tactics, much to the fury of Cyril Washbrook, the former Lancashire stalwart batsman and captain and now into the second year of his contract as the team manager. Washy had been appointed to ensure that the Blackledge fiasco was never repeated, but even during the days of his own captaincy, it had become apparent that his old-fashioned disciplinarian ways were not welcome in the dressing-room.

Washbrook had grown up in the fierce atmosphere of the Championship-winning side of the 1930s. As a youngster then, his views were not welcomed and he was forced to listen to those of his elders and betters, like Ernest Tyldesley and George Duckworth. In the less formal times of the post-war climate, much of that original discipline had disappeared. The result of the Lancashire committee's desire to be helpful was to drive the talented spinner Roy Tattersall back into league cricket and transfer Alan Wharton to Leicestershire.

The committee backed Washbrook's decision to discipline Clayton by dropping him for the Roses match against Yorkshire, which followed immediately after the semi-final disaster. Lancashire lost by an innings and 131 runs after forty minutes' play on the morning of the third day. The county club was in crisis. They bumbled on for the last month of the season, finishing in fourteenth place, fourth from the bottom.

On 31 August, in the middle of the MCC v Lancashire game at Old Trafford, arranged to celebrate the County's centenary, it was leaked to the local paper that Clayton, the captain Ken Grieves, the hard-hitting batsman Peter Marner and my old hero Jack Dyson were all going to be sacked. The club initially denied the rumour, then confirmed it in an official statement a few days later. Marner went on to join Wharton at Leicestershire; Grieves, who had been a stalwart at Lancashire since 1949, and the ex-City forward Dyson both retired.

The saddest loss to Lancashire cricket was Geoff Clayton, whose gritty fighting displays had scraped Lancashire out of a hole of their own digging more times than I could remember. He was only twenty-six. He went to Somerset, where he kept wicket in the first match of the 1965 season – against Lancashire. Somerset won crushingly by nine wickets. Lancashire were to remain a poor team until they found a class wicket-keeper in the Indian Test player Farokh Engineer.

The cricketing side of my dreams for 1964 had taken a hammering, but the political expectations of the autumn remained high. I rather shamefacedly recall that I had supported the Conservative Party in the election of 1959 for two reasons. The first was that Jeffrey Edis's father had solemnly warned that his stocks and shares might go down if the Conservatives failed to win their third consecutive election victory. Mr Edis owned a huge house off Hilton Lane with a large outhouse in which Jeffrey Edis, Michael Chadwick, Jeff Cohen and I played endless games of table tennis. Somehow, the implication was that a Conservative victory would interfere with our table tennis. I certainly hoped it might interfere with the Edises' dog – a slobbering, bad-tempered boxer called Major who, along with a dog called Whiskey which lived at number 3 in our street, induced in me a lifelong fear of dogs and any other animal baring teeth. The second and clinching reason for voting Tory was that 'Conservatives' began with a 'C' and so did my name.

Over the course of the next five years, my grasp of politics became a little more sophisticated, although my views were not widely shared. In my second year at Bury Grammar School, a mock election was held in which, to my disbelief, the Tory candidate romped home. The Communist campaign clearly split the left-wing vote and the Labour candidate was

143

left trailing. I found this a bewildering and slightly alienating state of affairs. How was it possible that these teenage kids were all voting Tory? We had no stocks and shares, no property values to protect. I could imagine voting for any candidate who promised, in *Blackadder*'s famous phrase, 'tougher sentences for Geography masters', but not for a candidate in short trousers who believed in hanging and flogging. We had enough flogging already in our school, thank you very much. Who were the loonies who wanted to continue it beyond the sixth form? Why did they vote the way their parents did, even though they were taking part in a secret ballot at school? It was my introduction to the mysteries of psephology.

As the election neared, Wilson promised that we would all be enlivened by the 'white heat' of the technological revolution. It seemed a good time to be young, for we stood then, it appeared, on the threshold of a new era of progress. The deferential society built on class privilege was disappearing, to be replaced by a meritocracy, a key buzz-word of the 1960s. Successive political disasters bedevilled the Tories, such as the Night of the Long Knives, when Macmillan sacked a third of the cabinet in order to preserve his own job, and the spectacular failure of the British independent nuclear missiles. In 1962, a minor official in the Admiralty, William Vassall, was convicted of spying for Russia and sentenced to eighteen years' imprisonment. A Tribunal of Inquiry was set up to sort out the mess, in the course of which two journalists declined to name the sources of their allegations. They were sent to prison for three and six months respectively, to the outrage of the press, who thus fell upon the much glitzier revelations of the Profumo Affair with cries of triumph. Profumo's great sin, it appeared, was not so much conducting a truly indiscreet affair but lying to the House of Commons.

This was the kind of politics I could relate to. A tired,

144

sleaze-ridden Tory government which had been in office too long and a bold new Labour administration in the wings, offering the promise of a new Jerusalem, presented a striking contrast. In 1960, the dynamic, charismatic young Senator, John F. Kennedy, had beaten off the challenge of more experienced politicians like Lyndon Johnson, Hubert Humphrey and Adlai Stevenson to secure the nomination of the Democratic Party and then to win the confidence of the country as a whole. Wilson modelled himself on this new political hero, adding the very British varnishings of his enthusiasm for HP Sauce and Huddersfield Town FC.

Despite the bizarre result of the school's mock election, I approached the prospect of the 1964 general election with enthusiasm. I was warned by one of the History masters who shared my political beliefs to expect a swing back to the government in the last few days before polling, because British women voters were essentially Conservative at heart. Prior to October 1964, transistor radios had been brought into school only on those Mondays when the draw for the next round of the Cup was made in the council chamber of FA headquarters at Lancaster Gate. During the deadly monotony of double Maths, somebody would have trailed the earpiece up through his blazer, inside the sleeve and thence into an ear covered by an insouciant arm. A whisper would instantly travel by schoolboy bush telegraph: 'West Bromwich Albion or Blackburn Rovers.' The problem was only in finding out whether the intelligence related to United, City or Bury.

On the morning of Friday 16 October 1964, the whole school was agog in a way that had not been matched by anything since two years previously when the Cuban Missile Crisis seemed to harbinger the end of the world and, with a bit of luck, the cancellation of gym on Wednesday afternoons. In addition to the general election, the morning had brought news of the entirely unexpected fall of Nikita Khrushchev, removed from his positions of power both as leader of the Communist Party and as prime minister. These posts were beginning to look as fraught with danger as those in the Conservative and Unionist Party. Moscow Central was a Brezhnev and Kosygin party gain.

Meanwhile, my hopes of a Labour landslide to equal 1945, and a triumphant 'We are the masters now' to be trumpeted to an audience that positively quaked before the prospect of comprehensive schooling, had already been dashed. Vote counting was much slower in those days and quite a few seats were still undeclared at breakfast on Friday morning. Although Labour was ahead, the remaining seats were concentrated in rural areas, which were traditional Tory territory, and the Celtic fringe, which had always belonged to the Liberals. The final result was Labour 317 seats, Conservatives 304 and Liberals 9, giving Labour an overall majority of just four seats.

My local constituency, Middleton & Prestwich, was a Conservative hold. Sir John Barlow Bart, the sitting member, distributed his election pamphlet on the front of which was a large picture of himself and his lovely lady wife in the grounds of their ancestral home. I noted grimly that his ancient seat was somewhere in Cheshire, beyond even the outlying provinces where Manchester United played their home games. To my irritation this anachronistic remnant of the landed gentry, who clearly regarded Middleton & Prestwich as some kind of twentieth-century rotten borough, retained the seat with a majority cut from 10,000 over Labour in 1959 to one of barely 2,000. The Liberals polled 13,000 – if only they had been aware of the delights that can come from tactical voting they could have helped in the Labour candidate. Indeed, it could be argued that but for the national Liberal share of the vote, which was virtually double that of the 1959 election, the Tories would have been returned to power. And if the disconcerting news of events in Russia had reached England before the polls had closed, it is almost certain that the electorate would have plumped for Alec Douglas Home's experience in foreign affairs and the maintenance of the *status quo*. Overall, it was a victory all right, but a muted one.

I would have settled for any sort of victory, muted or otherwise, in the depths of the awful 1964–65 football season, perhaps the worst in my lifetime with the possible exception of 1997–98. By the time I arrived back from Israel just before the publication of the 'O' Level results, the first four matches of the season had already been played. On the plus side, City had scored a very creditable ten goals. On the minus side, they had acquired only two points and were already in crisis. Three days after a thumping 6–0 win over Leyton Orient, City had crashed 2–0 at home to the mighty Northampton Town. Four days after that, they had hammered another three goals past the pathetic Leyton Orient but conceded four. It was clearly going to be one of those seasons. In the event, it wasn't. It was considerably worse.

We had invested many of our hopes in Derek Kevan and Jimmy Murray, who had struck up such a formidable goal-scoring partnership in the 1963–64 season. This season they never got out of the starting blocks. One or the other was usually injured and on the rare occasions when they did play together, they had been too long out of each other's company for the sparks to fly again. In defence, George Poyser was spoiled for lack of choice. He couldn't make his mind up between the man who replaced Trautmann, Harry Dowd, and the eighteen-year-old FA Youth Cup hero, Alan Ogley. Invariably one played until he had a bad game, after which he was dropped. When he returned after his rival had performed with similar incompetence, he knew only that the first mistake he made would ensure a similar fate.

147

In the centre of defence, the old stalwart Bill Leivers, who had played right-back in the good side of the mid 1950s and centre-half in the relegation season, had been displaced by the youth team centre-half Alf Wood. Unfortunately, after a bright beginning, Wood's form deserted him completely. Poyser even played him at centre-forward for a while, in a move that smacked of desperation.

In September 1964, to fill the troubled centre-half spot, Poyser bought the experienced thirty-two-year-old Roy Gratrix from First Division Blackpool for £5,000. His debut was at home to Derby County and, as all fans always are, we were mightily encouraged by the prospect of a new signing. Building a football team is like constructing an enormous and highly complex jigsaw. You are always looking for the magical catalyst, the one Alex Ferguson found when he signed Eric Cantona from Leeds. You always hope that the new signing will make all the other pieces slot instantly into place, even though none of them has previously shown the slightest indication that they will do so.

A home crowd can also spot a good or bad player in minutes. It was obvious from Best's first appearance that he was a supremely gifted footballer. After Colin Bell had been signed from Bury, he played poorly in much of City's promotion run-in, particularly against his former club Bury when he had the proverbial nightmare, yet such was Bell's innate class that we all knew it would only be a matter of time before he came good. Conversely, Michael Frontzeck, who played for Manchester City as a left-back during 1996, was spotted as an instant duffer. Rumour had it that he had apparently acquired some international caps for Germany, but that must have been his twin brother because the Frontzeck we saw playing for City would have been lucky to have scraped into a Sunday pub team. The fans knew Frontzeck's true worth long before it dawned on the management.

In the kickabout before the captains tossed up, Roy Gratrix looked fine. Yes, definitely, he could be the one we had been waiting for. As if inspired by Poyser's shrewd manipulation of the transfer market, City played really well in the first half and by the interval we were 2–0 up. The Derby forward line had hardly managed a single attack and Gratrix had looked a solid and reliable figure at the back.

In the second half, the plot changed. Gratrix, after all, might not be the Messiah we had been waiting for. Gnawing disappointment set in when the first cross from the right wing passed over his head and onto that of the opposing centre-forward. Maybe it was just nerves, we told each other. It's his debut, there's a crowd of over 16,000 people examining his every move. When the next cross also found Gratrix completely static as if his boots had been nailed to the turf, we wondered how it was possible that George Poyser, chief scout, assistant manager and now manager of a major football league club, had failed to spot the fact that his putative centre-half couldn't jump.

City held on in that second half for a rare 2–0 home victory. Poyser was so delighted with his new signing that he stripped the real Bobby Kennedy of the captaincy and offered it in supplication to the non-jumping centre-half, who was gracious enough to accept. Even with the acquisition of Gratrix, in succeeding weeks results failed to improve. A 3–0 home defeat by Swansea was followed by a humiliating 5–3 reverse, again at home, against the might that was Mansfield Town in the first round of the League Cup.

Poyser couldn't understand it. Gratrix had been bought to fill the gaps, not create them. He was the rock upon which he could construct an impregnable defence. Against Huddersfield Town, Gratrix had the sort of nightmare match even Poyser couldn't fail to spot. After gifting the first two goals to the opposition, Gratrix, in the euphemistic words of the local paper, 'had the misfortune to crown an unhappy match by helping in Les Massie's shot for Huddersfield's third goal.' Against a lively Bolton Wanderers attack spearheaded by Wyn Davies and a cocky fair-haired little striker called Francis Lee, Gratrix surrendered completely. Davies and Lee each scored twice as Bolton humiliated us 4–2, easing off after the interval, by which time they were already four goals up.

Gratrix failed to solve the centre-half problem. Bought and paraded with such high hopes in September, he was playing in the reserves after the Bolton match at the end of November. He was replaced by Roy Cheetham, who had been in and out of the team as one of a number of interchangeably useless half-backs. Within weeks, Cheetham had asked for a transfer. It was readily granted. Cheetham remained at Maine Road for a further four years.

The atmosphere within the club degenerated still further. On Boxing Day, we had a home match against Bury. It leaked out that day that left-winger David Wagstaffe, one of the few assets we had at that time, had been sold over the Christmas period to Wolverhampton Wanderers for £40,000. David Green arrived in a filthy temper and proceeded to launch himself into the traditional threat of the outraged supporter. 'I am never coming to watch this team again,' he declaimed angrily, to the approving murmurs of the crowd around him. Always the demagogue, he carried on in similar vein with increasing justification as the match started. City and Bury drew 0–0 in a game that was as dire as the scoreline suggests. We yearned nostalgically, not so much for our old First Division status – that was long gone – but for an echo of the previous year's Christmas scoring spree. Our yearnings were to remain ignored.

We won the return game at Gigg Lane 2–0 two days later, but if we thought prosperity was just around the corner, the next match showed us we were mistaken. On 9 January 1965,

City were hopelessly outplayed at Maine Road in the third round of the FA Cup by Shrewsbury Town of the Third Division. In the last fifteen minutes, City managed to gather themselves sufficiently to launch a desperate assault on the Shrewsbury goal. Only a scrambled equaliser by Derek Kevan two minutes from time kept our Cup hopes alive at all, but such was our relief at our escape from near disaster that we flew back to the number 76 bus as if on wings. For the next few days, we comforted ourselves with the thought that the team was bound to have learned its lesson, wouldn't underestimate Shrewsbury a second time, particularly away from home, and couldn't anyway play quite as poorly again.

At half-time in the replay, with City leading courtesy of a Matt Gray header, such reasoning seemed entirely appropriate. In the second half, Shrewsbury realised they had underestimated City and wouldn't play as badly again. They scored three times without reply and could have had more. City returned to Manchester a well-beaten side. Well, we said to ourselves, this is it. It doesn't get any worse. We can only go upwards from here, and isn't it fortunate we've got a home game against relegation candidates Swindon Town on Saturday?

Wrong again. Among the faithful, the match against Swindon Town has passed into legend, principally because of the attendance. In a ground built to accommodate 63,000 people, a grand total of 8,015 showed up to see City lose 2–1. I was there and I have the programme to prove it, although judging from the number of conversations I have had about the game over the years, it appears that I have personally spoken to the other 8,014.

Swindon Town were not a bad side and included in their ranks Ernie Hunt, who went on to Coventry City, and Don Rogers, who, before following manager Bert Head to Crystal Palace, stayed at Swindon long enough to win the League

Cup in a memorable final against Arsenal. However, despite other Cup humiliations including the abysmal double-defeat by Lincoln City in 1996, the Swindon Town match still retains its ranking as the nadir of Manchester City's post-war history. We live, however, in interesting times, and it is perfectly possible that by the time this book is published, another name will have been added to the lengthy roll of dishonour.

The winning goal in the 1965 debacle was scored by Swindon's centre-forward, who skipped past the recalled but doggedly statuesque Roy Gratrix to fire home. The goal-scorer's name was Mike Summerbee and the next time he came to Maine Road, seven months later, it was one of the most auspicious days in the club's chequered history. He was one of the first signings made by Joe Mercer, and arguably the best, but when he drove away from Manchester with his Swindon colleagues in January 1965, he left behind a club that had almost ceased to function. The *Manchester Evening News* noted grimly:

> The shadow of Old Trafford will gobble up Manchester City, because there is nobody connected with the club who can bring back its greatness.

This has been our greatest handicap for the whole time I have been supporting Manchester City. The shadow cast by the other club in town is indeed a large one, and during the years 1964 to 1968 when the Best, Law, Charlton side was at its peak, we could barely free ourselves of it even when we were successful. Less than three weeks after we won the League Championship, United won the European Cup. No doubt there will be those who will denigrate any attempt to see Manchester City in terms of its relationship with its illustrious neighbour. I am sure that to those people, this book will appear another spineless submission before the Red Menace, but certainly in 1965, as in 1998, it is hard to write of sport in the city of Manchester without being aware of the stark and unpleasant contrast.

Calls were started for City to merge with United, although I could never understand how this would work out to the benefit of either team. Manchester United certainly didn't need any of our players, and a merger, it was soon realised, would simply mean the end of Manchester City.

In the Woody Allen film *Stardust Memories*, Woody finds himself trapped on an old dingy train crowded with silent losers, a balding fat man, a man crying and wiping his nose with his sleeve, two gypsy women with kerchiefs over their heads, staring at him sombrely, disapprovingly. He glances out of the dirty window and sees on the parallel track a sparkling new train crammed with beautiful people, drinking champagne and partying. A gorgeous woman holds a trophy up to the window and flashes a dazzling smile at Woody. She kisses the window, leaving the imprint of her lips on the glass with her lipstick. Her train starts to pull out of the station. Woody realises he is on the wrong train. He tries to get off the train, but he can't. I don't need to labour the analogy, do I?

United raced for the First Division title in 1964–65, doggedly pursued by Chelsea and Leeds. Chelsea, managed by Tommy Docherty, were inspired by the arrival of Peter Osgood, who sprang from obscurity to stardom as quickly as Best had. Over Easter, however, eight first-team players were discovered to have breached club discipline and Docherty had no qualms about suspending the lot of them. Among the infamous eight were Terry Venables, John Hollins, Eddie McCreadie and, interestingly enough, George Graham. Docherty's action, admirably strong and decisive as it might have been, cost Chelsea the League title. Leeds and United were left to wrestle each other to exhaustion.

Round one, I was delighted to observe, went to Leeds in a

notorious brawling FA Cup semi-final at Hillsborough. Billy Bremner, Johnny Giles, Norman Hunter and the now unjustly neglected Bobby Collins launched an assault upon United in which the football played a secondary part. Jack Charlton almost tore Denis Law's shirt off his back. Law, Crerand and Stiles were not intimidated by these battling tactics and responded in kind. Under the rules of conduct practised by referees in 1998, it is likely that such a match would have finished as a five-a-side. Almost irrelevantly, the first match ended as a draw, the replay as a victory for Leeds by a single goal. Despite this triumph, the season was to leave Leeds without a trophy. They lost in the FA Cup final in extra-time to goals by Hunt and St John which enlivened what had previously been a dire match.

After the semi-final and the dust had settled, there were seven games left in the race for the League title and Leeds, following their victory, were regarded as the psychological favourites. Leeds eventually became more than just an efficient side, but in April 1965 they had been promoted less than a year and Revie was still feeling his way in the First Division. Bob Stokoe spoke on television recently of Revie's attempts to bribe him when Leeds were due to play Bury in a match vital to Leeds' promotion hopes. Stokoe had been a manager for only a few weeks and wasn't sure if this was common practice.

Revie was a thorough professional, unwilling to leave anything to chance. In his golden years, this amounted to sending flowers to the wives of his players to mark special occasions and throwing Christmas parties for the children of the Elland Road staff, as well as handing the team comprehensive dossiers compiled on all members of the upcoming opposition. In his early days, it appeared to extend to sticking £5 notes in the boots of the opposition. The team he constructed to gain promotion from the Second Division was built around Bobby Collins, a tiny, skilful but highly combative Scottish inside-forward, Billy Bremner and Johnny Giles, who eventually assumed Collins's role in both the creative and aggressive sense. It was, in 1965, a journeyman outfit and Revie knew precisely how to cut his coat according to his cloth.

If Revie sensed that Manchester United were a beaten side after the FA Cup semi-final defeat, he was mistaken. Three days after being knocked out, they went to Ewood Park to face a difficult away match at Blackburn Rovers, whose side still contained the former England internationals Ronnie Clayton and Bryan Douglas. Best was injured that day and Stiles, Law and Crerand subdued, but one man dominated the game. Bobby Charlton carried United that afternoon, scoring a memorable hat-trick, and his side came away with a 5–0 victory which restored their battered morale. A fortnight later, United went to Elland Road and gained revenge for the Cup defeat by beating Leeds 1–0. In fact, of the closing seven games, United won six, losing only anti-climactically on the last day of the season at Villa Park. That defeat meant that United claimed the title from Leeds on goal average, and they must have greatly enjoyed the Yorkshire side's discomfiture as they went down to Liverpool at Wembley.

United were back in the European Cup for the first time since those tragic weeks after Munich, and Busby could renew his quest for his personal Holy Grail. Living in Manchester in 1965, you could sense the dawn of a new age of optimism. It was clear to all of us that we had only seen the start of this exceptional United side and they had won the League Championship with a flawed goalkeeper, Pat Dunne, signed from Shamrock Rovers for £4,000 in the summer of 1964. It was one of the few areas in which we could take comfort. Early in the 1966–67 season, Busby spotted his mistake and signed Alex Stepney from Chelsea. It was like replacing Jim Leighton with Peter Schmeichel. Now there was no chance.

City, too, had had an interesting run-in to the end of the 1964–65 season. While United were embroiled with Leeds in the challenge for Cup and League honours, City were unable to recover from the hammer blows of those defeats in January against Swindon and Shrewsbury. The Saturday before Easter, we went to Burnden Park to watch the return derby match against Bolton Wanderers. It was a nasty, spiteful game of which the referee soon lost control. Wyn Davies and Francis Lee again were rampant, Bolton won it 4–0 and City, as the score suggests, were never in it. On Good Friday, the Easter Bunny brought George Poyser his P45. Along with Poyser, City also sacked the trainer, Jimmy Meadows, who had been injured in their cause in the 1955 FA Cup final.

Hitler made a habit of invading countries at the weekend, concluding that defence systems operated less efficiently at those times. The Arab armies certainly attacked Israel in 1973 on Yom Kippur because they knew the Israeli army would be at its lowest state of preparedness on the most holy day in the Jewish calendar. The First World War erupted over the August Bank Holiday in 1914, and fifty years later, Manchester City appeared to be following an identical policy.

David Wagstaffe was sold to Wolverhampton Wanderers on Christmas Day 1964, when there were no newspapers. George Poyser was relieved of his duties on Good Friday 1965. His place was taken on a caretaker basis by old Fred Tilson, who had scored the winning goal in the 1934 Cup final. He was now the reserve-team trainer and, according to Fred Eyre, one of the graduates of his academy, he spent every day sleeping when he wasn't picking horses. A recent caller to a radio phone-in on football offered the memory that when he was younger, he had always imagined that the phrase 'caretaker manager' meant that the man who had previously worn brown overalls and cleaned out the toilets had suddenly been promoted to run the club. In old Fred Tilson's case, this might have been true.

At the very same time, Lancashire appointed as their new coach for the 1965 cricket season the seventy-year-old Charlie Hallows, who had scored a thousand runs in May in 1928. Without being ageist about this, it must be admitted that neither appointment exactly filled the hearts of the supporters with optimism. How were we to know that, at least as far as City were concerned, the wheel of fortune had now reached the bottom of its circle? So often we had clung to a particular victory or a new signing as the harbinger of great things. Invariably they turned out to be a chimera. In July 1965, just before I finished my first year in the sixth form, Manchester City announced that they had appointed the former Sheffield United and Aston Villa manager, Joe Mercer, to be the new team manager.

Miraculously, the wheel of fortune was starting its long-awaited upward cycle. What followed was a Jewish Manchester City supporter's idea of the real meaning of the Resurrection.

Chapter Eight

The four friends were starting to separate. The close ties of pre-pubescent childhood were loosened by our different responses to the challenge of adolescence. Michael Chadwick began the process. He was one of the unlucky losers in the lottery of the Eleven Plus and his failure shocked us all. Eschewing the delights of Heys Road Secondary Modern, he went to the local Jewish King David School, where he revelled in the co-educational culture. We still saw him at City games, but it wasn't the same as it had been at Park View. The shift from primary to secondary to tertiary education is always accompanied by a sad fall-out in friends.

Mike saw David Green more often, as the two of them were staples of what passed for Jewish teenage society in north Manchester in the 1960s. Their friendship was cemented when they played for Habonim, a Jewish youth club, for a season in which David as goalhanger exploited the referee's hazy knowledge of the offside laws to finish as top goalscorer.

Jeff continued to play in goal for Prestwich Casuals, but at the age of twelve I seemed to retire from football outside school hours. Unlike the others, I was in a form taking 'O' Levels in four years and Sunday was a day of work. Manchester City absorbed the residue of my footballing interest.

As usual, I was falling between two stools. I didn't feel I

fitted in with the Jewish kids, which might sound surprising but then I didn't really fit in with anyone. I certainly wasn't included in the non-Jewish party gang which haunted Bury on Saturday nights either. My home was at Maine Road or Old Trafford, or in the darkened cinemas and theatres of Manchester.

The parties, whose debaucheries were relayed with such gusto in school on Monday mornings, terrified me. My fears of these teenage rituals were no more than a sense of social awkwardness, particularly with girls. It wasn't that my nights and daydreams weren't filled with the traditional thoughts of them; it was simply that I'd grown up without a sister, which made them seem strange beings; and the general instruction to be 'good' which my mother had issued, and which remained with me despite her death, was too overwhelming to ignore. Single-sex secondary education didn't help, either. Although there was a Bury Grammar School for Girls next door, the frontier between the two schools couldn't have been more daunting had it been surrounded by barbed wire and manned by guards with machine guns in watch towers.

I had no desire to smoke, having spluttered over a cigarette at the age of eleven and never wished to repeat the sensation, and the desire for alcohol was terminated abruptly by an early introduction to kosher wine. I had no great moral antagonism to drinking, smoking and sex, but only the last of these appealed to me – and as it appeared to be only approachable through the other two, I held onto my virtue more successfully than Lancashire held onto their slip catches off Statham and Higgs.

My shyness didn't prevent my wanting to become an actor. At the age of eight, I had stunned Mrs Newlands's class with a sensational recital of Longfellow's poem *Hiawatha*, long passages of which I had learned off by heart for the sheer pleasure of it. At Bury Grammar School, I had won the

Openshaw Verse Speaking Prize in my first year with a quite incomprehensible poem by Laurence Binyon. In succeeding years I was never to win it again, to my intense irritation, coming second or third for the rest of my time at school.

My brother had led the way onto the stage with a series of portrayals ranging from 'Boy On Scooter' in a thirty-minute play to 'Boy' in *Henry V*, Puck in *A Midsummer Night's Dream*, culminating in Mosca in *Volpone*. Rehearsals for the school play took place on Friday nights, which caused a certain amount of heart searching in the management, but were eventually approved on the grounds that they were 'culture'. At Park View, I had been forbidden from taking part in the nativity play by the combined weight of 5,000 years of persecution and my mother. Instead, I was permitted to be a stage hand, which didn't quite satisfy my dreams of stardom.

I started at Bury Grammar at the same time as a new young History master called Martin Booth, who introduced a dash of contemporary theatre to the school's somewhat staid choice of school play. At the age of twelve I was playing Mrs Martin in Eugene Ionesco's *The Bald Prima Donna*, wearing my cousin Sheila's size 6 dress. I enjoyed getting the laughs but the appeal of cross-dressing was limited; sitting with knees firmly together I found particularly difficult, and I decided to turn down any future calls for my services in the female department. Such had been my success, however, that Bert Asquith, senior English master and chief play producer, cast me as the young Prince Arthur in the rarely performed *King John*.

This was probably my first introduction to the fraught tensions of show business. The sixth-former playing the title role dropped out, for reasons which were never made clear to the rest of the cast but which in the trade papers would have been described as 'irreconcilable artistic differences', i.e., the producer suddenly realised he was crap. He was replaced by another of the English masters. The part of Constance, mother to Arthur, was played by a girl from the neighbouring Derby School whom I hated with an intense passion, for reasons now, alas, completely forgotten.

Asquith's elder daughter Carroll played Queen Elinor, mother of the King, but on the second night was struck down by illness and replaced by her own real mother who unavoidably, but disconcertingly for her fellow actors, stood on stage in full mediaeval costume reading from the book. The youngest Asquith daughter Lyn played Blanch, niece to King John, and I transferred some of my adolescent yearnings to her. They were returned in a metaphorical envelope marked Not Known At This Address.

Making his debut in the insignificant part of French Herald was D.I.S.Green, who was particularly proud of those three initials. He believed it exalted him, like P.B.H.May and D.C.S.Compton, and he would use the pages of Jeff Cohen's exercise books on which to practise his autograph, experimenting with the 'D' which was written with a great flourish, looping around the rest of the signature. In *King John*, his only speech, 'You men of Angiers, open wide your gates/And let young Arthur Duke of Bretagne in,' I can remember now better than he could at the time.

I was comfortable with his token appearance that year but worried by his sudden elevation to stardom the following year, when he played the eponymous hero of *Everyman*. In a very short space of time, David Green had brown-nosed his way past me into Asquith's favours. In the other half of the double bill, I was appearing, somewhat to my own surprise, as Johann von Staupitz, Vicar General of the Augustinian Order, in Martin Booth's production of John Osborne's *Luther*. Martin tried hard to convince me that it was a brilliant piece of casting against type, but the niceties of the theological argument were lost on me and in any case, the monk's habit I had to wear was uncomfortably itchy. I was starting to doubt my commitment to the acting profession.

In our final year together, Asquith cast David as Bottom and me as Flute in his own version of *A Midsummer Night's Dream* (again!). Asquith's reverence for Shakespeare did not extend to performing his plays as they were written. In *King John* he had added, to his own huge delight and the incomprehension of everyone else, a new scene in an abbey in which King John is poisoned. His justification was the same as W.C.Fields's defence of his insertion of a juggling routine into his performance as Mr Micawber in George Cukor's 1935 version of *David Copperfield*. When challenged by the producer, David O. Selznick, as to why he thought Dickens had omitted any reference to juggling in his novel, Fields replied that Dickens had probably forgotten about it. Had he remembered, the author would no doubt have included it.

Asquith claimed that Shakespeare would have been thrilled by his reworking of the stale old plays. He turned the court of Theseus into a nightclub and included as Master of Ceremonies the delightfully named Irishman, Phil O'Strate. Given the fact that we had the best parts and the funniest pieces of business, it was unsurprising that David Green and I battled each other in full view of the audience for their affections. Asquith was shrewd enough to take note of our competitiveness, and the Pyramus and Thisbe slapstick was imbued with some heartfelt upstaging.

A few weeks after this farewell performance, I auditioned for the National Youth Theatre and was rewarded with a place in the newly formed Manchester Youth Theatre. Its first production was to be *Richard II* and I was cast as Bushy, one of the 'caterpillars of the Commonwealth'. Struan Rodger played the King; Paul Seed, the director of *House of Cards* and other prestigious television dramas, was the usurping Bolingbroke; and David Schofield, another adornment of Equity, played the banished Duke of Norfolk. Bearing in mind the percentage of youth-team footballers who graduate to the first team, the NYT and the MYT have nurtured some fine egos in their time. An introductory meeting for the cast was held at the director's house in south Manchester. My initial impression was obscured by the dense cloud of cigarette smoke which hung over the proceedings. All my old feelings of antipathy to parties were aroused. Within ten minutes of entering that room, I knew I was not going to become a professional actor. During rehearsals, which coincided with the final Test match of 1966 between England and the West Indies at The Oval, the suspicion grew. Endless sitting around, waiting for my tiny scene to arrive half an hour before the end of the working day, was not my idea of a good time. The sense of alienation was increased when John Arlott on my transistor radio was telling me that Tom Graveney and J.T.Murray were scoring centuries, and John Snow and Ken Higgs were putting on 128 for the last wicket. To my dismay, nobody in the entire cast was interested to know that Higgs was out two runs short of the highest ever tenth-wicket partnership, between Wilfred Rhodes and R.E.Foster at Sydney during the 1903–04 Ashes series.

Maybe I was in love with Shakespeare rather than acting. I was certainly greatly influenced by events during the summer of 1965, when I was seduced by the season of Olivier's Shakespeare films presented in London at the old and much-missed Academy cinemas on Oxford Street. Before they knocked the building down and turned it into another Marks & Spencer store, those green-baize movie theatres gave a grounding in cinema education to thousands of people. Academy Two, which played *Henry V, Hamlet* and *Richard III* in repertory, was located below street-level, and even in the middle of Olivier's Crispin Crispianus peroration you could still hear the noise of the tubes as they rumbled their way between Oxford Circus and Tottenham Court Road. Academy

One, courtesy of Raymond Rohauer, whose credit was more ubiquitous than the star's, screened an annual season of glorious Buster Keaton classics, from *Our Hospitality* to *Steamboat Bill Jr.*

I was in London in the summer of 1965 because my brother Geoff had graduated from Cambridge, become engaged and moved to London for six months to study for his Solicitors' Finals. He found a room in a house in St John's Wood, where I stayed during the course of the Lord's Test match between England and South Africa. It was ten years since my first sight of Test cricket, and five years since South Africa had last played in England when Geoff Griffin was no-balled out of the first-class game and an unexpectedly feeble South Africa surrendered meekly to Cowdrey and Dexter, Trueman and Statham.

The match I saw at Lord's was universally remembered as Bland's Test. Colin Bland, the brilliant South African cover fielder, ran out Ken Barrington on the Saturday afternoon and was hailed as the finest cover point of all time. On the Monday morning, just to show that it had been no fluke, he did it again, this time running out Jim Parks. The match was eventually drawn, but South Africa won the series 1–0 after the Pollock brothers had destroyed England at Trent Bridge.

To add to the excitement of the summer, the following day Edward Heath defeated Reginald Maudling in the first round of the contest to elect a new leader of the Conservative Party. Like John Major in 1997, the defeated Alec Douglas Home had retired from the fray with evident relief. Now that R.A.Butler had also left the politics of Westminster for the politics of Trinity College, Cambridge, it was no longer considered necessary for the party to disappear into conclave before the new leader 'emerged'. The previous system had certainly appeared to be designed solely to prevent Butler's accession to the office of Prime Minister.

It was probably because I had been with Uncle Laurence and my cousin Ronnie to watch the England v South Africa Test match that I became gripped by the Conservative Party election. Laurence could be quite spellbinding as he ranted on during the cricket about politics, and he made both candidates seem fascinating. A television executive in my later life pronounced judgment, I think as a way of putting me down: 'The trouble with Colin is that he's a great enthusiast.' I wouldn't quibble with the judgment, but I wouldn't regard it necessarily as a putdown either. I think enthusiasm is one of the great virtues of life. There is no question that I acquired most of these enthusiasms, for sport, music, books, politics and so on, from my Uncle Laurence.

I wish we could have maintained the closeness we had when I was a child and he was still living in Manchester. He owned a large house in Broughton Park with a wonderful garden in which Ronnie and I played endless hours of cricket. Unfortunately, the garage which ran parallel to the garden contained a window which was infuriatingly positioned at short midwicket. Too frequently Ronnie dropped short, tempting me to pull him through the leg side. It required only the slightest misjudgment for me to crash the ball straight through that window, which I did with embarrassing regularity. Auntie Ada was distinctly unimpressed but Laurence maintained an amused tolerance. Ronnie was told to pitch the ball up and I was warned to roll my wrists and keep the ball down in the future. Ironically, the street in which Laurence lived has become the preserve of the ultra-religious Orthodox Jews whom Laurence so mistrusted. I am sad that he is no longer around to drive his car ostentatiously up and down the street on the Sabbath in order to provoke these neighbours beyond endurance. It is exactly the sort of antic in which he took great pleasure.

Writing about him now, after all these years, I feel nostalgic for the many blessings he bestowed – and still angry at his ultimate betrayal. Although I continued to enjoy going to the cricket with Laurence, his behaviour after my mother's death had irreversibly soured the relationship. After the cricket at Lord's was over for the day, we walked up the Finchley Road to Camden Library, where Laurence introduced me to my first hearing of the Schubert Octet. He was still a cultural influence, but I had lost my reverence for him and he knew it. The next time we were to meet was to bring the curtain down for good.

After that Lord's Test, I travelled to Switzerland with Jonathan Marks, a boy from across the street who was also learning German for 'A' Level at Bury. His parents had been particularly kind after the tragedy at home and I had by far preferred to stay after school with them than with anyone else. The Marks family was considerably more religiously observant than I had become by this time and when we got to the Swiss–German border at Konstanz-am-See, Jonathan refused to cross it. He was under strict instructions from his parents never to enter Germany and while I understood and sympathised with the origins of the *diktat*, I found the dogmatism hard to accept. Instead, we progressed to Vaduz in Liechtenstein which we both found charming, if a little short of historical interest. Sadly, for all my consequent support of them, Liechtenstein have never achieved anything significant in the World Cup or the European Championships and thus join the long list of losers to whom I have given my heart, if not my brains.

In Frank Capra's *Mr Smith Goes To Washington*, there is a speech delivered by James Stewart which sends shivers down my spine every time I hear it. The corrupt Senator Paine (played by Claude Rains) has organised public opinion in the form of 5,000 telegrams which are wheeled onto the floor of the Senate, where James Stewart as the young idealistic Senator Smith is facing humiliating defeat at the soiled hands of Paine. Paine had been Smith's father's best friend before he was murdered for attempting to expose dishonesty in high places.

Smith's essential decency and honesty appears to be in vain. Wearily he picks up a handful of telegrams, gazes at them in despair and lets them drop. He walks over to Paine, who has betrayed his own youthful idealism and is squirming inside as Smith reminds him and the watching gallery in the packed Senate of the man who had started them both on the road to a noble and honest public life.

I guess this is just another lost cause, Mr Paine. All you people don't know about lost causes. Mr Paine does. He said once they were the only causes worth fighting for . . . You knew that, Mr Paine, and I loved you for it, just as my father did. And you know you fight for the lost causes harder than for any others. Yes, you'd even die for them, like a man we both know, Mr Paine.

I wonder if Manchester United supporters can shed tears at that speech. What do they know of lost causes? The nearest they came to a lost cause was on the runway at Munich airport in 1958, and their tears were joined by everyone who loves sport and saw in that terrible accident the tragedy of young men of promise cut off before their prime. For Manchester United, Munich wasn't so much a lost cause as a cause delayed. Busby might have won the European Cup in 1958; we shall never know. What we do know is that he did win it in the end, and deservedly so. Manchester United supporters have been spoiled by success. It has bred in them an arrogance that has made them equally deservedly unpopular throughout the game. What do they know of lost causes, who only trophies know?

It requires very little perspicacity to realise that Manchester City have always been my lost cause. I'm no masochist. I don't enjoy losing, but it breeds in those whose lot it is to experience more than their fair share of disappointments a more rounded view of the world than is apparent from what used to be called the Stretford End. You can argue that in the years from 1968 to 1992 when United failed to win the League Championship, their supporters knew what it was like to walk in the shadows, particularly those cast by Liverpool.

Up to a point, Lord Copper. United regarded the lack of a League Championship not as a sign that something was wrong with the playing staff but as a sign that there was something wrong with the world. If United don't win the League (or Yorkshire the County Championship), the time itself is out of joint. (O curse and spite that ever Wilf McGuinness, Frank O'Farrell, Tommy Docherty, Dave Sexton and Ron Atkinson were ever born to set it right.) The earth is not spinning on its axis, the universe has been disordered. United are supposed to win things. It is a sign that God is in His Heaven and all is right with the world. United not winning the League Championship is an offence against Nature herself. That's why the FA should rearrange fixtures at United's convenience. It is divinely so ordered.

I like lost causes. I always have, I make no bones about it. My wife, being American, does not share this silly view. I explain to her that it all originated at Headingley in June 1956, when I was nearly seven years old. England won the toss and batted, but the Australian new-ball attack of Lindwall and Archer quickly removed Richardson, Cowdrey and Oakman to leave England struggling on 17 for 3.

Australia had won the second Test at Lord's to go one-up in the series and Laker's historic nineteen wickets in a single match had not yet been taken. The Ashes, regained after nineteen tortuous years in 1953 and retained so gloriously Down Under in 1955, were threatening to return with the Aussies again when out of the Leeds pavilion strode Cyril

169

Washbrook, Lancashire captain, six years retired from Test cricket and brought back to face the Australians at this moment of crisis by his fellow selectors in a desperate gamble. Washbrook joined May and together they took the score to 204, a magnificent partnership of 187. May was out just before the close of play for 101, leaving Washy 90 not out overnight. Although he fell lbw to Benaud the next morning for 98, two runs short of the century the whole country ached for him to achieve, his innings has become immortalised as one of the great Ashes knocks. May's 101 is far less memorable than Washbrook's 98, and the reason we remember the latter is not only because of the way in which he turned the situation around, but because he *failed* to make it to three figures. The triumph of the underdog is always going to be more appealing than another machine-like success of the over-privileged. 'Why does everyone hate us?' asks Alex Ferguson plaintively. 'They're just jealous,' whinge his adoring fans in adulatory explanation. They just don't 'get' it, do they?

My other lost cause, Lancashire, had come close to City's nadir before the 1965 season opened. Having sacked Ken Grieves, the Lancashire committee were divided as to who should become their next captain. Brian Statham, now approaching the twilight of his great career, was the only logical choice, but A.C.Smith, the Warwickshire wicket-keeper, was touted in some quarters. There was widespread surprise and dismay when the following advertisement appeared in *The Times* on 24 November 1964.

A First Class cricket club invites applications from persons with First Class cricket experience for the position of captain of a county Eleven.

The Lancashire committee eventually admitted the error of its ways, not by anything written or spoken but by appointing

Brian Statham captain for the 1965 season.

The romance of the lost cause and the triumph of the underdog are two of the themes which link my love of sport with my love of film and theatre. Brecht said that sport is the ultimate theatre. Manchester United fans call Old Trafford the Theatre of Dreams. Stuart Hall says that Maine Road is the Theatre of Comedy. They are linked by a love of drama. What you remember in sport are not just the goals, but the magic moments – Gordon Banks clawing away Pelé's header in that best of all World Cup matches, Bobby Moore wiping his hands on the velvet cloth before shaking hands with the Queen and lifting the Jules Rimet Trophy, Gazza's tears, Gary Lineker being substituted in his last match.

What you remember in movies are not plots but the magic images – John Ford's wagon train plodding through Monument Valley, Fred Astaire dancing 'Cheek to Cheek' with Ginger Rogers, the change of seasons in *Dr Zhivago*, Lawrence on his camel lost amid the vastness of the Arabian desert, images accompanied by outstanding movie music. The drama is also in the brevity of the great lines mixed with the image – Vivien Leigh grasping a handful of earth from Tara and vowing, 'I'll never be hungry again'; Bogart telling Claude Rains, 'Louis, I think this is the beginning of a beautiful friendship,' as they walk off into the mist of the Casablanca airport.

It was Olivier, both as actor and director, who crystallised my love of movies and theatre. I still find his *Henry V* and *Richard III* definitively satisfying. William Walton's music for all three of his Shakespeare movies was so moving that I eventually located the original soundtrack in Gibbs, a wonderful second-hand record shop near the Central Library in Manchester. I would play it over and over again, to the irritation of my neighbours, seeing, as I heard those melodies, the bold primary colours and sweeping panning shots

171

of Agincourt and Bosworth. I appreciate that Kenneth Branagh's *Henry V* has its admirers, and I was much struck by McKellen's interesting update of *Richard III*, but Olivier came first. He broke fresh ground and he deserves to be remembered as such.

In these days of video shops and movies on television, it is hard to convey quite how difficult it once was to see movies, once they had left the circuit for the first time. *Henry V* had been made in 1944 and *Richard III* in 1955, so to find them in 1965 was almost impossible. The Academy cinemas ran them every summer, but I wasn't in London very often and I was forced to change buses three times to get to places like Gatley or Chadderton, outlying suburbs of Manchester where, once a year, one of these films might play a schools matinee on a Wednesday afternoon. I hated the noise made by kids who didn't want to be there, but if I concentrated hard enough I could will myself back to 1415 or 1485, or, more interestingly, onto the set as the movie was being made.

Education, reading, call it what you will, can sometimes have an oddly divisive effect. I became obsessed with the history of film and theatre, but I never found a reciprocal interest from any of my friends who liked acting or going to the theatre. For them it was strictly a contemporary event. Together we would go to see out-of-town previews at the Manchester Opera House or national tours by the RSC or the National Theatre, but they had no interest in discussing how Olivier's 1937 performance of *Henry V* differed from his film version, or how his 1938 *Hamlet* at the Old Vic was influenced by the Freudian psychoanalyst Dr Ernest Jones. Here was something else to separate me from the rest. I could recite the history of productions at the Old Vic or the West End in the 1930s as easily as I could (and still can) name all the results of the FA Cup finals since 1946. There wasn't a point to it, although both sets of trivia came in useful later when I appeared on *University Challenge*.

In the opening moments of each *University Challenge*, I used to introduce myself as, 'I'm Colin Shindler from Manchester City, reading History,' to the amusement of Bamber Gascoigne and the boredom of my fellow team-members. This worked well enough till we reached the semi-final, when the members of the Churchill College team responded with, 'I'm John Smith from West Bromwich Albion, reading English,' etc. Bamber found this considerably less amusing and I was still working out how I could retort appropriately when I looked at the scoreboard and found we were losing by 165 points to nil.

By 1970, when these insignificant events took place, Manchester City had come to dominate my life. It all stemmed from the announcement in July 1965 that Joe Mercer was taking charge at Maine Road. Within a few days, for the princely sum of £30 a week, Mercer had lured Malcolm Allison from Plymouth Argyle to join him. Mercer's wife had been opposed to Joe taking the job at first, because he had been in poor health after his stressful times at Bramall Lane and Villa Park. The idea was that the dynamic Allison should work more closely with the players and take some of the pressure off Mercer.

It was a vain hope. Allison caused far more stress than he relieved, with his rantings at officials, his disciplinary record with the FA, his touchline bans and his high-profile media encounters. At the same time, it soon became clear that he and Mercer were forging a unique partnership, and their effect on the club was, initially at least, wholly beneficial.

School broke up in the summer of 1965 with City mired in the sloth of post-Poyser inertia. With the arrival of Mercer and Allison, the playing staff underwent a rapid transformation and by the time I started my last full year at school, significant progress had already been made. Ironically, Mercer's first signing proved one of his least successful. Ralph Brand, bought from Rangers for £25,000, had been one of the leading scorers north of the border for the past few seasons and had the reputation of being Scotland's answer to Jimmy Greaves. Unfortunately, the football in Scotland must have been played at a much slower pace, because Brand looked sluggish even in the Second Division in England. When he came, he was slow but he was a deadly finisher. By the time he was transferred to Sunderland two years later, he was considerably quicker but had no idea where the goal was any longer. The day after Brand signed, Derek Kevan, aware that his face didn't fit in with the new regime, packed his bags and left.

The day before the new season started, Mike Summerbee, according to legend, left his summer job supervising deck-chairs on the beach, hopped into his sports car and tootled up from the West Country to sign for Manchester City for a fee of £35,000. The following day he was the star man in a team which gained a creditable 1–1 draw at Middlesbrough, and over the next ten years he was to be consistently the star performer. On days when we lost comfortably by three goals to one, Summerbee would have scored the consolation goal and provided a stream of crosses which had been missed by the rest of the forward-line. He would probably also have been involved in a dust-up with the opposing left-back and been booked for it.

Summerbee was never a great finisher. If he was through the opposition defence with nobody to beat but the goal-keeper, it was a reasonably safe bet that the ball would finish at the back of the stand behind the goal rather than in the back of the net. Summerbee was fast, skilful, hard and, above all, humorous. He had a rapport with the crowd with which perhaps only Gazza, of today's players, can compare. I saw Summerbee once take a helmet off a policeman stationed by the corner flag and play with it on his head for five minutes.

One of his favourite tricks was to take a throw-in by

hurling the ball hard at an opposing defender's back so that the ball would return to him and he could continue down the wing. It was a practice much used in the school playground, rarely on the professional field. Summerbee could nutmeg a full-back, get scythed down, throttle the offender and kiss the referee as he strode thunderously towards him, all within the space of twenty seconds. He never quite established his place in the England team, but then Alf Ramsey's aversion to wingers was notorious.

A few days after the Middlesbrough game, Mercer made his third signing. The balding George Heslop came from Everton reserves for £25,000 and instantly claimed the centre-half spot for his own. It meant an end to the endless succession of rotten number fives stretching back from the days of the own-goal specialist John McTavish, through Jackie Plenderleith, Bill Leivers, Roy Cheetham, Mike Batty and Alf Wood, to the *reductio ad absurdum* of Roy Gratrix.

You couldn't accuse our new hero of being a footballing centre-half. My favourite photograph of George is of his wrapping both arms round John Radford of Arsenal, himself hardly the epitome of speed, in an attempt to prevent the centre-forward getting past him. George could jump, however, unlike many of his predecessors, and he was our best centre-half for ten years since the receding hairline of Dave Ewing was in its pomp.

The great quality Mercer gave his first team was a sense of continuity. He decided Harry Dowd was a better goalkeeper than Alan Ogley, and Dowd was to remain in goal for the next two years unless injured. The real Bobby Kennedy settled in at right-back, the gazelle-like legs of Cliff Sear at left-back, and the half-back line read, as it would for the next four years, Doyle, Heslop and Oakes.

In terms of goals conceded, it wasn't an immediate success. In its first eight games the defence leaked seventeen goals, but we only lost one match and when we went away to play the two sides which had started better than we had, Southampton and Huddersfield Town, we won one and drew one and Harry Dowd kept a clean sheet on both occasions. It was a beginning. Ironically, it was the match which ended that opening unbeaten run which convinced me we were going to win promotion.

I had been to Old Trafford to watch United play Chelsea. It had not been a particularly enjoyable afternoon, despite an early goal by Terry Venables. Charlton equalised and then Law scored a devastating hat-trick of headers to give the champions a crushing 4–1 victory in front of their adoring fans. The City match must have kicked off slightly late, because by the time I had barged my way out of Old Trafford and onto Warwick Road North, the result was not yet in. I had my transistor radio clamped to my ear as the crowd approached the bridge over the railway line. As invariably happened, the crush was so great that I was lifted off my feet and carried along by the tide of humanity. By the time they regained contact with the earth's surface, the result had been announced: 'Cardiff City 4, Manchester City 3.' Although we had lost, I felt that scoring three goals away from home for the second time in a week (we had also drawn 3–3 at Norwich) was a good sign and as soon as the defence settled we would start to pull away from the pack.

The front line of Summerbee, Crossan, Pardoe, Young and Connor also bore a settled look. Johnny Crossan, oddly enough, had been signed by George Poyser from Sunderland after the Shrewsbury and Swindon debacles, although his impact, like that of the rest of the team, was minimal on City's abysmal finish to the 1964–65 season. It must have been a strange but pleasant sensation for Mercer and Allison to find such a good player on the books of such an unpromising club. He was the logical team captain. Neil Young was converted from a left-winger to a striking inside-forward, his place at outside-left going to the youth-team winger David Connor. As City headed towards December, the goals started to dry up and after three successive away defeats, Malcolm Allison came up with the first of his great tactical plans, some of which were brilliant, most of them insane, but all of which were original. Mike Doyle was strong in the air but rarely had the opportunity to display it at half-back. Glyn Pardoe, who had started out as a goalscorer, wasn't making much of an impact on defences. Allison decided to swap them around in the middle of the match *without changing the numbers on their shirts*.

The move was instantly successful. A 5–0 thrashing of Leyton Orient was followed by a useful 2–0 away win at Crystal Palace. On New Year's Day 1966, 47,141 crammed into Maine Road to see the top of the table clash with Huddersfield Town. Johnny Crossan gave us the lead with a fortunate penalty, after which the game disintegrated into something just short of open warfare. David Connor blotted out the ex-United wing-half Jimmy Nicholson and Summerbee had his nose broken in two places – an occupational hazard for a combative winger with a proboscis large enough to provoke the refrain, 'We'd walk a million miles to the end of your nose, Mike Suuuuummerbee!'

The vital goal was scored midway through the second half by Mike Doyle. When City beat Rotherham 3–1 at home ten days later, Doyle scored his sixth goal in four games. The bandwagon was rolling. We went to First Division Blackpool in the FA Cup third round and were unlucky to come away with only a draw. Over 52,000 saw the 3–1 win in the replay at Maine Road, and nearly 40,000 watched a comfortable 2–0 victory over Grimsby in the fourth round. At home to Leicester City in the fifth round in front of 56,787, we opened nervously and were two down by half-time. Two goals in the second half, though, brought us a deserved replay and on the following Wednesday we went to Filbert Street where Neil Young scored the only goal for a famous victory. It barely rated a line in the newspaper because United had beaten Benfica in the European Cup on the same night.

I didn't go to Leicester, because I was in the middle of my mock 'A' Levels. Work apart, I couldn't afford to go to most of the away matches anyway, so I still made my bi-weekly treks to Old Trafford to watch United, courtesy now of my brother Geoff's season ticket in the new cantilever stand. Sitting without friends in a stand overwhelmingly red in allegiance was an exercise in diplomacy. I could never bring myself to stand and applaud a United goal, but I would clap fiercely if Best shot just past the post or Law headed over with the goalkeeper beaten. I experimented with applauding like a decent fair-minded Englishman a good (i.e. any) goal scored by the opposition, but since it was soon apparent that I was not surrounded by any other decent fair-minded Englishmen, I soon desisted.

Besides, in the mid 1960s those occasions arose very infrequently. There were times when Charlton would hit forty-yard crossfield passes with the outside of his boot for George Best to collect and wriggle past three or four defenders. There were numerous occasions on which the ball streaked across the opposition's penalty area with the predator Law inches away from turning it in. At those times, United seemed to be invincible. Every time Charlton collected the ball in midfield the crowd's roar began to gather in volume, Best would cause it to increase and Law would inevitably provoke the crescendo. I felt helpless, watching in awe as United rolled forward, intimidating the opposition defence, seemingly able to score at will.

The United crowd jeered good-naturedly at half-time if City were losing. It was a matter of no great consequence to them whether City were down 2–1 at half-time to Cardiff or winning by that score. Then, as now, they had their sights set on the European Cup and City's pathetic fumblings in the Second Division were a complete irrelevance. Occasionally you'd get one of the arrogant sods mouthing the platitude, 'It's always better for the city of Manchester when United and City are both doing well.' It's not a belief I share, and I think most United supporters can't stand even the possibility that there could be another team in Manchester who might do well enough to deflect some of the glory from their own magnificence.

Frankly, I prefer that view. It has the merit of honesty and, in my own way, I can confirm it because when United were relegated in 1974 after losing at home 1–0 to City, I was truly delighted to see them in the Second Division. In fact, had they slipped through the divisions in turn and arrived at the bottom of the Fourth I would have been even more delighted, so I simply don't believe all this patronising guff about what is better for the city of Manchester. In due course, the wheel will come full-circle again and at some point in my life, City will be top dog in Manchester again. It is a prospect to be savoured and, as with all deferred gratification, sometimes you can think yourself into a situation where the historical knowledge of the inevitable turning of the wheel of fortune is enough to keep you sane in the darker moments.

Manchester United, high on the aroma of their own legend, progressed serenely through the opening two rounds of the 1965–66 European Cup, then as now, the only competition they considered worth their winning. In the quarter-finals they met Benfica and at the end of the first leg, I felt there was some hope. United had blown a 3–1 lead by conceding a goal in the last five minutes and were fortunate not to lose another. A single-goal margin was little enough to take to the Stadium of Light. Benfica had been in four of the five previous European Cup finals and in Eusebio they possessed one of the great players of his day. At the back of my mind also was the comforting thought of what had happened to United on their previous trip to Lisbon, when they had been in possession of a 4–1 lead from the first leg.

As all the world knows, my hopes were cruelly dashed – 9 March 1966 was the day on which the talented young Irish footballer George Best became Georgie Best, superstar. He scored twice as United tore Benfica apart in front of 75,000 stunned spectators. They settled for 5–1, Sporting Lisbon dishonour avenged. A semi-final tie against Partizan Belgrade held no terrors. United were already mentally riding round Albert Square in an open-top bus displaying the European Cup to their adoring fans.

Now came the part that really infuriated me. It was bad enough that United should dominate the back pages of every newspaper, relegating City's heroic FA Cup fifth round victory at Leicester to the status of an also-ran. But when George Best returned from Lisbon the following day, he was photographed by the tabloids wearing a large sombrero, provoking the inevitable caption, 'El Beatle.' Manchester United, led by George Best's sexuality, had entered the world of show business. Fortunately, Mr Best's libido was to cause the odd chortle or two on the other side of Manchester in due course, but for the moment it was time for us to be stoic in the face of adversity. Our time would come.

Indeed, our time had nearly arrived. During the Mancunian spring of 1966, City's Cup run, allied to their consistent performances in the League, had led to rapidly increasing crowds and on 29 March, the first full house of 64,000 since the last derby match watched a mind-numbing goalless draw with Everton in the sixth round. It was just over a year since the day of the notorious 8,015 who had gathered to watch Summerbee playing for Swindon. Everton, it was gratifying to note, were as frightened of City as we were of them.

The following Tuesday, the four of us bunked school,

borrowed David's father's car and drove to Liverpool for the replay. This was by no means the easiest part of the day. David, being eight months older than the rest of us, had been the first to take his driving test. He had passed at his first attempt, in the amazing time of six weeks. We were all frightfully impressed until we actually got into the car with him and saw the way he drove. It was terrifying. The M62 had not yet been built and there were a lot of roundabouts on the East Lancs Road. David had either not encountered one on his foreshortened training or he had evidently developed a hatred for them, because his strategy was to ignore all roundabouts completely by driving straight over them. It's one thing to do this in a lorry or a jeep, quite another in a Ford Zephyr, especially at sixty miles an hour.

We arrived, emotionally drained, about three o'clock, played football with a tennis ball in the car park for two hours and got into Goodison Park as soon as the gates were opened. Half an hour before kick-off, Allison and the team emerged to wave at us, crammed into the swaying terraces. How we roared our approval at these heroes, Allison, Summerbee and the others, who had given us back our pride. David had enjoyed scaring us by relating stories of Scousers who peed into Fairy Liquid bottles then squirted the contents over the opposition supporters. It sounded like the actions of a deranged *Blue Peter* presenter, but we reckoned it was a small price to pay for the rediscovery of self-esteem, although, jammed onto the unsegregated terraces as we were, we kept a wary eye out for the first sign of a washing-up liquid bottle.

That heart-stopping Tuesday night, City came of age. Dowd and Heslop were magnificent in defence, Summerbee a constant source of inspiration to us and irritation to Brian Labone and his men. It was 0–0 again after ninety minutes, 0–0 after extra-time. We finally emerged from the ground after ten o'clock, having been incarcerated there since shortly after five, but we were so exhilarated by the game we scarcely noticed anything. We certainly didn't notice that David hadn't applied the handbrake and the car was rolling slowly down the slight hill of the car park, straight into the tail lights of the vehicle in front. Incensed, because his father used the precious car for picking up fresh food from the market for the Greens' small grocery shop, David leapt from his seat and fiercely berated the driver of the car into whom we had smashed for his idiocy. The driver, cowed by this pre-emptive strike, drove away in silence. It was only when David returned to the car that we pointed out the impossibility of the car in front having rolled backwards uphill into us. It took a good thirty seconds for the logic to sink in.

As sixteen- or seventeen-year-olds, the idea of repaying David's father by filling the car with petrol never occurred to us. Instead, we concentrated on how we could get back to Manchester in a car whose fuel gauge hovered menacingly on empty. The solution was to keep hitting the dashboard hard. After a second or two, the fuel-gauge needle would jerk unconvincingly towards the quarter mark, where it would stay, clinging pathetically for a couple of miles, before slumping back towards empty again. Frantic hammering would induce another feeble jerk, but eventually we crawled into Prestwich with the car still functioning. It had been a memorable day.

Irritatingly, the second replay at Molineux took place a week later, which was the first night of Passover. The ragings of adolescent rebellion were not strong enough to overcome the demand for our attendance at the traditional Seder night table. This year, particularly, the story of the Exodus from Egypt made more sense than ever. The previous year, we had solemnly intoned 'This year we are slaves but next year we shall be free men' and here we were, top of the Second Division and in the sixth round of the FA Cup, facing the prospect of a semi-final against United. The miracles the Lord performed to enable Moses to lead his people from Egypt were paralleled by the extraordinary transformation wrought by Mercer and Allison in a few short months. In addition, between the two replays, Labour had won a second consecutive general election, returning to power with a real working majority, and my old bugbear the sitting, not to say comatose member, Sir John Barlow, had finally lost the rotten borough of Middleton and Prestwich.

Unfortunately, the last of the plagues hit us that Seder night as well. Everton, outplayed by all accounts for the first thirty minutes, weathered the City storm and scored twice just before half-time. Mike Doyle, in a number nine shirt and playing as an orthodox centre-forward, made no impact at all and City desperately lacked a goalscorer.

Cup-tied for that game was City's recent signing from Bury, nineteen-year-old Colin Bell. Bury had initially refused to sell Bell to another Second Division club and then priced the player at a prohibitive £60,000. Allison would go to Bury matches, surrounded by scouts from other clubs, and would keep up a negative running commentary, 'He's got no left foot, he's useless in the air,' and so on, just to keep them at bay until City could raise the £45,000 Bury eventually accepted.

Over Easter we played Bury twice, winning an awful game 1–0 on Good Friday and losing 2–1 at Gigg Lane on the following Tuesday. Fortunately, we didn't go back to school for another two weeks and by this time I was in the middle of final revision for 'A' Levels. Bell, predictably, had a stinker for us in both matches. But none of that mattered on 4 May when he scored the only goal in a 1–0 win at Rotherham which clinched promotion.

Life was getting better and better. On 20 April, United had beaten a mediocre Partizan Belgrade side 1–0 but it was not enough to eradicate the two-goal lead Partizan had brought with them from the first leg in Belgrade, which had been wrung from an over-confident United side lacking Best. United were now out of the European Cup and, finishing a poor fourth behind Liverpool in the First Division, would not be back in the competition next year. A few days after the Partizan disappointment, a forlorn United were beaten by a Colin Harvey goal in the FA Cup semi-final at Burnden Park.

Twelve months before, a managerless City had staggered dazed into the close season, looking on from afar as United proudly displayed the League Championship. Now United, trophyless, had to slip away as City, temporarily, became kings of Manchester. For the final match of the season, another Maine Road full house gathered to acclaim City as Second Division champions in a meaningless last League match of the season against the other promoted team, Southampton. We gathered again as the gates opened, looking for the best seat in the Platt Lane Stand, on the front row above one of the staircases and away from the two pillars which blighted the views of 5,000 spectators. We were in fine verbal form as Jeff, David, Mike and I sat there, like four old men, reminiscing about the old days, i.e. last year. It was a party atmosphere, and as David Green noted brightly as he spotted the gleaming bald pate of the Southampton inside-right, 'Jimmy Melia's been up all night polishing his head for the big match.' When you're not quite seventeen, that kind of wit is hilariously funny. The match wasn't. It finished in a boring 0–0 draw, but we didn't care. We were up. United, beware!

Chapter Nine

It is impossible, in a book about football, to write about the summer of 1966 without mentioning the World Cup. It warrants but a brief mention in this one because it has been covered in such exhaustive detail elsewhere. My awareness of football had begun at a time when England were still frozen in the shocked state induced by the Hungarian victories of 1953 and 1954. The first World Cup I can remember is the 1958 tournament, in which England, recently deprived by the Munich disaster of Edwards, Byrne and Taylor, lost disappointingly in a play-off to Russia before the quarter-finals.

In 1962, there were only fuzzy television pictures from South America as England were dispatched 3–1 by Brazil. It wasn't the fact of the defeat or the margin of it that was so depressing, but a sense, fuelled then as now by press speculation, that the gulf between England and the better foreign teams was unbridgeable. Brazil had Garrincha and Vava; we had Bryan Douglas (Blackburn Rovers) and Gerry Hitchens (Aston Villa). Our team was respectable but in some way unequally matched.

Alf Ramsey restored to England a sense of the possible. In 1966 it was Brazil's turn to struggle, as they failed to reach the quarter-finals. Everyone was shocked but, clearly, relieved. If the 1966 World Cup was going to be a trial of physical strength rather than diabolical ball-skills, we could be seriously considered as a possible winner of the competition. That was the way it worked out. A deadly dull scoreless draw against Uruguay in the opening match of the tournament was followed by three scrappy, unconvincing victories over Mexico, France and Argentina.

Although I wanted England to win, I maintained a sense of ambivalence about the contributions of the Manchester United players, Bobby Charlton and Nobby Stiles. Charlton's goal which broke the deadlock against Mexico I saluted with joy, but Stiles remained a controversial figure in the England side, until the semi-final in which he marked Eusebio almost out of the game. Now it is possible to play both David Batty and Paul Ince in the England team without attracting adverse comment, but Stiles's selection for England was a naked admission that he was there to spoil the game for the opposition and take out their chief playmaker.

In the fortunate 2–0 win over France, Stiles crashed into their most skilful player Jacques Simon from behind, long moments after Simon had laid the ball off, leaving him writhing in agony. Since it happened directly under the gaze of the referee, it was a miracle Stiles wasn't sent off. Over the next few days, a storm of controversy built up in which FIFA told the FA that if Stiles were to repeat his actions, he would be banned from the tournament. The FA leaned on Ramsey to drop Stiles for the match against Argentina. Ramsey refused to do so, and made his support for Nobby plain for all to see.

I quite enjoyed Stiles's discomfiture because it was a reminder to the Manchester United worshippers that their idols' success owed something to brute force as well as sublime skill. In any case, if Ramsey saw Stiles as a vital element in a victorious England team, who was I to disagree? I took refuge, along with many others, in the story that suggested Stiles's fouls were a result of his contact lenses not working properly. The excuse had an attractively comic edge, which fitted the toothless grin Stiles exhibited off the field.

I cheered Bobby Charlton's two goals against Portugal despite the fact that since our meeting in the Blackpool hotel in January 1963, I had always believed that he was a miserable bugger off the pitch. I was relieved to note that the heroes of the final triumph came from West Ham United. That, at least, prevented Charlton's canonisation, though it only delayed his knighthood. I still think it is scandalous that Charlton was knighted and Bobby Moore wasn't.

Surely, *surely*, the Royal ante-chamber isn't covered in posters of David Beckham and Ryan Giggs? I feel pretty sure the Queen doesn't go to bed with her crown on, but it would hasten the end of the monarchy in this house if I felt she did so wearing a Sharp nightshirt with a number 7 on the back. This is not so far-fetched as it might seem at first sight. The Royal family fits perfectly the classic demographic breakdown of out-of-town Reds. They live nowhere near Manchester, they know nothing about football, they've never been to Old Trafford but they go to the Cup final. We have been told that Prince William and Prince Harry are Manchester United supporters. They would be, wouldn't they?

I am inevitably led to speculation about the murder of the Princes in the Tower. We know that Richard III was a Yorkist and we may assume that he supported Leeds United. In this fantasy, Sir James Tyrrel's actions can be seen in a completely different light. Perhaps the Manchester United marketing strategy has not yet penetrated the fifteenth century, although it seems clear to me that if a time machine were finally invented, the Manchester United sales staff would be the first people in it. They would be selling replica strips to the Romans as soon as they landed in Britain, as well as the specially designed ones which can be glued to the back of a chariot. Can't you just see Caesar's legions, riding into battle against the woad-covered warriors of Boadicea with their

Manchester United Double Double Winners stickers on their chariots?

The World Cup was a triumph for England rather than Manchester United. It was succeeded for me in that summer of 1966 by my own triumph in the somewhat less glamorous arena of the Manchester Union of Jewish Societies' Under-16 Tennis Tournament. I won the final 6–4, 6–4 after having been 4–0 down in the second set. It was a reward for sticking rigidly to a game plan which involved hitting deep to my opponent's backhand and pressurising the return by attacking the net. The only alternative strategy I had developed was to stand with my back against the wire netting at the back of the court and hit enormous, moon-ball lobs until the other player lost his temper and smashed the ball out.

In the semi-final, I was reduced to this tactic early on, because my opponent was Michael Chadwick. Now, I knew Mike well. I knew he was better than I was in almost every department of the game. He had a better serve, he moved more quickly around the court, he volleyed better than I did and he had a more reliable backhand. I slowed the game down. I tied and untied my shoelaces, I bounced the ball ten times before each serve. I could see Mike getting more and more impatient.

When I lost the first two games, I went immediately to Plan B. Mike scarcely won another game, although the match lasted forever. Every time the ball went up in the air, Mike tried a smash and netted it. He tried to copy my tactics, but he didn't have the patience and the ball would eventually drift out over the baseline. Next time he figured he might as well die gloriously, so he went back to the smash, but by now he had lost confidence in himself and every time he netted or hit the ball out, his confidence drained away still further.

I'm afraid I rather disgraced myself, because I found his frustration and fiery temper hilarious so I started laughing, which of course held the game up again. The more I laughed, the angrier Mike got. It finished something like 6–3, 6–1 and as he stormed off towards the dressing-room, he yelled over his shoulder that I was the most boring opponent he had ever faced and he was never going to play me again. And he never did.

After the excitement of seeing my photograph in the *Jewish Telegraph*, holding the trophy as if I were Bobby Moore displaying the Jules Rimet World Cup, it was back to the drudgery of rehearsals for the Manchester Youth Theatre's version of *Richard II*. By this time, I knew I was either a good actor acting poorly or, probably more accurately, a poor actor. A few days before the opening night, we went to school to collect our 'A' Level results, in the form of a tacky computer print-out without even a brown envelope to cover its dignity. I was delighted to discover I had managed an A in History and two Bs in German and English, together with a Distinction in an 'S' level paper on the Russian Revolution. In the fierce 'A' Level world of today, such a sequence of results would be barely better than average, but to me they were as good as anything I could have anticipated.

I had filled in my UCCA form, listing my preferred university choices, but I knew I didn't want to go anywhere but Cambridge, for which I needed to spend at least another term at school. Oxbridge places were then awarded after 'A' Levels and an interview, rather than, as they are now, on the basis of an interview and a conditional offer dependent on stated 'A' Level achievements – invariably either three As or, at the very least, two As and a B. On that basis, my results wouldn't have been good enough.

My interview took place on a crisp, bright September day. I had arrived by train the previous evening and walked into Tree Court of Gonville & Caius College, responding instantly to the sense of utter tranquillity and harmony the architecture created. I was intrigued to be woken up the following morning by a college servant (I'm afraid that's what they were called, however politically incorrect it may be now) bearing a huge jug of warm water and a bowl which my mother would have denigrated with the Yiddish word 'schissel'. The college servant explained painstakingly that there was no running hot water in the building. I assumed there had been a temporary fault in the boiler, until it was explained in an even more bored voice that there was no hot water in the building *ever*.

I had two interviews, one with Neil McKendrick, Director of Studies in History, my chosen subject, the other with Jeremy Prynne, Director of Studies in English. Although my brother graduated in 1965, he had returned to Cambridge for the summer term of 1966 to take his LL.B, so his recent presence made the opening exchanges pleasantly informal. McKendrick, who was to become such a significant influence in my life, soon progressed to an attack on my widespread interests, which I had naively assumed to be the reason I might be accepted into the college in the first place.

I was soon made aware that McKendrick felt that every hour not spent working in a library towards the goal of achieving a starred First in the Historical Tripos was an hour wasted. Since my avowed intention in coming to Cambridge was to spend a lot of time on the college sports ground and the rest of it in the theatre, I could see that we were instantly facing a conflict of interests. I left McKendrick's room in a state of confusion – something I was to repeat many times in the future.

Jeremy Prynne was considerably less frightening and we spent a happy half-an-hour talking about Shakespeare on film. I congratulated myself on my skill in twisting the interview to suit myself, but I suspect that after a week conducting such interrogations, Jeremy was only too pleased to let someone else lead the conversation. In the end, it would be Neil McKendrick's choice whether I was accepted or not. The only disconcerting note was the noise on the stone-flagged floor made by Jeremy's shoes, which sounded like the German army goose-stepping into Poland. I wondered whether I should change from History to English, but decided it probably wasn't a good time to tell McKendrick.

In the event, it all turned out satisfactorily. I was offered a guaranteed place for entrance as an undergraduate in History starting in October 1967, but I was strongly advised to take the Cambridge University Scholarship exam in November 1966. If I failed, I still had my guaranteed place; but if I did well, I could win an Open Scholarship (worth £60 a year) or an Exhibition (worth £40 a year). This was the sort of gamble I liked, and it compares favourably with the pressure created by the current system, which has abandoned the seventh-term entry. It was felt that the old way favoured independent schools, which had the resources to teach a seventh term.

Backed by my strong showing at 'A' Level, I enjoyed the History papers, feeling confident that I could perform in them on the day. Indeed, such was my confidence that I dared to take the David Green approach and wrote one essay on 'Religion is the opiate of the masses' with reference to the spell cast by football on the proletariat. I backed up the argument with as many facts as I could muster, including the famous story of the religious poster in Liverpool which asked simply, 'What happens when the Lord cometh?' The scribbled answer underneath was, 'Move St John to inside-left.' I then discussed in some detail how although this was witty, it would mean that Shankly would have to drop Roger Hunt, a tactic scorned by Alf Ramsey. The thought flashed through my mind that this was precisely the tactic that had backfired so disastrously with Manchester Grammar School, but I contented

191

myself with the knowledge that I had cunningly concealed from the Cambridge examiners my love of Manchester City. If they were all United supporters, it shouldn't affect me adversely. I was more worried by the Languages paper, in which I was now particularly weak.

A fortnight or so later, I returned home to find a white-faced cleaning woman pointing at a telegram on the table. I had never seen a telegram before, at least not one addressed to me. To the cleaning lady, it meant only one thing – someone had died in Flanders Field or the Western Desert. I tore it open to find a cryptic message, which read: AWARDED EXHIBITION CAIUS COLLEGE CONGRATULATIONS NEEDHAM MASTER.

I was in. Alas, the £40 was not paid, as I had fondly imagined, in gold sovereigns in an ancient ceremony. A third of the amount was simply deducted from the bill each term.

There was only one part of the experience which disappointed me: I seemed to have nobody with whom to share my delight. My father appeared to take this sort of success for granted. My brother was understandably more concerned with the imminent arrival of his first child, and my friends were now embroiled in their own 'A' Level run-up and were not going to enjoy seeing the gates of freedom swinging open for me. I learned instead to repress my feelings. 'Well done, Shindler,' said my History master, Mr Hodgkiss, kindly. 'I must say, I never thought you had it in you.'

Never mind, there was one place which loved me unconditionally. I took my Cambridge entrance as another mark of respect for Manchester City. I identified with the team so closely that, just as I celebrated their triumphs, I knew that they would be celebrating mine. I toyed with the idea of dropping a note to Mercer and Allison, but decided against it. I didn't want to break the illusion. That would come later.

The 1966–67 season had opened full of promise. There

was just one player of significance added to the staff – Tony Book, a thirty-year-old ex-bricklayer who had played at right-back for Plymouth Argyle, Allison's previous team. Seventeen thousand pounds seemed quite a lot to pay for someone of that advanced age. It would have been regarded as highly improbable that Book would still have been at Maine Road thirty years later, after the Kippax Stand, in which we stood to watch him make his home debut, had been razed to the ground.

After another draw away to Southampton, we beat Liverpool, the League Champions, 2–1 at Maine Road and scraped a 1–0 win over Sunderland, so that after eight days of the new season, we were top of Division One. It seemed only right, somehow. Clearly, we had been forced to suffer in the misery of the Second Division so that we could enjoy the taste of the nectar that was to follow.

When school started again the following week, I was asked to captain the Third XI. Bearing in mind that I had never played football for the school, this was quite an honour, particularly as I was told that the appointment was being offered to me based on my sterling work with a young cricket Second XI the previous summer. I had enjoyed working with that young and inexperienced team, seeing the side grow in confidence as it learned how to turn defeats into draws, draws into victories.

Jeff Cohen was my opening bowler, but I had placed my faith in youth. At seventeen years of age, Jeff wore the face of a grizzled veteran and I considered it my duty to encourage the youthful fifteen- and sixteen-year-olds. Consequently, Jeff was always taken off long before he thought he should have been, and when the words 'Thanks, Jeff, take a rest' wafted over to him from first slip, he would stand with hands on hips, replying, 'What? Already?' before mooching down to third man, pondering the injustice of the world in general and my perfidy in particular. He explained his erratic bowling by blaming the state of his new boots. Every delivery stride jarred his left big toe against the steel toecap. His appeals for clemency made no impact on my captaincy.

The prospect of returning to the football field as captain was very enticing. At seventeen, I was clearly too old for a lot of running around, but I could use my experience to guide the graduates of last year's Under-15s, much as Tony Book was already doing at Maine Road. To my regret, I allowed David Green to talk me out of it. 'Are you crazy?' he asked rhetorically. 'All those Saturdays watching Swindon and Cardiff and Leyton Orient, and now you want to blow the chance of watching Arsenal and United and Chelsea?' School away matches, in particular, would return me to Prestwich after the bus had left for Maine Road.

I had to admit he had a point. In the end, my love of City was greater than my love of school. The latter was expedient, the former permanent. I turned down the captaincy of the Bury Grammar School Third XI (not without considerable mental turmoil) in favour of my continued attendance at Maine Road. And how did they reward me? By losing 4–1 at home to West Ham and their World Cup heroes, by the same score to Osgood and company at home to Chelsea, and the following week to Tottenham Hotspur.

I saw the Chelsea defeat again recently on Sky Sports Gold and was surprised how much of the atmosphere of that game I had remembered. It was poisonous. The City crowd chanted 'Osgood No Good' with increasing fervour and jeered the cocky Cockney show-off whenever he touched the ball. Osgood allowed himself to become affected by the constant cries of derision and finally gestured in Churchillian manner at us.

We were incensed, particularly as it coincided with his scoring the fourth goal. It was the first time I can remember a crowd turning ugly in the way it was to do with nauseating frequency over the next twenty-five years. Prior to that match, I had been witness to ugly moments, infuriating refereeing decisions, the usual panoply of unfortunate incidents which can incite a crowd to violence, but I had never felt unsafe until that day.

City's bright start was threatening to turn into an autumn of anguish, although the Chelsea defeat had one redeeming virtue. Glyn Pardoe had been given such a runaround by a combination of the Chelsea attack and Allison's tactics that it was decided thereafter to try him as a left-back. Although his first game ended in a 2–1 defeat at home to Tottenham Hotspur, Pardoe distinguished himself at left-back and remained there successfully until his career was effectively ended by a broken leg, caused by a wild tackle from George Best.

In the midst of this bad run, we resumed the derby battle with United, who had also shot out of the blocks. On the first day of the season, Best was simply unstoppable as he initiated a 5–3 defeat of West Bromwich Albion. By the time they met City six games later, United had already scored fifteen goals compared to City's eight. Defensive frailties alone held United back, and Busby finally moved to solve the goalkeeping problem when he bought Alex Stepney. David Gaskell and Pat Dunne were out. John Connelly was sold to Blackburn and three members of the successful youth side were drafted in – Aston, who replaced Connelly; Sadler, who took over from Herd at centre-forward; and the tough-tackling Bobby Noble, who displaced Shay Brennan.

City, too, had turned their attention to their leaky defence. When they returned to Old Trafford for the first time for four years, it was with a forward-line of Connor, Bell, Summerbee, Pardoe and Young. Connor tried to man-mark Best, with limited success, Pardoe was withdrawn to bolster the defence and Bell could never get forward often enough to support

Summerbee and Young. It was one-way traffic. Denis Law, inevitably, scored the only goal, but it was plain for all to see that United ran out comfortable winners.

It wasn't as clear then that the United side of 1966–67 was going to be one of the greatest teams in their history. The success of England's 4–4–2 in the World Cup was already having an impact on domestic football. Wingers became obsolete, midfield players were auxiliary defenders and only two attackers were left up front. United were the non-conformists. Best, Law and Charlton obeyed no known pattern of play. They didn't need to, because they were so good. United's Championship success in the spring of 1967 was one of the final triumphs of attacking flair before the inevitable emergence of sides like Revie's Leeds United and Mee's Arsenal, teams built on the foundation of an impregnable defence.

On 29 October 1966, City were second from bottom. The previous week, we had been beaten 2–0 at Newcastle, a defeat which had followed two home losses in eight days. If City now lost at Burnley, they would be rooted to the bottom. We drove to Turf Moor in serious vein. Surely we hadn't wandered in the desert for so many years and been shown the Promised Land only to be sent once more into exile?

Admittedly, Burnley were no longer the power they had been at the start of the decade, when the team of Jimmy Adamson, Ray Pointer and Jimmy McIlroy had been the only real competition for the Spurs Double-winning side. However, they were at that time third in the table, and for the first twenty minutes they played like it. The ball barely got out of City's half before it was returned with interest. Dowd performed heroically to keep Andy Lochhead and the rest of the rampant Burnley attack at bay. His opposite number, Adam Blacklaw, touched the ball only once in the first half – and that was to pick the ball out of the net after Crossan had put City ahead, completely against the run of play.

Burnley equalised early in the second half and we could have been forgiven for thinking we were heading for our fourth defeat in a row. Crossan put City ahead again after seventy minutes but Willie Morgan made it 2–2 with six minutes to go. It was desperately disappointing to have come so close and been denied at the death. However, this wasn't the fragile City I had grown up with, shoulders collectively drooping as they bemoaned the cruelty of fate. The City I knew would collapse if the opposition scored first – and would tremble if we scored first, in case the opposition got really angry and gave us an even worse hammering. This was New City, Mercer and Allison's City, the City of Bell and Summerbee, and it was the latter two who sealed it.

With two minutes to go, Summerbee set off on another mazy run down the right wing, Bell shadowing him in the middle. Summerbee forced his way past his marker, Elder, centred and Bell found half a yard of room in which to control the ball. It seemed to take forever for that ball to come down before Bell drove it conclusively past Blacklaw for the winner. It was a joyful drive back over the moors to Manchester. We recognised that this 3–2 win was not like the rather flukey 3–2 win at Old Trafford the year we were relegated. City were now an altogether more talented, cohesive unit. We were going through a brief period of struggle, but we had the players, the team spirit and, more important, the managerial tactical awareness to get us through it. So we fondly believed.

However, by the time the return derby match was played at Maine Road in January, results had not improved. We had only won three of the eleven games played since the match at Burnley, partly because the week after that heroic drama, Summerbee was sent off against Newcastle and received a lengthy suspension. Malcolm Allison was in trouble with the FA and had been banned from the touchline for excessive coaching and comments made to officials. Relegation was in the air again. Johnny Crossan had lost form and favour and was dropped for the United game. On the Monday morning, he applied for a transfer. Crossan was a talented player and had contributed significantly to the promotion season, but he always seemed a man apart, a stranger to his environment. He left at the end of the season.

City played well on a day when the wind drove the rain into the stands horizontally. We might as well have been standing in the open Scoreboard End, such was the discomfort we experienced at the bottom of the covered Platt Lane Stand. Only Denis Law was missing from the United side which was storming towards its second Championship in three seasons. Struggling City matched them for endeavour, and we in the crowd played our part by roundly booing Nobby Stiles (like Summerbee, returning from a lengthy suspension after having been sent off).

Stiles, however, appeared to revel in the notoriety and snuffed out every City attack before it could threaten Stepney's goal. Fifteen minutes from the end, Bill Foulkes rose above the straining fingers of Alan Ogley, got his head to a corner by Jim Ryan and the ball looped into the net. It was a sickening blow, made worse by the gyrating United supporters. The City attacks increased in desperation but not in quality. With a minute to go, Colin Bell, who had never stopped running all afternoon, got to the bye-line and pulled the ball back across the face of the goal. Stiles, as usual, was first to the ball, but instead of heading it out for a corner, which was presumably his intention, he hurled himself at the ball and sent an unstoppable header past Stepney into the roof of the net. The Platt Lane Stand erupted. No Cambridge Entrance exam result could match the sheer joy that own goal created.

From the restart, City went at United again; Doyle broke

through, the goal at his mercy. Surely we weren't going to win, were we? No, we weren't. The indefatigable Stiles reappeared and swept the ball to safety. The referee blew for time. I wondered how it might be possible to convey to English teachers and examiners that the true sensation of catharsis is not to be found at the end of a Greek tragedy by Sophocles but at the end of a derby match against Manchester United, with an equaliser in the last minute courtesy of a mistake by United's best defender.

My time in Manchester was running out. Ever since the arrival of the telegram from Caius, I had felt I was living on borrowed time. According to Woody Allen in *Annie Hall*, a relationship is like a shark. It has to constantly move forward or it dies. My relationship with Manchester was getting to be a dead shark. I knew I was going to Cambridge in the autumn. It would have been easy merely to have stayed at school, seen plays and films, played for the First XI at cricket, been in the school play, maybe had another go at the Manchester Youth Theatre.

I knew I shouldn't do that. The very fact that it was so attractive and simple confirmed that I mustn't allow myself to take that easy option. Memories of Washbrook and May rescuing England from their position of 17 for 3 at Headingley constantly troubled me. I would have to go to London. I didn't know anybody in London, but I felt sure I had to test myself by living there. I would be desperately sorry to leave City, but I could see them in London when they played there and it wasn't like it was a permanent upheaval.

I found a job easily at Foyle's, the famous bookstore on Charing Cross Road. (It was still believed at that time that it was possible to achieve full employment, and when the unemployment figures crept over the half-a-million mark, the government was bitterly attacked in the House and in the press.)

I would be paid the grand sum of £9 10s a week. My father answered an advertisement in the *Jewish Chronicle* which offered full bed and board for £8 a week. I felt instinctively that the gap between my income and committed outgoings was too small, but I allowed myself to be persuaded (eventually, poverty drove me to rent a room from my uncle in Edgware) and one Sunday, we drove from Manchester to London and turned right off Cricklewood Broadway. We stopped outside a modern tower block and crammed ourselves into the tiny lift. My father helped me unpack, turned the car round and headed back north. I was on my own.

My landlady was relatively young, a divorcee, I think, and my hormones combined with a feverish imagination concocted a scenario which played better in Hollywood than Cricklewood. But it was disappointing, as Ron Atkinson would say, no doubt about that, Brian. Cut off from my friends and from Manchester City (the London-based newspapers carried reports on their local teams, instead of the northern reports I was used to), I knew I needed some kind of emotional sustenance. I picked up the phone and dialled HAM 6363. Uncle Laurence, a prime mover in the Socialist Party of Great Britain, had a telephone number which matched the JCK 636 registration plates on his Bentley.

Laurence used silly puns which we echoed happily. Those I always remember were 'Pass the Tom Graveney', in reference to the gravy boat on the dinner table, and 'Peter May I have the butter, please?' I started doing it with my own children when they were of an age to appreciate the delights of 'Chicken DeFreitas' rather than Chicken Fajitas. Laurence would intersperse these little word games with tirades of invective against the *Manchester Guardian*, which he read avidly so that he would have the material for his next letter of complaint.

His particular bugbear was the *Guardian*'s chief cricket correspondent Denys Rowbotham, known familiarly and inevitably in Laurence's household by the Yiddish corruption 'Denys Rowtochas'. Laurence hated poor, innocent Rowtochas, whom Matthew Engel, one of his distinguished successors, later described as 'a rather Olympian writer of great cricketing depth and integrity, much loved by his colleagues.' I suspect some of Laurence's contempt was cloaking the anger he felt against the world for not recognising his own unique gifts. Anybody with half a brain could see that he, Laurence Weidberg, should have been the cricket correspondent of the *Manchester Guardian*. Every day during the cricket season, Laurence would scour the paper, hunting for Rowtochas's mistakes. He wasn't interested in mere *Grauniad* typographical errors. He was compiling a dossier on Rowtochas's incompetence.

The list was eventually published in Laurence's article which was printed in the *Cricketer* magazine in September 1965. It began harmlessly enough by praising the *Manchester Guardian* as the very best kind of local paper. It paid tribute to the felicitous prose poetry of Neville Cardus, before launching its first assault. Rowtochas had written, 'Titmus square-cut a six.' Laurence claimed to have watched the whole of the match in question. Titmus did not hit a six of any description. Rowtochas wrote, 'Snow was dismissed by Higgs for the second time,' but from the attached scorecard it was clear that Snow had been run out in the first innings and bowled by Ramadhin in the second.

Laurence picked up pace. How could it be that 'the South African openers Goddard and Barlow were affected by Bland's loss of form' when Bland batted at number four? How could a Worcester crowd 'walk home happy across the Avon' when the nearest point of that river to Worcester was some thirty miles distant? 'Even in the Golden Age, the crowds and cricketers never walked that far,' Laurence observed, 'and if they did, I should not think they were very happy about it.' Note the grammatically correct use of the word 'should' rather than 'would'. Not bad from a boy whose father wouldn't allow to attend a university, and who went straight from school into the factory.

Laurence's final point was his best. Don Kenyon, the veteran Worcestershire captain and former England opener, guided his county to victory in the Championship in 1964 for the first time in their history. Rowtochas wrote movingly, 'For the first time in his life, Kenyon had a lump in his throat.' Laurence retorted thus: 'Two questions arise. What make of binoculars could detect a lump in the throat at a distance of one hundred yards? Having detected it, how did our author know that Kenyon never had one before?'

Uncle Laurence was extremely proud of the article and I was very proud for him. He was cleverer than 'they' were and he had just proved it. I was thinking of how much I admired him, and how much I wanted things to be as they had been between us, when I picked up that phone and dialled his number in Hampstead. Laurence told me it was inconvenient to see him. I was devastated. I had wanted his love and support so badly. I remembered ruefully his words to my brother when he excommunicated him, too. 'I'm finished with you,' he intoned as he pronounced judgment. My brother tried to protest but Laurence dismissed the appeal: 'I'm the Prosecutor, Judge and Jury,' he stated bluntly. Laurence Weidberg was not a mean-spirited man. He could be capable of great generosity. He gave Geoff and me an enduring love of music from Mozart to Gilbert & Sullivan, a love of theatre and books and, above all, a love of sport, particularly cricket. But it came at a price and, in the end, that price was too high for either of us to pay. So now I was on my own again.

Well, not entirely on my own. Every Saturday, I managed to persuade Foyle's to let me take my lunch-break from 4pm to 5pm so that I could sit in Soho Square and eat my sandwiches while listening to the 'second-half commentary from one of today's top League matches.' It was about a month after I started work at Foyle's when I heard the report of the sixth round FA Cup tie between Leeds United and Manchester City at Elland Road. The last match I had seen at Maine Road before leaving was the disappointing fifth round 1–1 draw with Ipswich, but City had gone to Portman Road three days later and made my third night in London a happy one by winning 3–0.

In the League, City were still struggling and although they had managed to climb to a position fifth from bottom, they were still only two points clear of West Bromwich Albion who occupied the second relegation place. Everyone expected a dour battle with Leeds on a par with the scoreless draw City had obtained at Elland Road in a League match only two weeks previously. I sat on the hard wooden bench in Soho Square, transistor radio glued to my ear, to hear a very different scenario unfold. Eric Todd, as ever, gave the best description.

> Not since Elijah dealt so summarily with those from Baal and those of the groves who ate at Jezebel's table, has anybody routed more prophets than Manchester City . . .
> They played splendidly but, being City, they just had to lose 1–0. Seldom, if ever, can outstanding teamwork have received such scandalous reward or underdogs been thus maligned more wrongly.

Translated into less heightened prose, City were all over Leeds like a cheap suit and went down to a goal scored in controversial circumstances. Jack Charlton, who had originated the tactic of standing in front of the opposing goalkeeper when Leeds had a corner, obstructed Dowd and headed in for the only goal of the game. City lost, but it proved a significant harbinger of what was to come.

On the last day of the season, I paid my first visit to Upton Park to see City draw 1–1 with West Ham. The outstanding player on the field was Colin Bell, who equalised Martin Peters's first-half opening goal. The pitch was rock hard, the sun was hot, the players listless after a long season and both sides were safe from relegation. It sounds like a recipe for a boring 1–1 draw. It was nothing of the kind. Led by Bell, who would surely be capped for England before long (Summerbee had been awarded his first cap that spring), City created enough chances to have won the match easily. I liked the look of the new outside-left Tony Coleman, a £12,000 buy from Doncaster who, according to legend, had arrived at Maine Road with his boots wrapped in a sheet of old newspaper. Next season, I thought as I left the ground, just wait till next season.

Unfortunately, there was a downside to City's strong finish to the season – United won the Championship by a street. Chelsea and Spurs pushed them hard before Christmas, Nottingham Forest and Leeds carried on the pursuit till Easter, but, rather like the state of the Premier League today, United were simply better than any other team and whenever they needed to, in David Coleman's infamous phrase, they opened their legs and showed their class. The week before City unluckily drew 1–1 with West Ham, United had clinched the Championship at Upton Park with a 6–1 win over the Hammers. They had scored four times in the first twenty-five minutes and presumably could have made it double figures had they been sufficiently motivated.

It was to be a constant factor in my life. Whenever City achieved anything, United were around to ruin it. When City became a really good and exciting team and United were trading on their past glories, the television companies still adamantly rejected City in favour of United. In the days when there was only *Match of the Day* on BBC 1 on Saturday nights and *The Big Match* (or local variation) on ITV on Sunday afternoons, City were almost never on, United never off. Canonisation by the media was to become a far bigger problem in the 1990s, but it had its roots back in the monochrome tones of the Sixties. During the Championship-winning season, City were on *Match of the Day* just three times – two defeats at Arsenal and Leeds and the home victory over Spurs. On the last day of the season when, if City won at Newcastle the title was ours, the *Match of the Day* cameras went to Old Trafford in the expectation that United would beat Sunderland and retain their crown. United lost 1–2. Ha! I hope the BBC ratings plummeted that night.

It was impossible to share these feelings about football in general and City in particular with anyone else at Foyle's, which contained a high percentage of immigrant workers – the only other idiots apart from students like myself who would accept the exploitative wages. I contented myself instead with staring intently at one of my co-workers in the paperback department. Her name was Maggie and she wore fashionably short skirts and provocatively long straight hair. She lived in Broxbourne, Hertfordshire, and was due to start at the University of East Anglia in October. She was uninterested in me but too polite to state as much, as a consequence of which I clung to the belief that she was as shy as I was and it needed only a combination of fortuitous circumstances for me to get off the mark.

I might have been tongue-tied around Maggie but I was very eloquent politically. I deeply resented the patronising and rapacious management for which I worked, and made a great show of buying the *Socialist Leader* and leaving it on the desk where I was working. The time-clock which we were required to punch every time we entered and left the shop was a source of constant irritation, and on my final day I took

205

great pleasure in disfiguring the cards of everyone in the building. Early in my career, I had been hauled in front of the manager – an oily, repulsive man called Rush – and told brusquely that if I persisted in wearing my lapel button which read 'KEEP THE POPE OFF THE MOON', I would be dismissed. I said I thought it was funny. He said a sense of humour was not the prerequisite for a sales clerk in a bookshop, and in any case Christina Foyle, the owner, was a practising Catholic and found it offensive. I removed the button like I was one of the Tolpuddle Martyrs.

The spring and summer of 1967, the so-called 'Summer of Love', was the very centre of that nebulous cultural concept, 'Swinging London'. Like everyone else, I read about it in the newspaper and magazine articles which proclaimed it, but I could never quite lay my hands on it. I blame nobody but myself. Ever since the trauma of the tracksuit at Park View Primary School, I had been unable to take pride of ownership in my clothes. Clothes to me were what my father brought home at the end of the day – large brown boxes tied with string, which had to be schlepped out of the car and into the house. As a consequence, Carnaby Street and the fashion revolution made no impact on me.

I enjoyed the pop music of the Sixties but I was never 'into music' as many of my contemporaries were. My dominant memory of the current Member of Parliament for Bury North, apart from the incessant combing of his hair into a quiff, was his high-pitched falsetto rendition of 'In the jungle, the mighty jungle, the lion sleeps tonight.' By the time I had gathered sufficient courage to buy my first single, 'Bobby's Girl', it had peaked and slipped out of the Top 20 altogether, provoking in those to whom I confided my purchase nothing but roars of derision. I was a Beatles fan rather than a Stones fan and as the Beatles lost interest and were replaced by less melodic bands and an altogether heavier sound, so I lost interest, too, although I cling with pride to my copy of the Beatles' first LP, *Please Please Me*, bought after school one rainy December afternoon in 1963.

Swinging London offered me little in the way of music and fashion, and my lack of a girlfriend kept me away from dancing and nightclubs. My contact with the hip cultural life of the capital was therefore restricted almost entirely to an avaricious consumption of films and plays. At the southern end of Tottenham Court Road stood two 'art house' cinemas, the Berkeley and the Continental. It was in one of them that I saw Antonioni's *Blow Up*, which reiterated the myth of Swinging London. They were reasonably priced cinemas which showed Truffaut and Jean-Luc Godard as well as Losey's *The Servant* and *Accident*. They were the London equivalents of the Manchester art-house cinema the Cinephone, which was situated at the top of Market Street, opposite what was the Arndale Centre until the IRA blew a large hole in it. The Cinephone started my love of foreign movies and it was there that I saw for the first time *Les Quatre Cent Coups*, *Une Femme est Une Femme*, *Masculin Feminin*, *Jules et Jim*, *Alphaville* and *Naked as Nature Intended*.

There seemed to be two contradictory scheduling policies at the Cinephone. One encouraged a love of all that was best and innovative in contemporary European cinema. The other screened nudie films for men in raincoats. Whereas my taste for the cinema was broad enough to encompass both *Nudists at Play* and *L'Année Dernière à Marienbad*, devotees of the genre represented by the former movie tended to find the Alain Resnais film something of a disappointment. Endless shots of empty hotel corridors and a story which plunged the viewer into a strange world of anonymous characters beyond the reach of time and logic created a fascinating analysis of the ambiguities of love. Unfortunately, the man at the end of the row where I sat found this very difficult to masturbate to, and

207

after complaining loudly about the scarcity of naked female flesh on display, he would, as a true Lancastrian, eventually demand his money back.

The theatre in London in 1967 was in a particularly healthy state. It was the heyday of Olivier's National Theatre at the Old Vic, where he led a brilliant company including Maggie Smith, Joan Plowright, Derek Jacobi, Albert Finney, Robert Stephens and Frank Finlay. I saw everything the company produced, usually a number of times because it was possible to buy day seats, which were nothing more than a wooden bench at the back of the balcony, for only two shillings. I saw Olivier as Othello and Tattle in *Love for Love*, I saw Robert Stephens as Atahualpa in Peter Shaffer's *Royal Hunt of the Sun*, and Finney in John Mortimer's adaptation of the Feydeau farce *A Flea In Her Ear*. Best of all was Zeffirelli's enchanting Italian cartoon version of *Much Ado About Nothing*, which I must have seen half a dozen times.

None of this really got me much closer to Swinging London than did working in the bookshop. Penguin dominated the paperback market and what they published each month led the fashion in writing and philosophy. If you were to ask me to describe the period now, my first inclination would be to point to the books on my shelf. The Penguins of Margaret Drabble, the New English Dramatists, the expanding Pelican list, encapsulate the period for me just as well as the plastic clothes, mini-skirts, multi-coloured shirts, beads, white lipstick, transparent blouses and Vidal Sassoon haircuts, all to the sound of 'It was twenty years ago today' on the portable record-player in the corner. They say if you can remember the Sixties, you weren't really there. I can remember the Sixties all right. I was at Maine Road.

Chapter Ten

Virginia Woolf believed it was necessary to have money and a room of one's own before one could write. When I opened the door of my room in Harvey Court on the day I arrived in Cambridge as an undergraduate, carrying my grant cheque, for the first time in my life I now had both. It was a heady moment. Growing up, my brother and I had shared a bedroom, a practice I ensured my own children would not have to follow. The money I earned at Foyle's was blown on a six-week camping trip in Italy, so I determined to replenish the bank account with a summer job in Manchester.

The best I could do was to drive an ice-cream van round the urban wastelands of Salford. The van was one of two owned by an excitable Italian and his hugely overweight, clinically depressed English wife. She and I went out together as the Italian felt he could cope by himself. It immediately became apparent that his reason for so doing was to avoid the need to sit in the same vehicle as his wife for ten hours a day. Unloading a dozen heavy cartons of books from Goods Inwards at Foyle's seemed like a party in comparison.

The most painful moment came on a Saturday afternoon when City were playing at home. There I was, watching half a dozen kids removing the wheels from a new Ford Cortina as the sound of 'Greensleeves' rent the air, knowing that three miles away, the lads in blue were playing Nottingham Forest.

Every minute in that van was torture, because I knew that City were on the verge of a breakthrough.

I had returned from Italy in time to watch a dull 0–0 home draw against Liverpool on one of those hot August afternoons when football seems an irrelevant exercise. The match was enlivened only by a penalty miss by Tony Book. Early-season optimism started to evaporate when we unaccountably lost 3–2 at Southampton on the following Wednesday night. David drove Jeff and me to Stoke on the Saturday, where David, already in a bad temper because he had been pulled over by the cops on the M6 for nothing more than driving without due care and attention, refused to stand up with Jeff and me and decided he would sit down by himself.

City were dire that afternoon. Within minutes of the kick-off, Summerbee had involved himself in a fight with Bentley, the Stoke City left-back. It wasn't the usual testing-out which Summerbee performed on his opponents on the occasion of their first tackle, but a genuinely vicious moment. The bad temper spread quickly to the stands and in those dear far-off days when crowds were unsegregated, it soon erupted into violence. A young man was led past us with blood pouring from a cut to his face. On the field, City looked inept. Stoke scored three times without reply and in a mirror image of the start to the previous season, when we had taken five points from the first six, City were bottom of the table with just a single point.

David arrived back at the car in a steaming rage. He wanted to sell most of the team on display, which indicated a lack of judgment, but he was forceful in his demand that City buy Francis Lee, who had recently been placed on the transfer list by Bolton Wanderers. It was certain that changes needed to be made, and they were. For the next match at home to Southampton, City moved Summerbee to centre-forward and brought in Paul Hince on the right wing. Like

Pardoe's move to left-back, which had also been the product of a succession of poor results, Summerbee's move to the middle was an instant success.

We hammered four goals past Southampton in the return midweek game and on the Saturday, when I desperately wanted to see what turned out to be a similarly conclusive 2–0 win at home to Forest, I was instead driving a menopausal fat lady round the council estates of Salford and Manchester. By the time the day finished at 7pm, I was as depressed as my companion. No job in the world was worth missing the renaissance of Manchester City for. Certainly not one that paid two pounds a day. At the end of its day's work, the ice-cream van had to be reversed into a garage which was precisely six inches wider than the vehicle. I was so upset at missing the Forest game that I reversed a little too quickly, producing that unpleasant sound of paintwork on unforgiving concrete. To my intense relief and the disgust of my father, I was sacked on the spot. Never had unemployment been greeted with such a bewildering effusion of thanks. The ice-cream business and I parted to our mutual satisfaction. Coincidentally, Jeff Cohen and Mike Chadwick were fired from their equally unglamorous jobs – cleaning copper wire machines at the Smith & Nephew factory near Belle Vue – at the same time that I collected my P45. The siren call from Maine Road was too strong for us to resist.

As if in confirmation, City continued their excellent form with a comfortable 2–0 home win over Newcastle. Something significant had happened in the past week because, sitting in the Platt Lane Stand, I knew, even before the match had started, that we were going to win. This foreknowledge was quite different from the previous belief that we could win if we played well. Something magical had happened with Summerbee's move to centre-forward, and I wasn't to lose the unshakeable faith this engendered for years to come.

Match by match, the team's confidence grew visibly as their goal tally increased. Three went in at Coventry, four at home to Leicester in a League Cup match, five (including one by debutant Stan Bowles) at home to Sheffield United. Summerbee was leading the line quite brilliantly. Against Sheffield, with his back to the United goal, he controlled a long punt upfield from the goalkeeper with the outside of his right foot and, in the same movement, turned and went past the centre-half, glided a pass out to the wing and raced into the penalty area to meet the cross, which he headed past Hodgkinson.

Six straight wins were brought to a halt at Highbury. I have been watching City at Arsenal for thirty years and only once ever seen them win there. This match at the end of September 1967 was a typically attritional game in which John Radford caused George Heslop more trouble than any centre-forward I had previously seen. Harry Dowd broke his finger and Mercer and Allison responded with one of their less impressive forays in the transfer market. For £25,000 they signed Ken Mulhearn from Stockport County, who was to City in this season what Pat Dunne had been to United three years earlier. Peter Schmeichel has been such a major factor in United's recent success that he has re-emphasised what Brian Clough claimed the day he bought Peter Shilton – good goalkeepers win Championships. Dunne and Mulhearn proved that in certain circumstances, exactly the opposite can be true.

It didn't help that Mulhearn's first appearance was yet another disappointing defeat at home to Manchester United. Such had been the confidence generated by the twenty goals scored in our six consecutive victories that we approached the first derby match of the new season convinced that this was the game wherein we would finally demonstrate to the world that we had arrived as a major footballing force. To add credence to this belief, Colin Bell scored after five minutes, taking a short pass from Doyle in his stride before shooting past Stepney. It was only Stepney's brilliance which denied Bell twice more from putting the game beyond United's reach altogether. I was due to move from Manchester to Cambridge the following day. This was the perfect leaving present.

Unfortunately, Bobby Charlton completely ruined the party. Against the run of play he equalised and just before half-time he robbed Doyle, who was dawdling with the ball on the edge of the penalty area, and swept it past Mulhearn. In the second half, City's poise deserted them and United held on with ease. It was desperately disappointing. Ever since that controversial penalty decision which had effectively relegated City in May 1963, I had been thirsting for revenge.

A year later, a weakened United team without Charlton and the infant prodigy Best had come to a storm-tossed Maine Road to play a charity match for the Variety Club of Great Britain. This was the season when Kevan and Murray had scored freely, and I was desperately anxious for City to demonstrate the improvement we had made in a year. We lost 5–3 to a Denis Law hat-trick in front of a mere 36,000 people. This day at the end of September 1967 had been the best chance since then to show how far along the road to recovery we had come, but Charlton neatly deflected us into a cul-de-sac. Even the following week's defeat away to Sunderland wasn't as soul-destroying as losing at home to United. It was like Big Brother constantly reminding you what an inferior little weed you were. One day, one day.

I arrived in Cambridge with a grant cheque which paid the bills for room, board and tuition fees, and a cheque for £30 from my father which had to last for ten weeks. Even with my Grade 6 Maths 'O' Level, I could work out that meant three pounds a week during the university term. Three pounds wasn't much even then, so if I wanted to watch City I would clearly have to start economising. It was no sacrifice; City was my life. That team was as familiar to me as my own family – in many ways they *were* my own family – and I devoted endless hours to daydreaming about them. In the midst of a particularly dull lecture I would write down on the lecture notes the eleven players who had played the previous Saturday, and a list of results from the start of the season together with the names of the goalscorers, with their totals in brackets at the side.

This might account for the rocky start to my academic career. In school, I had been allowed to concentrate on nineteenth- and twentieth-century history. At Cambridge, I was suddenly confronted by a paper in Mediaeval European History, about which I knew nothing. I was appalled that I should be required to write about Philip the Bold or Philip the Mad or Philip the Fat, about early Christianity and Byzantium, about Charlemagne and the Dark Ages. I was lost and miserable, perking up only slightly when I heard that City had finally signed Francis Lee from Bolton for a record £60,000. My mind went back to what David had said after the Stoke game. Could Lee be the missing piece of the jigsaw?

He began with a 2–0 win at home to Wolves, and seven days later I caught my first sight of him in a City shirt, when I hitch-hiked down to London to see the match against Fulham. As I was getting out of the tube station at Putney Bridge, a fellow sufferer accosted me and demanded to know if I'd seen Lee the previous week. I confessed I hadn't. 'Fucking unbelievable,' he stated categorically before marching off, leaving me more worried than reassured. Such a statement could just as accurately have been applied to Roy Gratrix as to a player with a bright future ahead of him.

In the event, it transpired that Lee had had an immediate and favourable impact on the City crowd, and in a comfortable 4–2 win over Fulham that day he scored with a shot that nearly broke the back of the net, clarifying the relevance of that initial assessment. I liked the Fulham crowd and still do. They had a nicely judged sense of irony, in marked contrast to their neighbours across Fulham Broadway. Chelsea are to Fulham as United are to City, and I retain considerable affection for a crowd which turns up week after week, hoping for the best but, with a long history of disappointments behind them, fearing the worst. They went down that year and haven't been back in the top division since. Although we helped them on their way by firing nine past them in the two League matches, they gained a certain modicum of revenge by dumping us out of the League Cup.

After Fulham, it was back to struggling with Cambridge, which was both liberating and constricting at the same time. It was liberating because of the room of one's own. Nobody cared if I was dead or alive, as long as I ate five dinners a week in Hall and turned in an essay for my weekly supervision. The food I could cope with, particularly as I made my own breakfast and lunch, but the work was constricting and getting worse.

I was floundering desperately, a lone Jew wandering through the dark ages of mediaeval Christendom.

It wasn't a Europe I recognised – no Real Madrid, no Benfica, no Juventus or Moscow Dynamo for a start, though at least, fortunately, there was no Manchester United either.

There were no monks strolling through the land with pictures of Ryan Giggs stuck in their prayer books or T-shirts with Eric Cantona's face under their habits, no soaring cathedrals with Alex Ferguson holding the Premier League trophy etched into the stained glass window.

There were no frontiers, and every man who could speak Latin could traverse the Continent and find only his brothers in Christ. More to the point, he could break his fast or find a bed for the night in a tavern with no danger of running into a group of Manchester United fans wearing their replica shirts and looking for a fight.

McKendrick suggested I switch back to the paper on Modern European History, 1789-1939, and postpone the compulsory Mediaeval paper till my final year. He sent me off to see Norman Stone, who was then a Junior Fellow at Caius and not yet the prolific don whose provocative Thatcherite views would fill the airwaves and the press in the 1980s. Norman was a breath of fresh air but although I found his conversation fascinating, it made him a rotten supervisor because he was so clever that his teaching defied any sort of communication. He would look at the eight sides of A4 I had painstakingly handed in on the 1848 Revolutions and then pronounce judgment. 'It was all to do with Czech window cleaners,' he would chortle, highly amused at his own wit. I would chortle along in his wake, aware that I was sitting at the feet of a famous Cambridge intellect but still unsure how I was to translate this into action in the Tripos (the Cambridge term for the annual summer examinations).

My first forays into drama were only partially successful. I was disconcerted to discover that the gentleman with a shock of bright-red hair who appeared to be fast asleep throughout my audition for the primary acting club, the ADC, was also president of the Footlights, which, during my brother's time, had produced John Cleese, Tim Brooke-Taylor and Bill Oddie. He managed to remain awake during my monologue, but betrayed no emotion that could possibly be mistaken for laughter. I wasn't going to be a Footlights luminary after all. The gentleman has been Head of Light Entertainment for BBC Radio for many years now.

I found a more congenial home with the Mummers, a theatrical group with whom I was to remain during my years as an undergraduate. A second-year undergraduate called Lenny, who looked disconcertingly like a younger version of my Uncle Laurence, cast me in a series of Pinter sketches and an instant friendship based on a shared sense of humour was born. It was the first time I had ever played Pinter, but it was sheer delight to act. If you got the pause right, you got the timing right; and if the timing was right, an innocuous line like 'Sometimes the Star's the last to go' could rock the house with laughter – particularly late on a Saturday night when the entire audience was pissed out of its mind and would have laughed at somebody reciting the telephone directory.

I thought I ought to have a go at journalism and applied to join *Varsity*, the student newspaper, as a sports reporter. My first assignment was to write about the match Cambridge University soccer team had played the previous Saturday. I nervously pointed out that the previous Saturday I had been at Maine Road watching City against United, but this was regarded as nit picking. Fortunately, I found a match report in Monday's edition of the *Cambridge Evening News*, which I rewrote in a style that was a pale imitation of the *Guardian's* Eric Todd.

I thought it would add spice if I obtained a quote from the University captain, so I cycled over to Jesus College and banged on his door. A head was shortly stuck out, followed by a body which appeared entirely unclothed as far I could see it. I had clearly disturbed the captain during some extra training, though whether it was with a woman, a gentleman or his own trombone it was impossible to judge. In any case, the quote I obtained wasn't verbatim the one which appeared in *Varsity* the following Friday. I was starting to narrow down my professional options. Acting and journalism, which had appeared very attractive at the age of fourteen, were both losing their pall.

In compensation, I decided I might as well try playing football again rather than writing about it. I tentatively suggested as much to the College Second XI captain, who practically wrenched my arm off in appreciation. My first match was at outside-right. I was never particularly quick over anything more than five yards, so when I skipped past the Clare full-back at the first time of asking, I was very pleased. When I scored my first goal, I was elated. By the time I had scored my second goal after twenty minutes, I realised that none of these lads would have got a game on a patch of waste ground. It didn't diminish the pleasure I took one iota. I felt like a star. It's a nice feeling.

David wrote to me during the term, as he prepared to take his Oxford Entrance exam. He had decided on Oxford in preference to Cambridge because he was determined to make his own mark on student society and didn't want me around to blow the gaff. His letter was a detailed report on the City games I had missed (he saw all forty-two League games that year), together with an analysis of what City were lacking. 'City are one player (Brian O'Neill of Burnley?) away from greatness,' he wrote, the day after a respectable 1–1 draw away at Everton.

The following week, with the same team, City hammered Leicester City 6–0, and the week after that, we met up in London for a pulsating 3–2 win at West Ham. Francis Lee, rapidly repaying his transfer fee, scored twice, including a breathtaking volley from the edge of the area. The team was fully formed and would remain a fixture in my mind now for life. The only changes made between October and the end of the season were when a player was injured. Otherwise the team read: Mulhearn; Book, Pardoe; Doyle, Heslop, Oakes; Lee, Bell, Summerbee, Young and Coleman. The team which Book assembled in the mid 1970s to win the League Cup, including Dave Watson, Dennis Tueart, Joe Royle, Asa Hartford and Peter Barnes, was arguably man-for-man the better team, but my heart will always belong to the glory boys of 1967–68. They were my team, they belonged to me. I had suffered for them and they redeemed me.

Glyn Pardoe, Mike Doyle, Alan Oakes and Neil Young were particularly relevant to this argument, because they had made their debuts in the dark days of Les McDowall and George Poyser. Oakes had first appeared as long ago as 1959, a quiet, unassuming figure with only one leg. Nobody ever saw him use the right leg for anything other than walking on, and it was with a certain amount of relief that when I finally got into the bath with him, I could confirm to Jeff, David and Mike that he was indeed possessed of two normal legs.

Pardoe was Oakes's cousin – country cousins, they were usually called, since they lived in Winsford, outside Chester. Pardoe made his debut as the youngest player ever to wear the City shirt, at the age of fifteen; and when Allison, in desperation, played him at left-back, he finally found his best position. Doyle had battled with Stan Horne, the black South African, for the right-half spot and only really claimed it permanently at the end of the 1966–67 season. But Neil Young was perhaps the best symbol of how City had changed for the better.

When Young first appeared on the opposite wing to David Wagstaffe, we were all aware what a talented footballer he was. In the relegation season, he slipped in and out of the team, too frail and gawky to hold down a place in a side that had to scrap every match to stay up. When City briefly threatened to return to the First Division at the first attempt, they played a settled and successful forward-line of Young, Pardoe, Murray, Kevan and Wagstaffe. As times got bleaker, Young slipped from view once more and it needed Mercer and Allison to release his natural talent. Although he moved to the left wing when David Wagstaffe joined Wolves, he was now being challenged by David Connor, the new youth team outside-left.

Allison moved Young into the inside-left position and a

star was born. Around the penalty area, on his left foot, Young became as clinical a finisher as Denis Law, the best in the business. He remained shy and gawky, the butt of the crowd's humour for his lack of appetite for the physical side of the game, but they appreciated what he offered the side, particularly on the six occasions in the year when he looked positively world-class. Young, perhaps even more than the other three, symbolised the enormous change which had overtaken the club since Mercer and Allison arrived in the summer of 1965.

That's why we loved him so much, and why there was a justifiably large stink created when it was discovered in about 1990 that he was destitute. The club, under its then chairman Peter Swales, denied any obligation to help. The task devolved to better men, but it was entirely consistent with the character Neil displayed on the field as a young man that he should end up in such a hapless condition. By the same token, Francis Lee's success in the waste-paper industry was similarly predictable.

A week after victory at West Ham, City returned home to play Burnley. David wrote to me after the match, claiming that the first sixty minutes of it was the greatest football he had ever seen a City side play. On the Monday morning, I sat in the Junior Common Room in College and read every newspaper report. As usual, it was Eric Todd in the *Guardian* who caught the mood of the moment, so I cut out his article and kept it in my wallet, where it remained for twelve years. In 1979, somewhere on East 57th Street in New York City, I was mugged and my wallet disappeared. After cancelling the credit cards and informing the insurance company, the only real thing of value I lost was that report of the City v Burnley match in November 1967. Fortunately, I had read it so often I could quote the opening stanza by heart.

Old men dreamed dreams and young men saw visions on Saturday at Maine Road where for nearly an hour Manchester City justified every superlative. They scored four goals, might have had six ... Songs of praise and thanksgiving were borne by the breeze onto the congested streets of Moss Side and why not?

I hope the mugger who robbed me was equally moved by the description.

I was now living an emotionally rootless existence. My father had sold the house we had lived in since I was five and had bought a small two-bedroom flat in a modern purpose-built apartment block very close to where Uncle Laurence had lived. He had indicated his intention to marry again, which pleased me but left me with an impending sense of further isolation. Meanwhile, there was always City. For the Christmas holidays, I travelled back to Manchester, living almost exclusively for those moments when I could watch the boys in blue.

They rarely disappointed me that year. The first match in December was a home game against Spurs. It was played on a sheet of snow and ice on which the players could barely keep their feet, conditions in which no Premier League match would be allowed to start. I find this rather sad, not because today's footballers are mollycoddled but because we don't get the chance to see how they might respond to these unusual conditions. I'm also sorry that we don't get the chance to see how cricketers perform on uncovered wickets. There's nothing to beat the sight of a team battling to survive on a sticky dog of a wicket, with nine fielders round the bat and the ball spinning viciously.

Football pitches today have undersoil heating and the situation would therefore never arise. If the heating works, the pitch is playable. If the heating can't beat the ice and snow, the match is postponed. Had such a situation arisen in 1967, we would have been denied the spectacle of the City v Spurs match which became known as 'The Ballet On Ice'. Spurs went ahead after six minutes when Jimmy Greaves tucked away a ricochet from a free-kick because he was one of the few players able to stand upright. After that it was one-way traffic, with Neil Young outstanding. Bell equalised before half-time; Summerbee, with a brilliant header, Coleman and Young all scored in the second half, in which City were rampant. It was a thrilling performance on a miserable day when the temperature rarely rose above freezing. At the final whistle, Jimmy Greaves, in a gesture of memorable magnanimity, waited by the tunnel entrance and shook the hand of every City player as he left the field.

The four of us went to Anfield the following week, trying desperately to find a turnstile which didn't lead to the notorious Kop. We failed, because by 2.15 every turnstile requiring cash admission was closed except those at the Kop end. So we watched from the Kop, and it wasn't just natural self-preservation which caused us to keep quiet; it was the feeling that once the City attacks had failed to pierce the Liverpool armour in the first fifteen minutes, we were in for a terrible caning. It was like being back at Old Trafford. Backed by that extraordinary crowd noise, every time Liverpool swept downfield it seemed inevitable they would score. Ian Callaghan on the right wing and, in particular, Peter Thompson on the left gave the City full-backs a roasting. I couldn't believe that Ramsey had tried both players for England and rejected them. Liverpool were awe-inspiring that day, and it was no surprise when Hunt put them ahead with a simple tap-in from another blistering Thompson centre.

However, this City team were made of sterner stuff than their predecessors. A misdirected header by Emlyn Hughes fell to the feet of Lee. He barged his way past three defenders and thundered the equaliser past Tommy Lawrence in the Liverpool goal. The four of us clung onto each other to prevent premature, not to say suicidal, celebration. City not only held out for the draw but should have won it in the last minute, when Doyle shot wide instead of passing to the unmarked Lee. In response, a Scouser urinated on the back of my leg. It was, just about, a reasonable trade.

Now we got a bit carried away with ourselves. We expected to win every match, home or away. The following week, we were leading Stoke 3–1 with five minutes to go. David Green, desperate to beat the traffic, pulled me away from the ground despite my bitter complaints. When we got to the car and switched on the radio, we discovered City had won 4–2. Still, I preferred to go with David than Mike Chadwick, who could never remember where he had parked the car. The roads around Maine Road are jammed with cars on match days and every row of Victorian terraced houses looks like every other one. On the rare occasions when we took the bus and came home with Mike Chadwick, we had to wait until 5.30pm when all the streets near the ground had cleared before he could find his car.

The rows about where to park, which way to travel through the centre of Manchester, which turnstile to queue up outside, when to leave if the match was still in progress, got louder and louder each week. Life at home was so dull in comparison that a good row about which road to park in could become the highlight of the week. I like to think the bantering conversation was like a Neil Simon play but I suspect it was merely full of adolescent posturing. I wondered briefly if the rancour in the arguments was destructive, but we were all so tightly bound up with City's amazing renaissance that it didn't matter at the time. It would have repercussions in later life.

On Boxing Day we travelled to West Bromwich, to see

City, with a couple of enforced changes due to Bell's absence through injury, recover from two goals down and two catastrophic blunders by Mulhearn to be level at 2–2 with less than a minute left. Then Mulhearn was caught in no-man's-land and Jeff Astle scored the winner. We sat slumped in our seats, unable to believe this unscheduled departure from the script. All except David Green. He was up on his feet, gesticulating fiercely in the direction of Ken Mulhearn. 'I am never, *never*, going to watch this team again as long as that idiot is in goal,' he swore fiercely. Four days later with the rest of us he watched City, with Mulhearn still in the team, lose the return fixture limply 2–0 at home.

Meanwhile, Manchester United were progressing serenely. They had in George Best the best footballer in the world, which I always thought was an unfair advantage. They should have been made to play with nine men plus Best. Best didn't have a weakness. He scored goals and made them, he could pass, head and defend with equal dexterity. If United needed a moment of genius, he provided it. In Europe, United had glided past Hibernians of Malta and FK Sarajevo, the champions of Yugoslavia, during the autumn and were set to face Gornik Zabrze of Poland when the quarter-finals commenced in March. Then, as now, they were attempting to defend the League Championship and win the European Cup. As I write, history is threatening to create a disturbing parallel.

During my second term in Cambridge, I became widely known as a Manchester City obsessive. Generally speaking, it was a time of increasing radicalisation on the campuses of Western Europe and the United States. Posters of the martyred Che Guevara adorned the rooms of students, fighting for space with the poster of the girl hitching up her white tennis dress to scratch her bottom, revealing an exquisite behind and no knickers. My room was already covered in clippings of Manchester City. There was no room for anything else on the wall.

When Harold Wilson came to Cambridge to talk to the people in the Market Square, he was greeted with a bombardment of eggs and a storm of abuse. Most of it was directed at his policy of support for the American bombing of North Vietnam. At the back of the crowd was a lone voice singing, 'Joe Mercer, Joe Mercer, Take no heed what people say, You're gonna win the Football League.' Just before Easter, Denis Healey, then Minister of Defence, came to Cambridge, where his car was stopped and attacked by impassioned and undeniably inebriated students protesting at the Labour government's continued support for the war in Vietnam. I stood and watched as they rocked his car dangerously from side to side before the police could drag them away as the crowd chanted, 'Healey Out, Healey Out, Healey Out, Out, Out!' Though sharing their deeply held political beliefs, I couldn't help amending the words to 'United Out, United Out,' etc. It made me feel better and had no lesser impact on British foreign policy than the more direct action taking place in front of me.

The real cloud on the horizon was Maggie. Everybody needed a girlfriend in Cambridge, for reasons of status as much as reasons of health. The odds of ten men to every woman were stacked against most of us. I clung to Maggie whom I had fancied the previous year in London, even though she was marooned in Norwich at the University of East Anglia. I wrote to inform her that I was passing through Norwich, an unlikely state of affairs with Norwich in the Second Division, but it provided a satisfactory cover story. It took me hours to hitch-hike there one Saturday and by the time I arrived, I had become paranoid about being able to hear the City result. Fortunately, Maggie, evincing a disturbing lack of enthusiasm for my presence, found a friend with a transistor radio and it was in his room that I heard we had won at Burnley, courtesy of a Francis Lee penalty.

I had hoped that my casual air of wanting to hear the football results rather than get to grips with her might have made me more attractive, but the tactic was sadly flawed. Unable to face the return journey by thumb, I took an expensive train back to Cambridge having extracted a promise from her that she would come to my friend Bob Stone's twenty-first birthday party, a major social event in the summer term. It was sufficient for me to cling to for the next two months, while I returned to Cambridge and the task of making sense of the Tudors and Stuarts.

My supervisor was now a woman, Margaret Bowker, whose fierce intellectual approach and clipped speech was even more disorientating than Philip Grierson's Mediaeval Europe and Norman Stone's bewildering Modern Europe. I struggled to come to terms with the Reformation, feeling handicapped by my lack of any technical knowledge of Christianity. I kept hearing the sound of my parents and their friends saying, 'What is that boy doing reading about Church history and the Liturgy and the Prayer Book? The Reformation was just an argument among the *goyim*. What business is it of ours if the *goyim* want to fall out with each other? It's better for the Jews they burn each other at the stake than they should kill us.'

No matter that I had effectively moved from the Manchester Jewish community to a community of students 200 miles away, no matter how far I strayed from the Prestwich Hebrew Congregation synagogue, no matter how hard I lusted after *shiksas*, I was still the captive prisoner of the thinking of my early years. I never tried to deny I was Jewish but if you had asked me to define myself, I would have done so in terms of Manchester City. Still the mental processes inculcated by my mother at an early age would rise to remind me of my Jewish heritage.

I felt my destiny calling as I travelled back to Manchester for the Easter vacation. Student radicalism was activating social unrest in France and Germany, but after beating Coventry 3–1, despite having Tony Coleman sent off, and then walloping Fulham 5–1, we had won six of the seven League games played since those dreadful Christmas defeats by West Bromwich Albion. We travelled over the Pennines to face Leeds United at Elland Road secure in the knowledge that we were deservedly joint top of the League. We were delighted, too, to see that, finally, we were considered good enough to be on *Match of the Day*. Now the world would see us for what we were. They did see us for what we were – on the day, not good enough to trouble the well-drilled Leeds team, who won 2–0. We had much of the possession in the first half, but failed to put away our two half-chances and after the interval, goals by Giles and Jack Charlton finished us off. We had no complaints and drove back contemplating the moment of truth – the return derby at Old Trafford against a United who had beaten Gornik and already claimed a place in the European Cup semi-finals against Real Madrid.

United and Leeds were now joint top, with 45 points from 32 games. Liverpool were third, two points behind but with a game in hand. City also had 43 points but had played a game more than Liverpool. The derby match by itself wouldn't settle anything, but United, heartened by the prospect of their European Cup win, had picked up form menacingly and if they beat us, they would open up a four-point gap. Psychologically, a defeat was unthinkable. United emerged from the tunnel preceded by the ball boys to the usual ear-splitting sound. We were standing in the Paddock, to the side of the Stretford End, trying to reconcile those conflicting emotions of optimism of what we might do to them and pessimism of what we feared they might do to us. My mind travelled back to my very first sight of these two teams, all those years ago, when only

Trautmann had stood between City and humiliation.

I tried hard to clear my head of such negative thoughts but as the pale blue shirts faced the blood red ones of United, I remained fearful. Tony Book got the ball trapped under his foot and half stumbled. Best quickly robbed him, ran on unchallenged into the City penalty area and thumped the ball past Mulhearn. Thirty-eight seconds had elapsed since the kick-off. We exchanged sorrowful glances, solemn shakes of the head. We were being found out. United were always the ultimate challenge and despite everything that had happened in the past six months, we still weren't good enough. O, ye of little faith!

Gradually, Doyle and Bell started to wrest control of the midfield away from Crerand, Stiles and Fitzpatrick. Bell, in particular, was majestic that night, and after twenty minutes he blasted a shot past Stepney high into the roof of the net. We were starting to dominate but at half-time, with the score still at 1–1, we were aware that a moment's genius from Law, Best or Charlton could still scupper us.

David was the most positive of us, pointing out that for the last thirty minutes of that first half, United hadn't managed a decent attack. The City forward-line struck terror into the United defence lacking Bill Foulkes. Constant pressure led to a free-kick to City thirty yards out. Coleman took it, sending the ball curling into the penalty area, where the unexpected balding head of George Heslop met it with a firm header to send it past the scrambling Stepney. It was Heslop's first and, I think, without recourse to the record books, only League goal for City.

United renewed their attacks but the City defence stood firm. Every time Law or Best threatened, he was surrounded by three City defenders snapping at his ankles. As United continued to press forward desperately in search of the equaliser, City counter-attacked once more. Bell, who had terrorised United all night, broke clear with the ball at his feet. Francis Burns, who was the only United defender close enough to catch him, pursued Bell unavailingly into the penalty area. As Bell drew back his foot to score his second goal of a famous night, Burns crashed into him. The referee blew his whistle and pointed to the spot. Today, Burns would have been sent off. I'm not sure he was even booked for that disgraceful tackle. Our joy was stilled by the sight of Bell prone and unmoving on the ground. After a lengthy interruption, he was stretchered off. Lee placed the ball on the penalty spot, stepped back ten yards and ran up like a fast bowler. He shot, as he always did, straight at the goalkeeper. Sensibly, Stepney dived out of the way.

At the end of Olivier's *Othello*, the great actor produced a small blade from a wristband and cut his throat, slumping over the dead body of the suffocated Desdemona. A group of actors stood around for a few minutes muttering about the future of Iago and who should now rule in Cyprus, but the audience paid little attention. The object of their fascination still lay on the bed, the body breathing as quietly as possible. So it was with the end of that match. Bell dominated that game so much that his departure effectively ended it, although there were still seven minutes to play. As Michael Parkinson wrote so accurately at the time:

> Sometimes in sport that rare thing happens and a game is burned on the brain. Those of us who were present at Old Trafford on 27 March 1968 . . . will never forget [it]. It was simply more than a game.

We raced back to the car before the United-supporting kids could begin their rampage round the streets of Salford visiting vengeance on the cars of City supporters. We were so happy, we paid even less attention than usual to what each other was saying. Our only anxiety was what would become of Bell. He was out for nearly a month. Our next anxiety was what would happen to City in the meantime. The answer was not long delayed. A few days later, we drove to Leicester. We sang our songs and anticipated another triumph. The team was quite unrecognisable from the heroes of that Wednesday night and they slumped to a depressing 1–0 defeat. What *is* it with Manchester City?

We recovered to beat Chelsea (just) and West Ham United (comfortably) on Good Friday and Easter Saturday, but still United, Leeds and Liverpool refused to give up the chase. The boys dropped me off at Manchester Piccadilly station after the West Ham game and I returned to Cambridge for a blissful summer term. On the Tuesday, I hitched down to London to see us lose again, this time to an Alan Birchenall goal in the return match at Chelsea. City played well enough to have wrested a point from the match, but ultimately it was another disappointing performance away from home on a par with the defeats at Leeds and Leicester. I wrote in sorrowful mood to David, giving him details of the Chelsea game. He wrote back by return of post, informing me that he had been at the game and bitterly contested my view of it. We arranged to meet in London for the penultimate match of the season, away to Spurs.

Meanwhile, to my enormous satisfaction, I was invited to Maggie's house in Broxbourne. It was exactly as I had imagined it – a large, attractive, detached house in the country. Her father could have been a retired colonel, her mother a stalwart of the local Women's Institute. Certainly they read the *Daily Telegraph*, a newspaper I had only previously encountered when searching for the detailed law reports of a notorious sex crime or, more often, when abroad and desperate for the county cricket scoreboard. There is a passage in *Portnoy's Complaint* in which the hero talks of a passionate interest in girls descending from the WASP aristocracy. He believes his desire is to penetrate their social background rather than their bodies. I suspect I might have been subject to the same emotion. Certainly, by half past four on that Saturday afternoon, faced with a choice between Maggie and a transistor radio I would have chosen the latter. I heard that we had given a dull, colourless display in a 0–0 draw at Wolves. Although Bell was back for the final run-in, expert opinion made Manchester United clear favourites to retain their title. They had just beaten Sheffield United 1–0, and with two home games against Newcastle and Sunderland and one away at West Brom, United had by far the easiest closing fixtures of the four teams still competing for the Championship.

Four days later, United beat a lacklustre Real Madrid 1–0 at home in the first leg of their European Cup semi-final. The nation prepared to celebrate. The following night, City scraped a fortunate 1–0 win against Sheffield Wednesday, but could make no real impression on United. Expert opinion still predicted that we would finish in third place behind United and Leeds.

Monday 29 April was the night of the College Football Club dinner. A bunch of teenagers in dinner jackets paid a high proportion of their grant cheques to eat rich food and drink fine wines while behaving in a manner best fitted to a Young Conservatives social event. After the drunken speeches, we filed out into the balmy air to play football, still in dinner jackets, on Parker's Piece, an open patch of land near Fenners, now the haunt of late-night muggers.

In the midst of this hilarity, God sent a message. I have no memory of his name or face, but the news he bore was my equivalent of the Annunciation. Not only had City won a vital 2–0 victory at home to Everton but United had gone down 6–3 at West Brom. Six-three! The prospective Champions of

Europe had been trounced, traduced, humiliated 6–3! Apparently, City had been so tense in the goalless first half that they had scarcely mounted a single attack of note. City kicked off that night at 7.45, fifteen minutes later than the match at the Hawthorns. During the half-time interval, a quivering announcer told the crowd that United were losing 2–0 at West Brom. With thirty minutes still to play at Maine Road, the air was rent with ecstatic roars as it was broadcast over the tannoy that United were now losing 6–1. A delirious City crowd now changed the atmosphere of the game. Roared on by the sense of beckoning destiny, City threw everything including Tony Book at the beleaguered Everton defence which, like West Brom's, had played in a winning FA Cup semi-final on the previous Saturday. It was the inspirational skipper Book who scored the breakthrough goal, Tony Coleman who doubled the score and sealed the win. We now had the same number of points as United, but a far superior goal-average. If City won their remaining two games, we would be Champions.

On the Friday night, Maggie was due to arrive in Cambridge for the twenty-first birthday party. She wore a long flowing gown and seemed to enjoy herself. Most of my bachelor friends were surprised that the girl I had long talked about actually existed. We danced and snogged with abandon. Tomorrow I was due to meet David at White Hart Lane, but tonight was going to be a spectacular curtain-raiser to the inevitable Championship triumph. Glued by the mouth to each other on a bridge over the Cam as all the clocks in the city sounded two o'clock in the morning, I was in a fool's paradise.

By the time we got back to my room, I was in a blue funk: what happened next? Books and movies were always reticent at this point. Did I make the first move and if so, what the hell was it? In the end, it didn't matter.

232

'Where are you sleeping?' asked Maggie brightly.

'Ermm,' I replied.

'You can have the pillow,' she said, chucking it onto the floor where I was supposed to curl up. I did so, trying to make out in the total blackness of the room what she looked like as she scrambled into my single bed.

In the tense silence which followed, I tried to reassure her that though we were both virgins, I knew what to do. 'I'm not a virgin,' said Maggie indignantly. I lay on the floor, transfixed by the information. If she wasn't' a virgin, what the hell was I doing lying on the floor? It was a troubled sleep I found, not aided by my bedder (the Cambridge term for a cleaning woman) who deliberately ignored the accepted sign of the wastepaper basket in the corridor not to disturb the student within by hammering on the door and yelling, 'Have you got a woman in there, Mr Shindler?' Well, I had and I hadn't, as it were, and I was buggered if I was going to be hung for stealing a lamb rather than a sheep. I threw Maggie her dress while negotiating at the door with the bedder. Maggie made good her escape (my room was on the ground floor, making climbing out of the window a simple matter even in a hitched-up ball gown) and I managed to save my undergraduate status. Young men had been sent down for smuggling women into their rooms quite recently. It would have been the final cruel irony had I suffered such a fate while preserving my virginal status intact.

The rest of the day was a nightmare. Maggie resented my proprietorial assumptions and talked of her boyfriend. I didn't quite know what the hell she was doing with me in Cambridge if she had a boyfriend. The conversation started at that point and went round in circles for about five hours. By the time she left, I was in a total daze. It was nearly three o'clock in the afternoon before I caught my breath. I had no chance of getting to Spurs now. David would simply go without me. He did. I went back to the room of my own and listened to a brilliant 3–1 City victory, with goals by Bell and Summerbee. For the second time that season, City had outplayed Spurs. Even the knowledge that United had thrashed Newcastle 6–0 didn't alter the prognostication.

Reading the papers the next morning, I came to a decision of profound significance. City were more important to me than Maggie was. I would continue to carry a torch for her, suffering nobly in the way young men do in romantic novels, but I knew now that my destiny was to be found not in her soft bosom but in Newcastle, where City had to go the following Saturday. If we won, we were Champions. And Newcastle had just been on the wrong end of a 6–0 battering by United. But if City lost or drew and United beat Sunderland at home, United would have retained their crown. Everything in the world was reduced to the battle for the League title. The only thing that mattered to me in the universe was the ninety minutes of football to be played at St James' Park on 11 May 1968. Elsewhere during this week, Enoch Powell was warning of rivers of blood flowing through the streets of England if immigration controls were not tightened. In Paris, *Les Evénements* had brought the country to a complete standstill. To me, nothing mattered except getting to Newcastle.

I left early on the Friday morning to hitch-hike all the way up the A1. It was a pleasantly uneventful trip and I arrived at six o'clock in the evening, found a cheap bed and breakfast and opened my copy of *The Age of Reform* by Richard Hofstadter, a brilliant Pulitzer Prize-winning book about American history between 1890 and 1940. It was like Tony Hancock trying to read *A History of Western Philosophy* by Bertrand Russell. Nothing made the slightest sense. The first chapter was on the agrarian myth and commercial realities. It sounded interesting. I wondered what Mike Summerbee would make of it. I wondered what Mike Summerbee was doing now. I wondered if Mike Summerbee was fully fit. He hadn't travelled with the rest of the party to Newcastle, so that he could have last-minute treatment on his injured leg. Would he score tomorrow? Would we win tomorrow? Pleeeeease!

I was torturing myself. I couldn't sleep. I opened *The Age of Reform* again and turned to a new chapter. It was headed, 'The Struggle Over Organisation.' I wondered how the City defence would organise on the morrow. How far up would Oakes and Doyle push to support that lethal forward-line? Would Neil Young have one of his awful away games or would he respond to the occasion? It was hopeless. I thought about Maggie. That wasn't a profitable line of enquiry either. I remembered Richard III lying awake on the night before Bosworth, tortured by visions of the ghosts of his murdered victims. Was Mulhearn lying awake even now, thinking of the points dropped against West Brom over Christmas? And so, eventually, I found my rest.

Next day, after helping Hyperion to his horse, I set out for the ground, sniffing the air. What was that awful smell? It turned out to be the brewery adjacent to St James' Park. I got there at 11. I wasn't due to meet David until 1.30. A couple of hours later, I started talking to an elderly man wearing a cloth cap. It transpired he was Eric Todd. My hero! With palsied fingers, I extracted my tattered copy of his match report against Burnley. He was definitely excited. He had exactly the right attitude to be a City supporter, a well-developed sense of the ridiculous – and what could be more ridiculous than this?

I met David and we took up our place, standing underneath the main stand just to the right of the halfway line. If you had written a storybook way to win the Championship, what now unfolded before us would have been discounted as unbelievable. Summerbee put City ahead, 'Pop' Robson equalised a minute later. Young hit a marvellous left-foot shot

235

to restore the lead, Sinclair seized on a mistake by Heslop two minutes later. Young scored again, but it was disallowed. Lee scored, same result. Bastards! Two-all at half-time. Five minutes after the restart, Young scored, we looked at the ref. Goal!

The news filtered through as it always does on the last day of the season, through some bloke with a transistor radio ten yards away. United were losing at home to Sunderland. Allegedly. Mike Doyle came near me to pick up the ball for a throw-in. I yelled the United score at him. Was there the faintest trace of a smile, did that noble brow ease, I wondered? He took the throw-in, Lee burst through the shattered Newcastle defence and thumped the ball past McFaul into the net: 4–2! It was ours. I could taste it. Lee stood on the wall behind the goal where he had just scored, arms aloft, waiting for the adoration. He got it from fans and colleagues alike.

Lee had another goal disallowed, and inevitably with five minutes to go, there was another mistake by Heslop and it was 4–3, United had pulled one back at Old Trafford. Every panicky thought that had ever crossed my mind came back to haunt me. If Mulhearn gives away two goals in three minutes and United equalise, I'm going to die. The cross is whipped in to the far post . . . and Mulhearn hangs on. The referee looks at his watch. I can't catch my breath. The players half stop, expecting the whistle. He waves play on, Doyle gives the ball away, here come Newcastle again. I'm going to expire with fright. I've gone into another world. I don't know where I am. Where is this world? Will City win the Championship in this world? And then David is holding me and jumping up and down. It's over, we've won. We've won the whole thing. I'm crying. I'm not the only one. This is mass hysteria, like the Beatles and their teeny-boppers. I wonder if Tony Book likes jellybabies? This is how the religious sects operate; they get their victims worked up into a state, then they baptise them. I wouldn't mind being baptised right now if Colin Bell were leading the service. Hang on. Hang on. It's me. It's over. The players have gone. David's gone back to Manchester. How, I don't know. I'm here, by myself, walking along with the City crowd and an overnight bag. What am I going to do? I haven't thought beyond five o'clock on this day for a week. I know I belong in Cambridge, but I've no idea how I'm going to get there. I'm walking along in a crowd of Blues, smiling stupidly, singing, chanting. This isn't me. I don't join anything. I'm an observer, an outsider, a Jew, an alien, *der Ausländer*. 'Can I have a lift, please?' I ask the guys I'm caught up with. Of course I can. A Blue will do anything for another Blue at this moment. We get into his van. He has no idea where he is. We listen to the radio. Allison's on. 'We'll terrify the cowards of Europe,' he boasts. Of course we will. These players, this team, my heroes, MulhearnBookPardoeDoyle-HeslopOakesLeeBellSummerbeeYoungandColeman could do anything. Where are we? We're in Consett. Where's Consett? God knows. They let me out. I have to find the A1. I find it. I get a lift to Weatherby. And then another to Huntingdon. Somehow I get to Huntingdon town centre around 11.30pm. The last bus to Cambridge leaves in ten minutes. I've made it. It's been a day of such strange, overwhelming emotions.

I walk into Harvey Court, singing. I'm drunk with emotion. All the City songs, like a familiar hymn sheet, are reprised tunelessly but with great feeling. Lights go out all over Harvey Court. Nobody wants to be around when the obsessive is at his most unbearable. I don't care. They're going to get the lot, from 'Sha La La La Summerbee' to 'Heigh ho, heigh ho, it's off to Mexico/For Bell and Lee and Summerbee and Glyn Pardoe'. Nice tune. Great lyrics. Who can object? Oh, this wooden floor is a nice place to lie down. I'm tired. So tired. Isn't that what they say in the movies just before someone dies? Maybe I'm dying. Maybe I'm going to meet my mother and tell her about City. That'll show her for making me change to United. Who the hell are United? This is one day where I just don't give a twopenny ha'penny about United. They lost. They're a bunch of losers. Yesterday's men. Tomorrow belongs to me, to us, to Manchester City. Goodnight world. I guess it finally all came right. Happy ending. Happy dreams.

Chapter Eleven

It lasted four days. Not just the euphoria, but also the sense of accomplishment. After all those years, desperately praying for our place in the sun, it was over. Four days after the momentous events in Newcastle, Manchester United drew 3–3 with Real Madrid in the Bernabeu Stadium. It was all they needed to move into the final of the European Cup. It was all the rest of the world needed. There was still only one team in Manchester.

A George Best goal had been the sum total of all they managed to achieve in the first leg at Old Trafford. The papers were full of contempt for Real Madrid who, like their ageing left-winger Gento, were only a pale replica of the great side that had dominated Europe ten years before. They did, however, warn that Real might be a different proposition in Madrid, and so, initially, it proved. At half-time, United were 3–1 down and all the old memories of Lisbon and Belgrade must have washed through the dressing-room. Then Sadler misheaded the ball over the line to force the tie into a possible replay and with fifteen minutes left, Bill Foulkes, of all unlikely people, scored to give United a draw on the night, a famous 4–3 victory overall.

The country was awash with happiness. After Celtic's ground-breaking 2–1 win over the ultra-defensive Inter Milan the previous year, the European Cup was coming to Britain for the second year in succession, to England for the first time ever. Benfica, who had beaten Juventus in their semi-final, might as well save the money for the air fare. There was really no need for them to show up. After all, the match was due to be played at Wembley. A terrible sense of inevitability, rivalling anything in a Greek tragedy, descended on me. It made me sick.

In the Junior Common Room in Harvey Court, there was a small television set, serving the needs of the hundred residents. To see anything, you had to get there early to bag a chair within watching distance of the set. The crowd started building up in the JCR half an hour before kick-off. The raging jingoism made the atmosphere like a re-run of the World Cup final. Surely some of these Arsenal or Liverpool supporters would want Benfica to win. Sadly, I was the only one in the room flying the Portuguese flag that night.

I suspect that, as and when United finally make it to the European Cup final after a thirty-year gap, that situation would not be repeated. The bitterness which has crept into football over recent years has left too many sour memories. If 1968 was about Munich, the boys who died, Busby and Charlton, Law (who was injured and couldn't play in the final) and superstud, superstar Georgie Best, 1998 will be about money, and power, and arrogance, and United's domestic domination.

The electric, emotional atmosphere of Wembley that May night in 1968 was transmitted by television. There was only one moment when I thought a miracle might happen. Charlton had put United into the lead and even when Graca equalised for Benfica with ten minutes left, one felt instinctively it was a blip. It was United's night. It was meant to be. Then a long ball forward caught Stiles out of position for the only time that night. Eusebio seized the moment to break clear of the United defence. The ball bounced nicely into his stride. In that split-second, I could see the prospect of a last-minute rescue – the tears of despair, the hunched bodies, the desperate feelings that it will never happen. There would have been no time for United to equalise before the end of normal time.

That split-second was all I had. Eusebio belted the ball straight at the advancing Stepney. The United goalkeeper couldn't have got out of the way even if he'd tried. The ball came to rest in the folds of his stomach. It was over. United scored three times in extra-time and a legend was born. The only redeeming feature is that it has hung over United for the last few years as the League Championship hung over them for twenty-six years. It is a truth universally acknowledged that the European Cup belongs to Manchester United. It is a travesty that clubs like Borussia Dortmund are too stupid to understand this and will keep beating them. Haven't they read *The Day A Team Died?* Are they too thick to be properly overawed by playing in the Theatre of Dreams? They'll learn. Everyone else has.

In an attempt to clear my head of this sickening anti-climax, I borrowed £35 from my father and flew on a student charter flight to New York. I had started a course on American History that summer term and instantly fell in love with the country. The summer would only confirm what the university library had already taught me. My future was in some way bound up with America.

I was met at the airport in New York by relatives about whom I had only heard. My maternal grandfather, the one with the raincoat factory in Bury, had left Galicia to join his brother in New York but, like many other Jews, had been ejected from the boat at Grimsby, having been told he was in New York City. I don't know if the two Weidberg brothers ever met; my great-uncle's family were simply referred to as 'the American relatives' with a mixture of pride that they, too, had been successful, and envy that the American scale was so much greater than the British one. My grandfather, despite selling-up in the late 1950s for over a quarter of a million pounds, continued to live in a small semi-detached house with a tiny kitchen for the rest of his life. Our American cousins, the other Weidbergs, lived in the affluent suburb of Yonkers in Westchester County and were as hospitable as I could possibly have wished.

In England, the concept of central heating was still new. Heat was provided by open fires or electric radiators. On winter mornings, it would be so cold we would have to get dressed in the bathroom with the door to the airing cupboard open. In America, I was confronted by the concept of the second bathroom. My aunt confided to me that she would rather divorce my uncle than allow him to share her bathroom. He was permitted a small bathroom of his own, oddly positioned off the kitchen. It was disconcerting when he disappeared into it while I was still eating breakfast. In order to make the experience a little more palatable, he would turn on a radio to disguise the sounds of his operation, as a consequence of which my daily Frosted Flakes were consumed to the accompaniment of marches by John Philip Souza.

After a couple of days searching, I found employment as a tennis counsellor at Camp Potomac – a summer camp for Jewish American princesses and princes outside Pittsfield, Massachusetts, in the Berkshire mountains. My job was to look after ten boys and, during the day, to teach the boys and the neighbouring girls' camp the rudiments of tennis. I had far more trouble with the girls, who had to be dissuaded from altering their hairstyles between throwing the ball up and serving. The sexual precociousness of the fifteen-year-old girls I was teaching terrified the life out of me and I clung resolutely to my virginity – which is a lot more than could be said for them.

The summer of 1968 was a remarkable time to be in America. Martin Luther King and the other Bobby Kennedy had been shot dead only weeks before. While I was still in Camp Potomac, the Russians invaded Czechoslovakia and a week later the television news showed endless replays of Mayor Daley's cops beating up the kids outside the Democratic National Convention in Chicago.

It was stirring stuff – not just the politics but the euphoria of America itself. I enjoyed almost everything about the country, from the baseball at Yankee Stadium, where I saw one of the last 'at bats' of the great Mickey Mantle, to the open freeways of New England. I recognised, even at the time, not only that I was a guest in the country but that my experience of America was a partial one. I might not have fallen in love with the country so readily had I been staying in Newark or the South Bronx.

I missed nearly the whole of the 1968 Ashes series, including the remarkable last day at The Oval when the crowd helped the groundstaff to clear the water away so that Derek Underwood could bowl the Australians out, taking four of their last five wickets in the last hour of play to square the series. More to the point, I missed the 6–1 hammering of West Bromwich Albion in the Charity Shield with which City began the new season. It seemed as if they would simply continue where they had left off at Newcastle, despite Tony Book's absence through a long-term Achilles' tendon injury.

I returned to England in time to see the home leg of the European Cup tie against Fenerbahce of Turkey. David Green couldn't make it that night. He had booked tickets to take his girlfriend Chrissie to see the Royal Shakespeare Company in Stratford. I warned him, not entirely seriously, that he might be missing City's only match in the European Cup. He reminded me of Malcolm Allison's cavalier boast that we would terrify the cowards of Europe, and set off for

Stratford with a light heart. With an equally blithe spirit, I watched Summerbee miss a goal he could have scored with his nose and the match ended in a miserable 0–0 draw. Two weeks later, just after the start of the Cambridge term, I listened on the radio as Tony Coleman put City ahead after twelve minutes but, backed by a fanatical crowd, Fenerbahce swarmed all over us, scored twice and that was the end of the European dream.

It was a most unexpected and unwelcome turn of events. The vivid drama of the last few weeks leading up to the Championship triumph was still fresh in the mind (and as you can see, remains so) and this reverse knocked the wind out of my sails. I had made my reputation as the only, certainly the only visible, Manchester City supporter in Cambridge. There was a defrocked don who constantly hurried around the town with a bundle of newspapers under his arm, looking as though he was being pursued by the secret police. This man was a known and familiar sight in Cambridge. My own fetish was slightly more hygienic but regarded as harmless eccentricity. If City were reverting to their old ways, I would become the object of derision, having nailed my blue-and-white colours so firmly to the mast.

I was glad to get back to Cambridge. My father had remarried and my brother had just gained a second daughter. I had no home of my own in Manchester any longer and although my heart belonged there (and still does), my body would have to be fed, clothed and sheltered elsewhere. The American History course became increasingly more interesting as I moved into the twentieth century. I knew my future life would somehow be connected to America, but I didn't know how. I knew City would get out of their slump, but I didn't know how. I knew I'd meet the girl of my dreams, but I didn't know who.

Everything happened together in the New Year. Cambridge out of term was miserable. I received special dispensation to stay in College over the Christmas vacation. The Cam froze over, the Hall where we ate dinner shut down. The staircases emptied and the heating barely worked. I returned to Manchester solely for the Christmas matches but City were already fifteen points behind the leaders, Leeds United, and had no chance of retaining or even competing for the title won so gloriously seven months before. I scuttled back to Cambridge as fast as I could. I was the main striker in our College First XI and we had a good chance of winning Cuppers, as the knockout competition is called.

In the first round, we beat King's College 9–0. We were 6–0 up before I scored, but I finished with a hat-trick. In the second round, we were unfortunately drawn against Fitzwilliam, by far the strongest side in Cambridge. Their central striker was called Peter Phillips, and apart from leading the University side, he had already had trials with Cambridge United and Luton. We trained hard, prepared well and fought like tigers on the day, but we lost 5–2 and I finished the game in Casualty at Addenbrooke's Hospital. Over the years, I finished so many games in those familiar surroundings that I was better known in Accident and Emergency than in our dressing-room.

Limping through injury to pride as well as calf muscle, I bumped into Rosemary, the girlfriend of Derek Hirst, another Caius historian. Rosemary, a thoroughly likeable, vivacious girl who died tragically young, introduced me to her companion, an attractive blonde girl reading history at Girton. Her name was Jenny and the moment I laid eyes on her, I knew she was the one. Jenny herself certainly had no such presentiments. We ran into each other again in the university library and went for a cup of tea – wild place, that university library. I was completely and utterly hooked. She played the piano to

245

a very high standard and she laughed at my jokes. There was
nothing wrong with this girl.

I finished playing in Shaw's *Man & Superman* at the ADC,
directed by my friend Lenny. I had enjoyed it, but had been
distracted on the second night because City were at home to
Newcastle United in an FA Cup fourth round replay. Goals
by Bobby Owen and Neil Young were enough to take us
through to a fifth round tie away to Blackburn where, after a
couple of postponements due to the icy weather, we eventually secured a 4–1 win. By this time Tony Book had returned
and we were starting to buzz as a team. On Saturday 1 March
1969, City were due to play Spurs in the sixth round at Maine
Road and the College football team had arranged to play
Queens' College in Oxford. I asked Jenny if she would come
with me. My heart was thumping fit to burst. She said she
would. I was as happy as I'd ever been.

The coach drew up in Oxford at lunchtime and I escorted
Jenny to David's rooms in Trinity College. True to form,
David had finagled one of the best sets of rooms in college
and in Bill Pill, the most corrupt scout (as Oxford bedders
were called) in the university. Jenny disappeared to meet her
Oxford-based friends as David and I went down to watch
Football Focus. The main interview was with Mike Summerbee. Over that particularly bleak Christmas, I had written a
long letter analysing the decline in Summerbee's fortunes,
which was published in a Manchester City magazine. During
the television interview, responding to questions about his dip
in form, Summerbee confessed he was puzzled. He had, he
claimed, received a letter about it from Cambridge University.
I sat stunned. I turned to David.

'Did you hear that?'

'What?' David had been gossiping to a friend.

'What Summerbee said. About me.'

'About you? What are you talking about?' To this day, I

don't know whether I dreamed it or not. Saturday 1 March was an extraordinary day.

We lost the match against Queens' 2–1 but I scored our goal and I was perfectly happy, particularly when I learned that Francis Lee had scored the only goal of the game at Maine Road. We were in the semis. Jenny and I had dinner and went to see *Elvira Madigan* in an art-house cinema in Headington, within 200 yards of the Manor Ground, home of Oxford United. We were high on our own emotions, mine heightened artificially by Francis Lee. The theme music to the Swedish love story is the second movement of Mozart's 21st Piano Concerto in C, K467. My relationship with Jenny had been initiated by a shared love of Mozart's piano music. This piece affected me so deeply that for three years after our eventual break-up, I couldn't bear to listen to it.

We wandered back to Trinity. The coach had already left for Cambridge with the rest of the team on it. David, oblivious of the somewhat delicate stage my relationship with Jenny had reached, disappeared into his bedroom, threw a pair of sheets at me and said he was tired and was going to bed. I looked at Jenny. She looked away. I started to move the two couches together and make a bed of sorts. I was waiting for Maggie's deathless line, 'And where are *you* going to sleep?' It never came. Jenny turned the light out and slipped under the sheets in her underwear. I followed immediately. It had been a hell of a day and it wasn't finished yet.

I'd like to pretend what followed was a practised seduction. Since neither of us had ever been in a comparable situation, that was unlikely anyway. What followed was a predictable fumbling and groping, and a recognition that bodies were awkward things and this whole exercise, which in my lurid imagination had interrupted many a session in the university library, was both more basic and more complex than I had imagined. After half an hour of trial and error, both

247

combatants retired from the fray without a decision. I awoke an hour or so later, immediately and acutely conscious that I was alone. I could hear the sound of sobbing in the distance. I opened the door to David's rooms, went out into the corridor and found Jenny doubled up in agony on the floor of the bathroom. She had been attacked by appalling pain, like the worst kind of menstrual cramps.

A few days later, we tried again in her room at Girton. This time the operation was a complete success, although I was conscious throughout that I was still wearing my socks, the only part of my body that was covered. We had both reached a fever pitch of excitement and though mine would certainly survive the three seconds it would take me to remove my socks, I wasn't sure that Jenny's would. If I were to disengage and remove my socks conventionally, I was terrified that she would abandon the game. I tried to remove them by curling the toes of my right foot inside my left sock, but it was in vain. My socks remained where they were.

During the summer, Dudley Moore came to the Arts Theatre, playing the Woody Allen part in *Play It Again, Sam*. Changing the dialogue to fit the English ear, the girl asks Dudley what he was thinking of while making love. 'Bobby Charlton,' he replies. (United again! I thought.) 'I wondered why you kept shouting "Shoot!" ' she says. In the original, American version, Woody is thinking of the San Francisco Giants star Willie Mays and Diane Keaton says, 'I wondered why you kept shouting "Slide!" ' I'm not sure why, but I think the American version is funnier. The image of a base runner sliding is less threatening than a footballer about to shoot.

My point is that I was thinking about Mike Doyle. I have a vision of Doyle, rather like Beckenbauer or Bobby Moore, breaking up an attack, bringing the ball out of defence, looking for the long ball out to Summerbee on the wing or to

Bell bursting through the middle. In the event that greater durability is required, I can then invent an entire City attack involving the ball hitting the bar, then the post, before being scrambled clear for a corner. As Woody rightly concludes in his monologue on this subject, in which he plays an entire inning of baseball, 'Bottom of the ninth, two men out . . .' etc. culminating with 'By this time, she's been in the shower five minutes.' City simply wouldn't leave my mind, even at the peak of ecstasy.

I had much to be ecstatic about at this time. A week after the Spurs match, City went to Old Trafford and won again. This time a solitary goal by Mike Summerbee was enough to claim both points. Clearly my letter had had a most salutary effect, although it is arguable that the upturn in City's fortunes was due more to the return after long-term injury of skipper Tony Book and the spirit engendered by a successful Cup run.

Two weeks after the victory at Old Trafford, the four friends met up at Villa Park for the FA Cup semi-final against Everton. Along with the Newcastle match which won the Championship, this match has remained in my mind more vividly than any other. The irony is that it was a poor match, a typical attritional FA Cup semi-final. Allison dropped Tony Coleman and detailed the dependable David Connor to mark Everton's danger man, Alan Ball. So seriously did Connor take his task it was rumoured that he had to be restrained from hanging onto his man during the kick-in.

Both defences were on top and there was scarcely a shot at goal for the whole ninety minutes. We had long resigned ourselves to another time-consuming and prohibitively expensive replay when City won a last-minute corner out on the right. Young took it, curling it temptingly into the area. Doyle won it in the air and nodded it down to Summerbee, who laid it into the path of the nineteen-year-old centre-half Tommy Booth. From a distance of less than six yards and with his left foot, Booth struck the ball firmly into the back of the Everton net.

I don't think I've ever known one particular moment of ecstasy as sharp as that. There have many better games, more exciting games, outstanding goals, satisfying victories over United, but nothing like Tommy Booth's goal for distilling the essence of a lifetime of football-supporting into one sublime moment. We all knew that Everton would hardly have time to kick off before the final whistle would blow, so we were certain that Booth's goal had won the game. It had also confirmed City as a major force in British soccer, not a one-trophy wonder. An FA Cup final appearance, the year after an exciting League Championship win, meant that we had joined the elite of the English game.

I arrived back in Cambridge satisfied rather than euphoric. Jenny was staying with me (illegally) in College. I didn't have to go home for Easter. I could continue to work hard for my First Class degree, I had my girlfriend living with me and City were in the Cup final. I could, romantically, see a vision in which this lifestyle simply continued. Jenny and I would marry and raise a family, I would carry on with my research into some area of recent American history, City would continue to win trophies and replace Manchester United as top dog in Manchester and therefore the world. My son would support Manchester City and come back to Caius and we would be a happy achieving family.

The dream lasted a good few weeks. Part One of the Historical Tripos in the summer term of 1969 examined us in all the papers we had studied to date. I think I worked harder that term than I had ever done before. I rose each day at six o'clock and rarely went to bed before midnight. Jenny, who had no exams herself that summer, was selfless in providing comfort of a physical and spiritual kind as I drove myself onwards towards the First, spurred by Neil McKendrick whom I was determined to show was mistaken when he said it wasn't possible to be successful in the Tripos and play as much sport as I did and act in the theatre as well. I might have added that the acting and sport with Jenny was also time-consuming, but I thought it best to let that pass.

A month before the first examination, General Historical Questions ('Better fifty years of Europe than a cycle of Cathay.' Discuss), I managed to get hold of my ticket for the Cup final. For years we had complained about the ludicrous ticket-allocation for the showpiece final. Supporters of the two clubs were allowed about 16,000 tickets each, with the remainder divided between the various societies and clubs affiliated to the FA. Fortunately, among the people who should never have been allowed anywhere near Wembley in preference to genuine fans, were the Cambridge University Football Club. A little prostration was all that was required. At least my reputation as a genuine, if somewhat evangelical fan counted in my favour. I later discovered that my brother had acquired his ticket for United's 1963 Cup final appearance from the same source.

The day itself was oddly anti-climactic, principally because the four of us had acquired our tickets individually for different parts of the ground and we never saw each other on the great day. I was sitting next to Peter Phillips who had scored against Caius for Fitzwilliam. He listened patiently as I extolled the virtues of every City player. 'Neil Young,' he said briefly. 'Young's the most talented player you've got.'

It was Neil Young, of course, who drove the ball past the Leicester keeper Peter Shilton for the only goal of the game. Summerbee had taken Lee's thrown-in, wriggled past his full-back, shaken off the attentions of the centre-half Woollet, got to the dead-ball line and pulled it back to Young, who was hovering around the penalty spot. Young hit it first time and the net behind Shilton billowed. 'Told you so,' said Peter

Phillips. Unable to articulate the emotions I was feeling, I kissed him. Phillips shut up for the rest of the game, fearing a repeat. I will never forget the sight of wise old Tony Book calming his team down even while the other ten players were going wild with delight at the goal. He knew how vulnerable we were to the counter-attack.

The game swung from end to end. Andy Lochhead missed spectacularly for Leicester, Allan Clarke went frighteningly close on three or four occasions. The City defence looked worryingly unstable but every time we attacked, I felt we would score. In the end it was a surprise that there was only one goal in the game. As Book went up to receive the Cup, I felt strangely calm; there was nothing like the euphoria of the Newcastle game or even the semi-final goal. The players seemed remote from me; physically, because Wembley crowds are a long way from the playing surface, and emotionally, because they had been swallowed up by an alien ritual. I wanted them back at Maine Road where we all belonged. Somehow they now belonged to the nation, not to me. It was a transient sensation, but it was enough to send me off that evening looking for a different sort of sustenance. I steered clear of Soho and finished up in the back row of the balcony at the Theatre Royal, Haymarket, watching Alec McCowen in Peter Luke's play, *Hadrian the Seventh*.

The Tripos Examination came and went. I felt I couldn't have given anything more. I was drained. Jenny and I went to the Caius May Ball together, finishing with breakfast on the riverbank near Grantchester. When we got back to Girton, we were shattered. We curled up together, seeking comfort. The contraceptive packet still lay in the inside pocket of my dinner jacket. We decided it wasn't worth getting out of bed for. We let nature take its course.

My relationship with Jenny had been like living through an Edwardian romance – idyllic settings, pretty clothes,

252

friendly faces. Jenny and I decided we would drive round Europe together. It had been six years since I'd done it with my brother and his friends, and I was anxious to share the experience with the girl I loved. At the end of the term, she stayed up in Cambridge with me until I got the results of my exams, even though she had to rent a room because she could no longer stay in Girton. One morning, we had arranged to meet for a walk before breakfast. She opened the front door of the house where she was staying in a simple white dress. The sun was shining, Cambridge was tranquil, only the birdsong broke the enveloping silence. For a moment, Jenny looked like an ethereal vision. A few weeks later, that was all she was to be in my life – but I have never forgotten that one pure, captivating image.

Chapter Twelve

I have always been a believer in the Elizabethan Wheel of Fortune. How could a life, having survived through some hard times, emerging to blossom as if divinely ordained, be reduced to despair so quickly? The first blow was the First blow. I couldn't have worked harder, no matter how hard McKendrick might have chided me. I had rediscovered a lot of my self-confidence in my second-year courses on American History, British Social and Economic History 1500-1800 and the Expansion of Europe. I knew I'd revised thoroughly, I knew I'd scored well on those papers. The question was, had I recovered from that disastrous first year?

For those who bother to remain in Cambridge for the eventual announcement of the results, it can be a harrowing experience. At ten o'clock, a man in official academic attire emerges from the Old Schools with a printed sheet of paper. He pins it on the noticeboard outside the Senate House and the waiting crowds surge forward, calling out names and results. I decided to skip the possible public humiliation and arrive at 10.30, after the initial surprises had been megaphoned round town. The various papers swam before my eyes: Law Tripos Part II, Mechanical Engineering Tripos Part I, Modern and Mediaeval Languages Tripos Part I, Architecture and Anthropology Tripos Part II, Historical Tripos Part I. Here it was.

My mistake was to start from the top and work down. I scanned that Class One list a dozen times. 'They missed me out,' I thought. My eyes slipped down. 'Class Two Division One, Shindler C Caius.' Failed, I thought. Nothing else, just 'failed'. How was it possible? McKendrick explained sympathetically. I had been right on the borderline. I had achieved five leading alphas out of my twelve marks; one more, and I would have been home and dry. The average number of Firsts given in Part One of the Historical Tripos at that time was nineteen. This year it was thirteen. I was number fourteen. Last-minute deflected winner past Trautmann in a game we should have won.

I wandered blindly through Cambridge for an hour or so, forgetting my promise to go back to Jenny. Eventually I sat down in a darkened arts cinema which was showing Frank Capra's *Mr Deeds Goes To Town*. It was a mind-bending experience. The story is of Longfellow Deeds (played by Gary Cooper), a plain, simple country man who inherits $20 million from his uncle. He moves to New York and is mercilessly exploited by the sharks of that noble town, particularly the newspaper reporter played by Jean Arthur, who pretends to fall in love with him but traduces him each day in her newspaper. They visit Grant's Tomb together. Jean Arthur wonders what Cooper sees in it. Cooper speaks in that unique drawl.

I see a small Ohio farm boy becoming a great soldier. I see thousands of marching men surrendering. I see the beginning of a new nation – like Abraham Lincoln said. And I see that little Ohio boy being inaugurated as President. Things like that can only happen in a country like America.

The post-exam audience dissolved into hoots of derisive laughter. Nobody talks like that, nobody even thinks like that.

I did. In that one moment, I found my vocation. I wanted to make films, and I wanted to make them like Frank Capra, full of warmth and comedy. I haven't always succeeded, but I've never lost the desire.

My failure as a scholar was followed sharply by my failure as a lover. Perhaps failure isn't quite the right word, but my inability to raise myself off the bed that fateful morning after the May Ball was to have dire consequences. It was only apparent that Jenny had missed her period when we had already left England for our European misadventure. Everything went wrong that could go wrong. She was terrified and moody, I was desperate and over-anxious. The entire six weeks passed by in a blur of stomach-tightening tension. Outside Salzburg, somebody told us that a man had walked on the moon and, perhaps more amazingly, England had beaten the West Indies in a Test series. In the grim streets of Communist Budapest, I saw a comfortingly familiar graffito. It read, 'Ferencvaros 1 Liverpool 0.'

More significant was my visit to an Austrian monastery somewhere off the main road between Salzburg and Vienna. There was a notice outside the walls next to the Holy Collection Box on which it was written that, for a very reasonable consideration, the monks would be prepared to pray for the donor's wish of choice. I suppose they would normally expect to be praying for the souls of various dear departeds, but I collected all my loose change and wrapped it in a sheet of paper before dropping it into the box. Although my deteriorating relationship with Jenny was a more immediate concern, I had decided that its future prosperity was out of God's hands so I had written on the paper, 'Please let Manchester City win the European Cup-Winners' Cup.' The monks, whom I had assumed would have been Rapid Vienna supporters to a cowl, came through big time. A symbolic nine months later Tony Book was holding the trophy aloft in the

Prater Stadium down the road. This was some religion! It was almost enough to persuade me to take Holy Orders. Almost, but not quite. In subsequent years, I have often wondered where that magical monastery is. Like Ronald Colman in Capra's *Lost Horizon* I feel I am doomed forever to wander the earth hoping desperately for another sight of that enchanted Shangri-La – or the FA Carling Premiership.

There was nothing remotely beguiling about the rest of that ill-starred trip. As soon as we returned to Cambridge, I went back into rooms in College and Jenny refused to see me. Whatever she was going to have to do, she was going to do alone. I had seen all those black-and-white Woodfall films – *Saturday Night and Sunday Morning, A Kind of Loving*. I knew it was up to me to offer to marry the girl. I did. It wasn't rejected, it was ignored. I retreated to the university library and my Part Two dissertation on the Historical Legacy of John F. Kennedy and to my comedy records. I played them over and over again, *The Goon Show*, Tom Lehrer, Bob Newhart. More than any other, I played the record of the BBC radio commentary of the Cup final. The description of Neil Young's goal has almost been obliterated because the groove has been worn away, so often did the stylus visit it. The despair I experienced reawoke those same feelings which had lain dormant just below the surface since my mother's death. Once again, Manchester City were my major, maybe my only source of comfort.

The new term eventually began, but my heart wasn't in it. Bob Stone directed me in the one part I had always longed to play, the title role of *Richard III*, which we performed in the august setting of the Senate House. It was to be the apex of my acting career – and it was my swansong.

Lancashire, under the inspiring captaincy of Jack Bond, had won the first ever Sunday League forty-over competition sponsored by John Player. I was obviously pleased, it was the first trophy we had won since I'd been born, but it still couldn't relieve the gnawing despondency that overwhelmed me.

David invited me to Oxford for his twenty-first. It was the same day that City overwhelmed United 4–0 in the most one-sided derby match seen for years. I didn't want to go to the party. I couldn't. That term, I was faced with my Mediaeval paper which I had postponed two years before. It was called Church and State in Mediaeval England, 1066–1272. It was a nightmare. Slowly, I began to haul myself out of it, helped by David who rented a flat for us in south Manchester during the Christmas vacation. He bought the Beatles' *Abbey Road* album and played it constantly for three weeks.

During that vacation, City faced United in a two-legged semi-final of the League Cup, the only domestic honour neither club had won. The first leg was at Maine Road, only three weeks after that 4–0 hammering. United began, as might be expected, nervously, and City dominated the first half-hour with their irrepressible fast-flowing football. They were helped by an early goal from Bell, who smacked the ball home joyfully when Stepney could only parry a fierce drive from Lee. Slowly, United roused themselves and in the second half, Best and Charlton started to make inroads into the City defence. Best and Kidd eventually combined to create a chance for Charlton, who side-footed the ball past Corrigan.

After eighty-eight minutes, just as it seemed certain that a 1–1 draw was all we would manage, Lee fell over Ian Ure's outstretched leg. Memories of Dowd and Law in 1963 instantly flashed through my mind. Referee Jack Taylor was about as far away from the incident as we were in the back of the Kippax, but he had no hesitation in awarding the penalty. Lee blasted it home and United went crazy. Things like this didn't happen to Manchester United. Best, who had a header cleared off the line in the last minute, petulantly knocked the ball out of Taylor's hands as they were walking into the tunnel, for which he was fined and suspended. It was the return leg which finally brought me back to life. In front of a full house at Old Trafford a week before Christmas, City seemed to have the tie sewn-up with an early goal from Ian Bowyer, but again United wouldn't lie down. Fullback Paul Edwards equalised on the night and when Law stabbed home after Corrigan had dropped the ball, United were threatening to snatch it from us. It was a sublime moment of incompetence from Stepney which gave it to us in the end. An indirect free-kick was awarded twenty yards out. Lee blasted it through the wall, and Stepney, understandably, felt he couldn't let it pass unguarded into the net, even though had he done so, it would have meant nothing more than a goal-kick to United. In trying to save Lee's powerful drive, the United goalkeeper fumbled the ball into the path of the onrushing Summerbee. In front of the transfixed Stretford End, 'Buzzer' crashed it high into the roof of the net. It was all over.

That victory perked me up no end. I still had the Jenny problem to deal with in Cambridge, but I had a League Cup final to look forward to, I'd won my way onto the College *University Challenge* team and I had discovered the seductive qualities of film history. I knew what I wanted to do with my life.

Jenny was undoubtedly still a problem. Despite her rejection of me and, I thought, by implication, all men, she was now living with a postgraduate Australian man in a house directly opposite where I now have my car serviced. Cambridge is a small town and student circles even smaller. I saw her far too frequently for my liking, since we continued to haunt the same locations. Every time we met, particularly when she had this tall Australian in tow, it was like a dagger had been inserted into my ribs. These feelings of loss, rejection and pain were to remain my constant companions for almost three years.

It was nearly a year before I dared to ask a girl out again. Even at the time, I realised I was trying to duplicate the events of that March day in Oxford the previous year. David was directing Pinter's *The Birthday Party* and was anxious to display his unique gifts to as wide an admiring audience as possible. Feeling badly that I had failed to join him for his twenty-first the previous November, I plucked up the courage to ask a pretty red-haired girl whom I had met when she had been the costume mistress in a production in which I had appeared. She was delighted to go with me to Oxford. So far, so good.

The party after the performance was a fairly typical event of its time. David had fallen madly in love with a leggy blonde called Nicki and was desperately trying to rid himself of the now unwanted attentions of Chrissie, who had loyally stuck with him since his days at Bury Grammar School. Much alcohol was consumed, as you would expect of any 'wrap' party. To all artificial substances, I have always had a somewhat Puritanical response. I maintained that my mood swings were dictated by Manchester City's last result and I didn't need anything else to enhance them. In addition, I enjoyed neither the taste nor the smell, and I was particularly disconcerted by the manner in which friends changed their character under their influence.

My friend Lenny, who had directed me in most of my Cambridge plays – including a famous production of *The Alchemist* in Jesus College Cloisters, in which the part of Pertinax Surly was taken by an unknown would-be writer called Salman Rushdie – was now a trainee director at Granada Television in Manchester. The weekend before the Oxford party I had spent with him, watching on television the 1970 FA Cup final, an exciting 2–2 draw between Leeds and Chelsea. I suggested that Lenny might enjoy coming to David's party. It was a fatal error.

261

There have been many worse moments in my life, but rarely a betrayal so spectacular. I could see them dancing together and put it down to two of my friends being very friendly. They later claimed that they hadn't meant to disappear into the bedroom but had been the helpless prisoners of what they had consumed. It certainly did nothing to increase my admiration for the stuff. Indeed, so strongly did I now loathe it that I am probably better fitted for public office, at least on that score, than the current President of the United States.

The night turned out to be a horrible mirror-image of the previous year. Instead of holding and comforting Jenny, I was wandering round Trinity College looking for a room in which to spend the rest of the night as far away from the party as possible. I would have preferred to have gone straight to the bus station, but I couldn't get out of the locked college. I caught the first bus back to Cambridge in the morning, frozen rigid with feelings of humiliation. The girl returned by the last bus and came straight to my room, where I was desperately but unsuccessfully trying to retain basic information about the incursions of the Ngoni tribes in Africa in the nineteenth century. She apologised for hurting me, but remained adamant that since we hadn't reached any kind of agreement prior to our trip to Oxford, she was a free agent entitled to dispense her favours where she wished.

Lenny rang the next day, full of apologies, again blaming the grass and the girl and his own weakness, encouraging me to try for the First that had eluded me the previous year. It was hopeless. I hadn't enjoyed my courses this last year and I relied on technique to get me through. It was a respectable Upper Second, but nothing remotely as impressive as the previous year.

Everything tasted sour to me. Just when I expected life to be opening up with a number of possibilities, the world seemed a cold and unfriendly place, with only Manchester City and Lancashire providing solace. After their famous victory over United at Christmas, City went on to win the League Cup final against West Brom on a pitch that looked like a cabbage patch. Corrigan stood rooted on his line after five minutes, allowing Astle to head West Brom into the lead, but led by a magnificent display from Francis Lee, City slowly fought their way back into it. Doyle equalised, and Pardoe grabbed the winner in extra-time. This time David and I were together again and the atmosphere was less alienating than it had been at the previous season's Cup final.

City's performance that day was all the finer because they had only returned from a European Cup-Winners' Cup quarter-final first leg at midnight, thirty-six hours before. Although League matches continued to be disappointing, City came alive in the Cup matches. The second leg against the Portuguese Cup winners, Academica Coimbra, was settled by a spectacular twenty-five-yard shot by Tony Towers in the last minute of extra-time. They were supposedly attached to a university, but they were a dirty side – there was none of the Corinthian spirit and 'Three cheers for Pembroke' with which we ended our games. 'They've all got Firsts in shirt-tugging and ankle-tapping,' observed David grimly. In the semi-final, a desperate rearguard action away at FC Schalke was disrupted by a goal from Libuda, but the second leg at Maine Road turned into a triumphant 5–1 rout of the Germans.

We made enquiries as to how we could get to the Prater Stadium in Vienna for the final against Gornik, but we simply didn't have the money. We settled down, instead, to watch it on television. City were on the verge of becoming the first English side to win a domestic and a European trophy in the same season. It would be their fourth major trophy in two years. But instead of Barry Davies commentating on the great game from Vienna, we were pre-empted by David Coleman and the FA Cup final replay between Leeds United and Chelsea. We were rewarded at the end of Chelsea's celebrations with a glimpse of the goals by Young and Lee which had won the game, and Tony Book holding up the European Cup-Winners' Cup to the muted applause of 4,000 drenched spectators.

Lee and Bell went on to Mexico, integral members of the best squad Alf Ramsey ever selected. Bobby Charlton was coming to the end of his career and Colin Bell was his natural heir. City were at least being given some recognition by the national side, although the inclusion of David Sadler in Ramsey's final twenty-eight for Mexico seemed yet another triumph for the myth of Manchester United. Had Sadler been wearing the red shirt of Nottingham Forest rather than the red shirt of Manchester United, it seemed highly unlikely he would have forced his way into Ramsey's thoughts.

That World Cup, which started with such high hopes, ended in the infamous 3–2 defeat by West Germany after England had been 2–0 up just after half-time. It is popularly believed that it was instrumental in the unexpected Tory victory in the general election which followed four days later. It was the first election in which I was entitled to vote, and I cast mine on the losing side. I can certainly confirm that I was desperately upset at England's unexpected loss and at the criticism directed at Bell, who had substituted for Charlton after Germany's first goal, but it would take more than the incompetence of Peter Bonetti to make me vote Conservative.

My Cambridge undergraduate career came to an end in an atmosphere of uncertainty and anti-climax. I decided not to remain in Cambridge to take my degree in person. I had applied for a Department of Education & Science grant to finance research for a PhD on the relationship between Hollywood films and American history between 1919 and 1941, but without a First it was highly unlikely I would get it.

Neil McKendrick, who had been sympathetic to my near miss the previous year but dismissive of my efforts in this last year, thought he might be able to persuade the Gonville & Caius College Council to provide the equivalent financial support. He wouldn't know for a few weeks, so I decided to go to Israel and work on a kibbutz until the decision was made. If the decision went against me, I had no idea what I might do with my life. I had always been a positive person, even during the dark days. I knew in my heart I would get to Cambridge, I knew City would emerge into the sunlight. Was my life really heading for oblivion?

I found a job on Kfar Hanassi in northern Israel, looking after the chickens. The hours of work were from 5am to 1pm, which was bad enough, but I grew to hate those chickens with a passion. Vicious little buggers they were, constantly nipping at my ankles like so many John Fitzpatricks, the aggressive little midfield player brought into the United side by the new manager, Wilf McGuinness, to replace Paddy Crerand and give the half-back line more bite. My boss was a Polish immigrant called Chaim, whose branded numbers were still prominent on his forearm.

Israel had altered in the six years I had been away. Immigration from the Third World was changing the demographic balance of the country and victory in the Six Days War had induced a climate of arrogance. It might have been a healthy change from the Jew as Victim mentality of previous years, but I felt alienated here as well. Government in the past had been composed of significant numbers of European-educated intellectuals like Abba Eban. Chaim Weizmann, first President of the country, had been a lecturer in Chemistry at Manchester University in 1917, when he had succeeded in persuading the then Foreign Secretary, A.J.Balfour, to declare that the British government favoured the establishment of a National Home for the Jewish people in Palestine.

The future, however, belonged to Menachem Begin and Yitzhak Shamir, men whose political support came from the dispossessed Third World immigrants, and Israel drifted inexorably to the right.

The only piece of mail I received during my two months on the kibbutz was a postcard from David, who was directing a play on the Edinburgh Festival Fringe. It read: 'See you Saturday 29 August, Players' entrance, Goodison Park 2.30.' It was all I needed to reaffirm that there was some vestige of hope left in the world. I arrived back in England on Friday 28 August. Saturday at 2.30, we met up again and our faith was rewarded when Colin Bell scored the only goal of the game.

It's amazing how an early-season victory can be as welcome as flowers that bloom in the spring, tra-la. On the Monday, I rang McKendrick who, in his typically understated way, conveyed the information that the College Council had indeed approved my request for a grant. My next three years were going to be spent researching into American film history. I was ecstatic. Everything turned round. The following Saturday, Lancashire bowled Sussex out for 184 in the final of the Gillette Cup at Lord's. Led by Harry Pilling, they cruised home by six wickets.

Eight days later, Lancashire clinched the John Player Sunday League for the second year in a row. Their two overseas signings, Clive Lloyd and Farokh Engineer, had proved invaluable. Jack Bond, an ordinary batsman but an inspirational captain, led a well-balanced attack with Peter Lever and Ken Shuttleworth, who were both to go with Raymond Illingworth to reclaim the Ashes that winter, and Jack Simmons and David Hughes, the parsimonious spinners and doughty late-order batsmen. This was the best all-round Lancashire side I had ever seen. Surely it presaged an upswing in my private life as well.

What private life? I didn't have a private life. I bought a Mini and began a year of commuting between Cambridge and London. I hooked onto a World Cinema course run by Professor Thorold Dickenson at the Slade School, part of University College, London. The National Film Theatre was my other principal port of call that year as I tried to learn the alphabet, grammar and history of film in the space of a few months. Before the days of video recorders, and Channel Four, and movies at all hours of the day and night on ten different television channels, there was no other place to go to see the old movies which were a fundamental part of my research. I had been made captain of football at Caius, but faced with a choice between a league match against Trinity College and a rare screening of *The Public Enemy*, I invariably chose the latter.

I was busy enough but out on the edge again. My contemporaries had all left the previous summer. I was still seeing too much of Jenny on the arm of another man and not enough of City. I drove to Oxford to pick up David en route to a match at Wolverhampton. Something significant invariably happened when I went to Oxford. As I arrived at the gates of Trinity College, he was deeply immersed in conversation with a skinny young man I'd never met before. David introduced me as a fellow City supporter to someone who had been at his primary school, Bowker Vale, when he had first arrived from London. The name of this skinny young man was Howard Davies.

The drive to Wolverhampton took far longer than we had anticipated. 'For God's sake, put your foot down,' demanded David sarcastically as we careered along the A449 with the accelerator pedal practically nailed to the floor. We eventually arrived at the ground five minutes before half-time. City were already a goal down. In the second half, Wolves scored twice more and could have had six. On the way back to the car, 5,000 City fans shuffled along into a claustrophobic pedestrian subway in almost complete silence, so abject was our misery. 'Bloody 'ell,' muttered somebody mournfully. 'Turn the bloody gas on.' Even the hypersensitive Holocaust-conscious Jews in the party could scarce forbear a wry smile.

This self-deprecating humour – quintessentially Jewish, you might argue – has long distinguished the City supporter. In September 1996, City played Crystal Palace the day after it was rumoured that Francis Lee would replace Alan Ball with the Palace manager Dave Bassett. City were even more inept than usual and soon found themselves 3–0 down. Feelings were so hostile that the crowd began to chant 'Bassett Out' before the Palace manager had even taken the City job.

In the event, the crowd got its wish. Bassett stayed at Palace and City took the Palace scout and former Manchester United player Steve Coppell, who had a nervous breakdown in less than five weeks; Bassett went to Nottingham Forest and Coppell, miraculously restored to health, took over at Palace. Five minutes from the end of that Palace game, Kavalashvili scored a consolation goal for City. The crowd around us started to sing, 'We're going to win the League.' The Palace supporters jeered us for what they considered the height of unfounded optimism. The man behind Howard stood up and bellowed at them, 'It's called irony, you stupid fucking Cockney twats!' Howard and I just smiled. This was why we supported them.

I liked Howard instantly, but I was soon made aware that early acquaintance had certainly not bred familiarity between him and David. They loathed each other politely and still do, though since I am friendly with both, they have learned to couch their language in the folds of diplomacy. 'Your friend Green . . .' Howard always begins, unable to dignify David with the use of his first name. 'Your friend Howarddavies . . .' replies David, running all the syllables together so that they should not defile his tongue.

Over succeeding years, I went to more matches with

Howard than with David. That first season was City's last significant attempt to win a European trophy. We had fought our way past the mighty Linfield (just), Honved and Gornik (again) before being drawn to face Chelsea in the semi-final of the European Cup-Winners' Cup. We had already won magnificently at Stamford Bridge that January, in a 3–0 victory that was so dazzling I was sure we were going to win the FA Cup again that year. In fact, I was more convinced we were going to win the FA Cup after that fourth round victory than I was when John Bond's team was ten minutes away from glory against Spurs in the 1981 Centenary final. Our name was on the Cup in 1971, I was absolutely certain. In the fifth round, we were drawn at home to Arsenal, who annihilated us 2–1 on their way to the Double. It was a shattering blow. I had been *so* certain . . .

All we were left with now was this return visit to Chelsea, with a team so decimated by injury that it contained seven reserves including Connor, Donachie and Mann, three left-backs; and neither Howard nor I had even heard of somebody called Johnson who had taken Summerbee's place on the right wing. We warmed up by going to see Dirk Bogarde in Visconti's *Death in Venice*. We were so powerfully affected by the Mahler *adagietto* we could scarcely speak, other than to wonder why the beautiful young boy playing Tadzio, the object of Aschenbach's romantic yearnings, had looked uncommonly like Derek Jeffries, City's utility defender. Since David Green had seized on Derek Jeffries, loudly proclaiming him as the best young player in the country, we wondered mischievously if David's admiration for Jeffries could have been prompted by anything other than his skill as a footballer.

Howard and I soon found we shared a similar sense of the bizarre. Four days before that semi-final at Chelsea, which we lost 1–0, we went to see City play at Leeds Road, this being during Huddersfield Town's brief stay in Division One. The City captain and right-back Tony Book had a particularly irritating mannerism in which, assuming he had the time and space, he would stop the ball, trot back a few paces and then centre as if he were taking a free-kick. When he did this, his shoulders invariably hunched, making him look, in our eyes, a little like Richard III. We happily developed this idea out loud, trying to see if other Shakespearean characters were applicable to City. An old Yorkshireman in a cloth cap, standing in front of us, turned round and quoth, 'Ah've been comin' ter this ground since 1926 and Ah've nivver 'eard so much rubbish in all me life.'

In 1982, David and I made an all-star version of the Victorian melodrama *East Lynne* for BBC2, which was transmitted on 29 December. We gave a publicity interview to the *Manchester Evening News* in which we pronounced our support for City as 'rock-hard'. On 3 January, they were due to play at Watford. City were a team in terminal decline and indeed were relegated that May. The night was bitterly cold, with snow flurries so biting you had to eat the snow flakes away to clear your vision. Howard rang, wondering if I was going. I rang David. He declined. I rang Howard back, attempting to find an excuse that wasn't too cowardly. Howard would have none of it. He was going and so, therefore, was I. He arrived on the doorstep, a large smirk on his face: 'Hello, is this the rock-hard Manchester City supporter?'

Howard lived in Rochdale, close to where my brother was raising his family. My brother bore the downturn in United's fortunes with commendable stoicism. Although a United fanatic since 1948, he had never indulged in excessive triumphalism, for which, during my dark times, I had been grateful. In return, although I exulted in City's continuing success over United and our rivals' visible fall from grace, I behaved with what I thought was similar decorum, although, quite unwittingly, I was responsible for an act of betrayal greater than anything I experienced in an Oxford college.

Geoff's first daughter was called Freya and she was born in December 1966, between the Second Division Championship and the First Division Championship wins. Naturally, I bought this little baby the things that were important – *Winnie The Pooh*, *When We Were Very Young*, *Now We Are Six*, *Miffy Goes to the Seaside*, *Looking at History* by R.J.Unstead, and trinkets and posters from the Manchester City souvenir shop. For the big matches, when I had to buy tickets in advance, I would take her down to Maine Road and let her queue up with me. By this time, the Jesuitical propaganda had worked its magic and to my brother's horror, he discovered he had 'lost' his daughter to an alien sect. It must have been worse than losing her to the Moonies, because as far as I am aware, Moonies encourage kids to run away from home rather than hang framed posters of Colin Bell over the bed. I am delighted to say that Freya, under extreme provocation, has maintained the faith. Her recent marriage to Ashley, a confirmed Arsenal fan, has meant that there is no chance of recidivism and future generations will also be immune to the Old Trafford poison. Strangely enough, I was never permitted much contact with Geoff's two other daughters.

If relations in the Shindler household were strained, those in the Green household resembled World War Three. David's brother, also Geoffrey and also a United fan, is younger by seven years than David. When City were thumping United twice a season in the late Sixties and early Seventies, Geoffrey was in his early teenage years and subject to constant abuse. David had long mastered the art of provocation he had initially practised on Jeff Cohen. It took Jeff two years of extreme irritation before he exploded at David. Watching David tease Geoffrey unmercifully became like watching bear-baiting. David had a very sharp tongue and he soon made it clear that he wasn't going to stop until Geoffrey was moved to violence. Cups of hot coffee (recently made by

271

Evelyn, their long-suffering mother) would be hurled across the room. On one infamous occasion, the clock which stood on the mantelpiece was flung at David. It smashed to pieces harmlessly on the wall behind him. Both Geoffreys have had their days in the sun since then, but in those years of City's ascendancy, a visit to the Green household was like watching Archduke Franz Ferdinand visiting the Bosnian army in Sarajevo – and we all, as Lady Bracknell says of another outbreak of violence, know what that unfortunate movement led to. David's father Louis was so inured to living in no-man's-land that he was perfectly capable of drawing my attention to some scandal he had read about in the morning papers while his two sons fired missiles at each other past both our faces.

The friends were splitting up again. David was coming to the end of his time as an undergraduate at Oxford and began putting feelers out for jobs in television. Howard was going to France for the next academic year as part of his joint honours course in French and History. I needed to get to Hollywood because my thesis required raw material which was only to be found in the film capital. In 1971, many of the key players in the movie industry of the 1930s were living in comfortable retirement, and any documents I needed would have to be retrieved from the studios themselves. The practice of depositing important papers in university archives had not yet begun.

Through the good offices of Thorold Dickenson at the Slade School of Fine Arts, I was awarded a Research Fellowship at the American Film Institute in Beverly Hills. I would start in October 1971, but before leaving England there was something I desperately wanted to do. I had been much influenced by the sports writing of George Plimpton, the American author who had spent time training as a quarterback with the Detroit Lions before writing *Paper*

Lion, a book on American football; touring on the professional golf circuit before writing about golf in *The Bogey Man*, and so on. Nobody yet had done anything similar on the subject of life inside a British football club. Hunter Davies was planning to spend a season writing about Tottenham Hotspur, but he wouldn't be training with them. This was my big idea.

I wrote to Joe Mercer outlining my proposal to write about the club, particularly my intention to shadow Colin Bell, and enclosed copies of the football column I had been writing for the Cambridge student newspaper *Varsity*, courtesy of a Manchester United-supporting editor, the rock music specialist Tony Wilson. Mercer must have liked the columns, or been distracted by the internal boardroom politics which, not for the last time, were threatening to tear the club apart. A week after the 1970–71 season finished with a meaningless but still weird 4–3 home defeat by United, Mercer wrote back in his affable style.

Dear Mr Shindler,

I have no objection to you training with the team here at Maine Road.
I suggest you contact Colin for further details, i.e. when training begins for next season.
Looking forward to meeting you.

Yours sincerely

Joe Mercer
Team Manager.

If Hollywood greeted me with a marching band, hot and cold running starlets and a fat contract for the rest of my life, it couldn't induce a greater thrill than that letter from Joe Mercer. The little boy who had worshipped at the shrine for fifteen years was finally being allowed inside the Holy of Holies. Once a week, the more observant Jews are supposed to go to the Mikvah, a communal bath, in which they immerse themselves in water and emerge cleansed both physically and spiritually. What spiritual effect would getting into the bath with Mike Doyle have on me, I wondered? I would soon find out.

Chapter Thirteen

Inevitably, things did not begin smoothly. When I arrived at Maine Road on 14 July 1971, the first day of pre-season training, Mercer was still on holiday in Torremolinos and Allison knew nothing about the arrangements I had made with Uncle Joe. At least, that's what he said. Relations between the two men, which had always had a certain degree of edge, had, by this time, disintegrated so badly that they barely spoke to each other. After Allison had campaigned to be made team manager, Mercer had been 'promoted' to general manager, but everyone knew the significance of the change. Allison wanted his time in the sun, and the fact that he was a brilliant coach and a rotten manager wasn't going to stop him. Relations deteriorated still further. If I was Mercer's man, Allison would mark his card accordingly.

The players, I was delighted to discover, were remarkably undefensive about my intrusion. The staff were not. Allison, Mercer, the trainer Johnny Hart, physio Peter Blakey and chief scout Ken Barnes all acted as if I had been sent by the tabloids to stitch them up. At twenty-two years of age, I was as fit as I had ever been in my life but the gap between the amateur and the professional soon began to show. On the first day of training, we did a half-mile jog to warm up, followed by eight bursts of 220 yards sprinting, followed immediately by four lung-bursting 100-yard sprints. I was labouring badly at the end of this, trailing everyone by a couple of yards.

At the end of the first week, the papers were full of speculation about the transfer of the big centre-forward Wyn Davies from Newcastle to City. There were various muttered comments about Douglas Bader, because Davies was reputed to be useless with the ball at his feet. Clearly, someone was going to be dropped to accommodate him, and an aura of indefinable tension hung over the training ground. During a practice game, Summerbee sent over a number of harmless centres to the far post, at which point Allison strode onto the field and boomed out, 'He won't be here till Monday!' The tension dissolved, though Neil Young, the logical candidate for the chop, wasn't laughing much. Davies eventually arrived for £52,000 at the end of July.

Summerbee and Lee were by far the brightest of the players. They were also the two most concerned with their outside interests. One day, Summerbee had set up an important meeting with a client of his shirt business, only to discover that the club had arranged the pre-season photocall for the same time. He tried to organise a boycott, but as soon as Allison arrived, the workers' solidarity collapsed. 'It's business, Mal,' he pleaded. Allison fixed him with a basilisk stare. 'This is your business, son,' he stated shortly. Summerbee cancelled his meeting at the shirt company.

Allison was arguably the most innovative coach in British football in 1971. One morning, I travelled with Heslop, Tony Towers and Derek Jeffries to the Physical Education Department of the University of Salford, where the players underwent testing for physical stamina. Blood samples were taken at the start and finish of each player's experiment, so that the acid-level change in the blood could be measured. No doubt in today's more enlightened climate every Premier League player undergoes something similar, but in 1971 this was unique in British football and, predictably, was regarded by the players as a complete waste of time.

The world of professional football was, and probably still is, a closed and naturally suspicious one. On my first day in the Maine Road dressing-room, I hung my shirt on Glyn Pardoe's peg, an act of sacrilegious folly equal to mentioning *Macbeth* in a theatrical dressing-room. The previous December, in the annual victory over Manchester United at Old Trafford, this time by 4–1, Glyn Pardoe's leg had been broken in a tackle with George Best. It was a bad break and Pardoe didn't play again for two years. In fact, such was the emergence of Willie Donachie as the new left-back that the match against United was effectively the end of Pardoe's career. Nevertheless, his peg in the dressing-room retained some kind of totemic significance and nobody dared touch it.

Allison eventually thawed sufficiently to give me the *de rigueur* nickname. Tony Book was known as 'Rocky' but also 'Booky', and Bell was known as 'the Baron' as well as 'Belly'. I never heard him referred to as 'Nijinsky', which was reportedly Allison's nomination. He called me 'Poet', which caught on rapidly and I rather enjoyed it. I couldn't be 'Colin', since there was only one Colin at Manchester City, and my surname sounded even more ridiculous when appended to the traditional suffix 'y'. 'Poet' seemed to have a positively Shakespearean connotation, as in 'The lunatic, the lover and the poet/Are of imagination all compact,' and the players seized on it eagerly, as in 'Give us that fuckin' comb, Poet.' Doyle weighed up the nickname carefully. 'Poet? Does that mean you read books an' that?' I affirmed that it did. I took the paperback I was reading out of my jacket pocket. It was Budd Schulberg's classic novel of Hollywood, *What Makes Sammy Run?* Oakes grabbed it out of my hands, read out the title and tossed it back to me. 'When he's got the shits,' he said shortly.

Initially, as the players struggled to 'place' me, I was somewhat intimidated by the cliquey atmosphere. As soon as they saw me vomiting on the side of the pitch after a particularly gruelling training run with Derek Ibbotson and Joe Lancaster, they started to warm to me, gave me rides in their cars to the training ground, played the usual practical jokes on me. On a scorching July morning, we trained for two hours and returned to the dressing-room dehydrated. I grabbed what I thought was orange juice. As the liquid hit the back of my parched throat, Mike Doyle grinned. 'I've just pissed in that,' he said casually.

Doyle was known as 'Tommy' to distinguish him from Mike Summerbee – which worked fine until Tommy Booth got into the first team. Mike Doyle was the City rep for the Professional Footballers' Association. He took his position seriously, as evidenced by the fact that I saw him holding Derek Jeffries upside down until he had shaken sufficient money out of the youngster's trousers to pay that month's subscription. Even more laudably, he also perfected the art of soaping his genitals in the bath with a bar of soap in such a manner that he appeared to be ejaculating. It was quite a frightening experience to be on the receiving end for the first time. I thought I might retaliate by telling him of the part he played in my erotic adventures, but I feared he might misinterpret the confidence and my credibility in the dressing-room would be shot for ever.

Lee once used me as a goalkeeper on one of the rare occasions we were permitted to train on the Maine Road pitch. 'Get in them nets, Poet,' he shouted, waving me towards the goalposts at the Platt Lane End where Jeff Cohen had once swung from the crossbar. I got in them nets quickly. Lee carefully lined up two balls, one behind the other on the penalty spot. I decided the one in front would be unstoppable, so I decided to go for the second ball. The first one sped into the left-hand corner, the other one travelling low to my other side. I dived, got one hand to it, but the ball still zipped into the net. I got the feeling back in that hand shortly after Christmas. It was the season of Lee One Pen.

One morning, Allison gave the first-team squad a pep talk about the coming season, telling them that the Championship was within their grasp. He rounded on Neil Young, who never spoke a word normally. 'You can have your best season ever,' Allison said, looking directly at the talented inside-forward, 'better than the Championship year. How many goals did you score that season?' Young looked blank. He had no idea. I couldn't contain myself. 'Nineteen,' I called out. 'And three in the Cup.' Everyone smiled except Allison. On a certain level, I knew them better than they knew themselves.

Inevitably, as I got closer to them I lost objectivity. One day, I walked off the pitch with Tony Towers and George Heslop. Towers was bitching about a newspaper report of the last match, which had taken him to task for sloppy defence. I waited till Towers left. Heslop took his position as Senior Pro very seriously. 'What was he supposed to write, George? You know Tony had a stinker.' Heslop thought for a moment. 'Well, he could have written, "Tony Towers wasn't his usual tower of strength in defence." ' I had a lot of time for George Heslop.

We played at Chester in a pre-season friendly on 28 July, winning 4–0, and I sat in the press box with Peter Gardner, the *Manchester Evening News* correspondent who reported on City affairs for thirty years. He was almost certainly the author of the report which had caused Tony Towers so much anxiety. On the way back, I persuaded the coach driver to drop me off at Old Trafford because Lancashire were playing a Gillette Cup semi-final against Gloucestershire. There had been a long interruption for rain and it seemed unlikely that Lancashire would finish their innings that night. At half past five, when I got there, they had made only 70 of the 230 they needed to overhaul the Gloucestershire total and Procter had already removed Wood, Pilling and David Lloyd. The match then became a gladiatorial contest between the white South African Procter and the black West Indian Clive Lloyd, who hooked 4,4,2,4,2 off successive deliveries.

The light got worse, the wickets kept falling and Lancashire's position rapidly declined. Our champion, Clive Lloyd, went at 160 for 6, Jack Simmons at 203 for 7. When David Hughes, batting at number nine, got to the middle, he complained that he couldn't see the bowling properly because it was pitch-dark out there. It was perhaps not surprising as it was nearly 9pm and the light from the Lancashire dressing-room pierced the gloom like the Eddystone Lighthouse. Arthur Jepson, the umpire, pointed to the night sky. 'What do you see there, David?' he asked.

'I can see the bloody moon, Arthur,' said Hughes.

'Well,' replied the umpire reasonably, 'how much further do you want to see?'

With five overs to go, Lancashire still needed 25 to win and there was only Lever and Shuttleworth, the fast bowlers, to come in after Hughes, so he decided he would have to attack the off-spin of John Mortimore. In one of the most famous overs in the history of one-day cricket, Hughes clobbered 6,4,2,2,4,6 – 24 off the over. In reply, Procter whistled four balls into Bond's rib cage. Off the fifth, they scrambled a single. City supporters, United supporters, Bolton, Blackburn, Everton, Burnley, Liverpool and Accrington Stanley men were united as one, as Old Trafford rose to acclaim an historic Lancashire victory.

They went on to win the final against Kent by 24 runs, in another memorable encounter. Lancashire, with Clive Lloyd, Simmons and Hughes again prominent, struggled to 224 for 7 in their 60 overs. Kent, after a nervous start which saw them reduced to 105 for 5, recovered thanks to a scintillating innings of 89 by Asif Iqbal. Kent needed only a further 28 runs off six and a half overs when Asif drove Simmons fiercely but uppishly through the off side. The thirty-nine-year-old Lancashire skipper Jack Bond launched himself at the ball and stuck up a despairing hand as it hurtled by him. He fell to earth clutching the ball in his right hand. The now-legendary catch turned the match. The last three wickets added only one run, and Lancashire had retained the Gillette Cup.

As my time at Maine Road came to an end, I felt myself at the apex of the sporting universe. My formative years had been spent justifying to myself, and others, why I expended so much emotional energy on supporting Manchester City and Lancashire. What had seemed an insupportable burden to carry at the age of thirteen became a garland of laurels seven years later. My pleasure in City's rise was intensified by the discomfiture of Manchester United supporters as they watched helplessly while their team, European Cup winners only a couple of years before, slipped into mediocrity.

United tried to promote from within, as Liverpool were to do with so much success in the 1970s and 1980s, but the choice of Wilf McGuinness to succeed Matt Busby was an unhappy one. The new manager, hamstrung by Busby's over-bearing presence at the club, could never replace the great man in the hearts of players or supporters. The 4–1 home defeat by City in December 1970 was followed by defeat for the second year running in the semi-final of the League Cup, this time by Third Division Aston Villa. A couple of days later, Busby summoned McGuinness to see him. 'Wilf, Wilf,' McGuinness later reported Busby had moaned as he shook his head in bewilderment, 'I don't know how we're going to do without you – but we're going to find out.'

Busby returned for the second half of the 1970–71 season and supervised United's climb away from the looming threat of relegation to a more than respectable eighth position, but he retreated to the back of the stage again when Frank O'Farrell (or Frank O'Failure, as David Green called him) was appointed as manager just before I joined the City playing staff. Worryingly, United started the 1971–72 season by storming to the top of the table, with only two defeats in the first fifteen matches. Fortunately, they came down with the Christmas decorations.

At Maine Road, that season started with a disappointing 1–0 loss at home to Leeds. Colin Bell was injured before the end of pre-season training. Young made way for Davies, as we had all expected, but regained his place for the next match at home to Crystal Palace after Summerbee had been hurt against Leeds. George Heslop was particularly unhappy at Allan Clarke's behaviour. Hunter, Bremner and Giles were well-known for their uncompromising physical aggression, but Clarke's mean-spirited ankle-tapping upset Heslop even more. Fortunately, Palace were dispatched 4–0 and the season was now deemed to have properly begun.

A satisfactory 2–2 draw away to Chelsea, in which Lee scored his fourth goal of what was to become a record-breaking season for him, was followed by a 2–1 defeat at Molineux. In the dressing-room the following Monday, Francis Lee rounded on the athletics coach, Joe Lancaster, and pointed the finger of blame for the defeat squarely at him. The training had been so intense that the players had simply wilted in the second half and couldn't pick their legs up. As so often at this time, City relieved the pressure with a 4–0 thumping of Spurs.

Allison pointed the finger of blame for the Wolves defeat elsewhere. Neil Young was dropped to make way for the return after injury of Summerbee. Colin Bell's season started at last, but at the expense of Alan Oakes because Heslop was being played as twin centre-half with Tommy Booth. City were playing a classic 4–2–4 with Doyle and Bell in midfield,

Summerbee and the teenage left-winger Ian Mellor out wide, and Lee feeding off Wyn Davies through the middle.

I saw Neil Young in the dressing-room before the Spurs match started, looking stunned and upset even though the writing had been on the wall since the day the rumours broke about Wyn Davies. I felt deeply sorry for Young, although in the previous season he had scored only one goal in twenty-four League appearances. He always looked like a lad who couldn't look after himself. I was not surprised to hear the story that he had once bought his wife a dog for £16 which had to be sold for £12 just before Christmas because he couldn't otherwise afford to buy the coal to heat his house.

Young started one more game for City, when Davies was injured in October, and made his final appearance as a substitute the following week in a 1–0 home win over Everton. In January, less than three years after he had won the FA Cup for City, along with the perennial twelfth man David Connor he was sold to Preston for £48,000, after which he slowly faded out of the game and his life took a predictably downward spiral.

I was sorry to see Young go. Although Tony Coleman had been the first member of the Championship-winning side to leave the club, Neil Young had been a part of my life for eleven years. He seemed as much a permanent component of Maine Road as the bricks and mortar. To read of his playing for Preston and Rochdale and Southport was painful. Alan Oakes, on the other hand, who hadn't shown up for that match against Spurs, eventually won his place back at the expense of first Heslop and then Derek Jeffries. In July 1976, after another League Cup winner's medal and 665 appearances over seventeen years, Oakes left to become player-manager of Chester and thereafter take an honourable retirement.

It occurred to me at the time, sitting in the dressing-room

before the start of the match against Spurs, how closely the worlds of show business and sport were related. You were only as good as your last game, and if you were dropped, you soon realised that the show went on without you: the crowd chants, the ball is kicked, the cameras turn and nobody really cares that you are no longer part of the scene – provided we win, of course. There was a nervousness in the dressing-room at 2.30 much like before a first night. There was very little air-kissing or embracing, but a lot of good wishes were conveyed by an army of hangers-on, people like me, I suppose. Mike Doyle dealt with it in his unique style. 'I'm going to the library,' he announced loudly, picking up a matchday programme and marching into the lavatory.

By the time I left, I was part of that family. On my last training season, I took part in a game in which one had to call, receive the ball, lay it off and sprint to the back of the opposite group. 'Yes, Wyn,' I shouted nonchalantly (I rejected 'Douglas Bader' as a possible nickname, though it was used often enough in conversation with David Green). 'Yes, Poet,' called Willie Donachie, with a lack of self-consciousness which pleased me enormously.

Colin Bell gave me a lift back to the ground. Surveying the world from the passenger seat of his E-type Jaguar, I commented that he must be a very happy man. On the contrary, he responded, he was deeply unhappy. I was so flabbergasted by the response that I failed to ask a further question for fear of trampling on sensitive ground. Instead, the conversation retreated to one of those staples of fan magazines, which attempt to discern players' favourite foods and favourite music. Bell's ambitions were to win the European Cup and secure a happy marriage, which at least showed a comforting sense of perspective.

I left City and England in ambivalent mood. In one sense, I was quite happy to return to my position in the audience.

There is a magic in sport, as there is in the theatre, and if you see how the trick is done, the magic goes. If you value the magic, you shouldn't seek to know how it works. In addition, much as I anticipated what a year in Hollywood might bring, I was conscious that I was closing a chapter of my life. There was nothing to keep me in England except Manchester City, and I knew that the unique privilege I had been granted by Mercer would never be repeated. Working in a football club is like working on a film. The pressure is intense and the working relationships reflect it. You feel closer to your colleagues than you do to your family, for the time that you spend together in mutual adversity or triumph. You can barely conceive of life without them. Then the film finishes, the transfer goes through and the ties are broken. Another film, another club means new relationships and the cycle begins again.

Of course, I remember every detail of those two months I spent with City, even though it's now twenty-six years ago. I assumed that the players might have remembered me, however vaguely – there couldn't have been all that many Cambridge PhD students training with them. In May 1997, courtesy of Howard Davies and Colin Barlow, I returned to the hallowed interior of Maine Road. Colin Bell, who had been monosyllabic in 1971, was now the youth team coach; he was fifty years old, wore lightweight spectacles and seemed in such great condition he could have pulled on a blue shirt and trotted out onto the pitch. (Would that he did, when I saw who *was* trotting out onto the pitch.) Kinkladze jinked past us in the corridor. Bell looked like the player, Kinkladze the apprentice. In conversation, Bell was now eloquent and charming – and had no memory of me whatsoever. I tried the chairman, Francis Lee, the cocky little bugger who had borrowed my comb, stuck me between the posts and confided he had a collection of Jean Harlow movies at home. 'Course I remember you,' quoth Francis with his trademark bonhomie. 'You had a beard, didn't you?' *Sic transit gloria mundi.*

Before I left England, I did a deal with the *Manchester Evening News* brokered by the helpful Peter Gardner. In return for three articles about training with City and life for an expatriate Mancunian in Hollywood, I would receive the *Saturday Football Pink* free for a year. I devoured the newsprint off those airmail lifesavers, absorbing everything from the match report of Altrincham versus Macclesfield Town to what was playing at the ABC cinema in Deansgate.

My body was in Beverly Hills 90210 but my soul lay mouldering in Manchester 14. Every Sunday morning, I drove to the supermarket on La Cienega to buy the *Los Angeles Times*. On the last page of the sports section would be the English football results. With trembling hands I would turn the pages, the eye running ahead of the brain as it looked for the line of newsprint that would dictate my mood for the week. The day I will never forget was looking at only half a line which read 'Manchester City 3'. It was a good five seconds before I went back to the end of the line: 'Manchester United 3'. What? How?

Apparently, it was one of the classic derbies. United went 2–0 ahead, City equalised with two goals in as many minutes, 'Yes Wyn' Davies had a goal disallowed for no apparent reason and Aston shot past Corrigan with the aid of a deflection off Gowling to give United the lead again. With a minute to go, Summerbee sent a screamer towards the top corner only for Stepney to bring off a magnificent tip over the bar. From the corner, the ball ricocheted to Summerbee on the edge of the area whence he dispatched it past Stepney, this time into the roof of the net. Meanwhile, I was in the UCLA library.

I wanted City to win the Championship again desperately and from the time I left England in late September 1971 until the end of February 1972, they lost only two matches. They had a settled squad of twelve players – Mellor contesting the number 11 shirt with Tony Towers – just as they had in the title-winning season four years previously. I was thrilled and bizarrely angry that I couldn't share in the delight. Jeff was a social worker in Leeds, Michael Chadwick was doing an MA in Sociology at the University of East Anglia, David Green was working for Hughie Green at Yorkshire Television, and Howard Davies was perfecting his French in Marseille.

Howard and David sent airmail letters packed with information, and I confess now that there was a worm of envy working its way inside me. How dare my team, the lads with whom I was on such intimate bodily terms, display their wares so promiscuously when I was stuck amid the palm trees of California? Manchester and England would rise to acclaim the success of the plans that were hatched when I was part of the club, and I couldn't be there to experience the euphoria. When Easter came, City had stormed six points clear. Allison's master plan was working to perfection . . . then he signed Rodney Marsh for £200,000 from Queens Park Rangers and the world exploded.

David bought the Allison PR wholesale, writing the new team out half-a-dozen times on the back of the air letter in the space where the return address should be written. The word MARSH was spelled out in capitals. At last, City had their own superstar to compete with George Best – or so it was felt. Personally, I shared Mike Doyle's downbeat view, with reference to Marsh: 'You don't win things with players like him in the side.' Maybe it was because I was in California, but I never shared David's sense of ecstasy at the Marsh signing. I couldn't see where they'd play him for a start, without breaking up that perfect 4-2-4 which had brought Lee twenty-nine goals so far.

Over Easter, City lost 2–1 at home to Stoke and 2–0 at

Southampton. It opened the door for the chasing pack. Despite another 3–1 victory at Old Trafford, in which Marsh, coming on as substitute, scored a cracker, we dropped a vital point at Coventry and lost at Ipswich in the penultimate game. Derby County skipped ahead and though we hammered them in the last game of the season, we missed the title by a point. I was miserable and relieved at the same time. At least I hadn't been stuck in a Hollywood apartment and missed the supreme accolade. The defeat at Ipswich somehow preserved the integrity of the miracle at Newcastle in 1968. After driving home from Ipswich, David sent an air letter with a drawing of himself as a miserable man with a large nose looking over a wall. An unhappy Joe Mercer left for Coventry City and that team would never challenge for the Championship again.

I enjoyed many aspects of Hollywood – the movie culture, the sunshine, the sheer physical ease of life – but nothing could replace the void left by the absence of my heroes. Although I had been busy enough, watching up to thirty films a week, trawling the archives for old films, old scripts, and talking to old writers, producers, directors and actors who had been working in the Hollywood studios in the 1930s, I remained lonely. I made few friends, though I did manage to meet Frank Capra and I became the only twenty-two-year-old Englishman driving an open-top red MGB in a town that was awash with impressionable and sexy young women to cling, unwillingly I admit, to celibacy.

The American Film Institute, to which I was attached, was then housed in a huge mansion in Beverly Hills. From my perspective, its value was in its close association with the major studios from whose archives it could acquire prints of classic movies, which I needed for my research but which were otherwise inaccessible. One day, a print of the MGM picture *Boys Town* starring Mickey Rooney and Spencer Tracy arrived for me. By common practice, all screenings had to be notified to all students, but since I only summoned old movies from the 1930s, I was usually the sole occupant of the screening room for my movies.

As *Boys Town* unspooled one sunny afternoon, four weeks and two days after the end of the football season, I was sitting in my accustomed position in the centre of the third row, my notebook open on my lap. I had just started to note the credits when the door opened, admitting a bright shaft of sunlight which obscured the words on the screen. It is always difficult to enter a darkened cinema directly from bright sunlight, as the eyes take minutes rather than seconds to adapt. Instead of standing quietly at the back of the cinema to allow this process to happen naturally, the new arrival decided to stumble onwards, groping for a seat. The hairs on the back of my neck started to rise. The idiot was making straight for me. Blindly, it headed for the middle of row three. There were thirty-nine empty seats in this theatre and it was coming straight for mine. It banged into an upturned seat two places away and sat down abruptly.

I was in a raging temper. Who was this interloper who was ruining my enjoyment? The power of the film then took over and the cloying sentimentality of the production worked its magic. I fought the rising tide, but a number of sobs escaped me. 'There are no bad boys,' intoned Father Flanagan as he comforted the distraught Mickey Rooney. The music rose to a climax, the end credits arrived and the bloody house lights came on too quickly as I was still fumbling for my handkerchief. The interloper sitting two seats away was intrigued. Who was this sobbing lunatic who thought he owned the cinema? The interloper turned towards me. She was breathtakingly beautiful.

We walked out to the car park together. I decided not to mention her breach of moviegoing etiquette. I pointed out that the main exit was now closed because it was after 6pm. She would have to use the upper exit, towards whose gates I motioned. She smiled that devastating smile, thanked me courteously and drove off towards the closed exit. I ran after her waving furiously, suggesting she followed me out of the top gate. She smiled again. I was mesmerised. I got into my car, drove slowly out onto the main road and came to a stop sign. In the hundred yards it had taken to travel that distance, I knew beyond a reasonable doubt that this was the girl I had to marry. If I continued to the next traffic light, she might turn right, I would turn left and we would never see each other again. I braked, got out of the car and strolled casually back to her. I suggested we patronised the nearby Hamburger Hamlet for a cup of tea. She was very impressed. A cup of tea was a new chat-up line in Hollywood.

Living as I was on $20 a week, courtesy of Neil McKendrick and Gonville & Caius College, I tended to run my cash-in-hand down to the last five cents before drawing another precious $20 from the bank. As we sat down in the coffee shop, I realised I had enough money for only one cup of tea. I claimed I was hungry rather than thirsty and would she like an omelette? I made a very good omelette in my apartment. (It was true. I lived off them.) It was another seduction coup. Things had never gone this smoothly before. I looked at the third finger on her left hand. I couldn't believe there wasn't a ring there. It was 22 May 1972.

On 4 July, Lynn and I became engaged. In the space of a few weeks Lynn had softened three years of hardening romantic arteries. Her influence was so profound, her impact so immediate that for the first time in ten years I even started to get to grips with my mother's death. Her family was welcoming and accepting despite the ostensibly odd pairing of a Jewish Manchester City supporter with an American blue-eyed blonde beauty queen. It turned out that in the same month in 1966 when I was accepting the tennis cup from the Manchester Union of Jewish Societies Lynn was being crowned Miss Santa Barbara. I was, as George Best would have been, highly impressed. I am delighted to say that our marriage has lasted rather longer than his liaisons with assorted beauty queens.

I had to return to Cambridge to finish my PhD thesis, and in four weeks City were due to play at Aston Villa for the Charity Shield – an odd arrangement since neither club had won either the Cup or the League the previous year. Lynn was a little disconcerted by the pace at which I was moving. I flew home because my ticket had been booked a year ago. I had arranged for Lynn to follow in a couple of weeks. After I left, Lynn had second thoughts; not surprising really, considering the emotional void she was being asked to fill.

I picked her up at Gatwick airport one blazing summer's day in late August. She was wrapped, and remained so for weeks thereafter, in a floor-length white camel hair overcoat. For her, it was an essentially practical solution to the problem of translating from a Californian to a British climate. To me, it was symbolic of her delicious eccentricity and her impeccable sense of style.

A week or so after I introduced her to Cambridge we met, as I knew we must surely do one day, Jenny walking down King's Parade towards us. We stopped and conversed quite normally and then parted and went our separate ways. To my great delight I felt nothing for Jenny any longer. My love for Lynn had grown so rapidly that it was all I ever needed. Lynn, of course, took the whole thing in her stride effortlessly, as she was to do with most of the triumphs and tragedies of the next twenty-five years. Though still lacking a sense of direction, for which I remain daily grateful, she more than compensates with a remarkable ability to adapt to changing circumstances.

This ability was called upon immediately to deal with the huge culture gap with which she was faced. Apart from the weather, which maintained a steadfast Manchester bleakness despite her arrival in the middle of August, there was the small matter of this blessed football team about which she had already heard too much. On her second day in the country, David and I took Lynn to see City at Crystal Palace. The new season had started badly, with four defeats in the first five matches. Recently promoted Palace extended the record to five defeats in six matches. Francis Lee missed a penalty and Lynn understandably failed to see what it was about the game and the team that exercised me so greatly. David and I decided to ban her from future City matches, a *sine die* suspension she accepted with equanimity.

We moved back to Cambridge while we decided what to do with our lives. On the first Saturday in September, I took her to the Graduate Centre, where we settled in comfortable armchairs in front of the television to watch the Gillette Cup final between Lancashire and Warwickshire. Lancashire were so badly hit by injuries, I explained, that Clive Lloyd, our star batsman, was having to open the bowling. Warwickshire, led by M.J.K.Smith and Alvin Kallicharran, had reached a worrying 207 for 3 before five wickets fell in the space of eight balls for six runs and their innings closed on 234 for 9. Lancashire made a poor start to their reply and were 26 for 2, with Barry Wood and David Lloyd back in the pavilion, when Clive Lloyd strode to the wicket. Lynn chose this moment to fall into a deep jet-lagged sleep and awoke some two hours later to find our hero still at the crease. 'Is that guy still at bat?' she wondered out loud. I tried to explain that she had slept through one of the great one-day innings of all time as Clive Lloyd hammered his way to 126, taking Lancashire to their third consecutive Gillette Cup final victory by four wickets with more than three overs to spare.

Despite Lynn's inability to absorb the fascination of cricket, I remained desperate to marry her. In my campaign to convince her, I was fortunate to receive the help of the bureaucracies. The Home Office made it clear that Lynn's three-month Visitor's Visa would not be renewed on the basis of our engagement. The College made it equally clear that the attractive one-bedroom flat in Harvey Road, overlooking Fenners, was only available to married couples. My family reminded me that Lynn wasn't Jewish, and what would become of the children of a mixed marriage? As Marshall Foch wrote in his order for the day during the first battle of the Marne in September 1914: 'My Centre is giving way, my Right is retreating. The situation is excellent. We shall get married.' It was the best decision I ever made. To my relief, she eventually agreed with it.

The wedding took place on a glorious Cambridge September day. The tourists had mostly retreated, the undergraduates had not yet arrived. The sun shone out of a cloudless blue sky that would not have disgraced California, and the bride, in Shakespearean splendour, was too lovely and too temperate to be compared to it. The wedding party, after the ceremony and lunch in College, decamped into punts on the river. It was a perfect day and as we wandered back to the cars, David, who had been my best man, and I reasonably assumed that God, who had so blessed this union, might possibly out of the goodness of His heart leave a little something on the plate for Manchester City.

We sat in David's car and turned on the radio at five o'clock for *Sports Report* and the familiar signature tune. I had always believed in omens, that good sporting results presaged success in other areas of life. The success of the marriage was bound up with what we would now hear. We waited with the usual tightening of the stomach muscles as the classified reading of the football results began in those

293

familiar measured tones. 'Birmingham City 2, Everton 1,' it started, and so on past 'Ipswich Town 1, Leicester City 1; Liverpool 5, Sheffield Wednesday 0; Manchester United 3 (groan), Derby County 0 (groan, groan); Southampton 2, Crystal Palace 0' until it reached the deathless line, 'Stoke City 5, Manchester City 1.' On the basis of those results, Manchester City were that night rooted to the bottom of the League table, separated from Manchester United on goal average. I looked at the the woman with whom I had pledged to build a future together. Oh, God! What the hell did this result mean?

Epilogue

On Sunday 5 May 1996, the four friends met for the first time in twenty-five years. The occasion was entirely appropriate. Manchester City were staring relegation firmly in the face again. They had to beat Liverpool at home and hope Southampton and Coventry dropped points. If all the results were identical, City would go down.

The intervening years had inevitably taken their toll. As Sam Goldwyn said so wisely, 'We have all passed a lot of water under that bridge.' Michael Chadwick and Jeff Cohen drifted apart in the late 1970s. Mike became a teacher in Lancashire before training as a psychotherapist. In 1984 he met his second wife Shelley, with whom he went on holiday to the United States. They decided to stay, opened a small school in Berkeley, outside San Francisco, and eventually moved into business, opening a string of successful lingerie shops known as Chadwicks of London – on the grounds that Chadwicks of Manchester wouldn't convey quite the same image of sophistication.

Jeff Cohen graduated from the university of Hull with a joint honours degree in Law and Sociology. He soon decided the Law was not for him and transferred his attentions to social work. In 1978 he married Lesley, who was a clinical psychologist in the same psychiatric unit in which he was working. Their two teenage sons, Ben and Simon, however, resisted their father's attempts to indoctrinate them and followed the glory trail by supporting Liverpool. Jeff hasn't given up hope and spent last summer decorating Simon's bedroom with Manchester City wallpaper in the hope the magic might work subliminally.

David Green and I remained close. I was best man at his wedding in Leeds in 1977, and again five years later when he married Jane. Only Michael Chadwick of the original quartet married a Jewish girl, an interesting microcosm of a wider problem besetting modern Jewry. David married outside the faith (a terrible crime), divorced (possibly a worse crime, depending on which rabbi's teachings you read) and then married out again (off the scale).

We started making films together at the BBC in 1981. I was the producer, he was the director and our first effort, called *Wilfred & Eileen*, was the moving story of a young couple who marry against their parents' wishes. Wilfred is shot in the head in the first weeks of World War One and Eileen travels to France and nurses him back to health. It was well-received, although the making of it was interrupted by City's unexpected appearance in the FA Cup final against Tottenham Hotspur. One day's filming was abruptly terminated when the director called 'Wrap' from inside his car as it headed down the A40 to Wembley, where the producer was anxiously awaiting his arrival for the replay – the one won by that Ricky Villa goal which the BBC replays *ad nauseam*.

We did everything together, writing, producing and directing, like Michael Powell and Emeric Pressburger. We made a documentary series on American Jews, an all-star version of the Victorian melodrama *East Lynne* and a movie for Yorkshire Television about cricket in a Yorkshire village during the First World War called *1914 All Out*. Eventually, we managed to get my movie script about the Great Train

Robbery, *Buster*, financed when Phil Collins agreed to star in it.

Buster contained the occasional Cityism. In one scene, Buster and Bruce Reynolds are reading the English newspapers in Acapulco. Buster reads something worrying. Bruce thinks the police are onto them, but Buster points instead to Charlton Athletic's unexpected win at Manchester City, 3–1. 'Eddie Firmani scored twice,' he adds unnecessarily. I remembered that match quite vividly. Firmani gave Roy Cheetham such a torrid time I thought it worthy of immortalising on film.

The two Establishment figures who decide on the infamous thirty-year prison sentences handed down to the Train Robbers were given the names of Sir Leslie McDowall and Chief Superintendent George Poyser. Not that anyone noticed, but David and I hugged ourselves quietly. For any PhD student of the future looking at the films of David Green, I suggest serious attention is paid to an early episode of *Emmerdale Farm* featuring Toke Townley wearing a Manchester City scarf.

Although *Buster* was the movie break we had both been seeking, the pressures drove the two of us apart. I thought he was exploiting my script to get to Hollywood, he thought I was holding him back, and I became increasingly unhappy with his direction. What should have been the realisation of a childhood dream became the basis of a horrible breakdown in relations. In the end, he moved to Hollywood and I remained in Muswell Hill.

Although he made one big action movie, things didn't go particularly smoothly for him out there and he returned to England in 1993. We got a change-of-address card but he was now making the successful *Hollywood Women* series for his own company, September Films, while I was doing battle with Ian McShane on the set of *Lovejoy*. McShane had cunningly established early on that Lovejoy was a Manchester United fan, to my intense disgust, so when I became the show's producer there was little I could do apart from the occasional act of sabotage. Whenever Tinker and Eric and Lovejoy were seen having a cup of tea, Lovejoy would be drinking from his Manchester United mug. I conspired with the prop boys to 'lose' the damn thing one evening, but next day, when Lovejoy went to make the tea, there was pandemonium on the set until it was 'discovered' again on the prop van.

It was City who brought us together in the first place and it was City who reunited us all. They had looked doomed to relegation from the start of the Alan Ball regime in 1995. My son, also called David, and I had been to see them lose miserably 3–0 at Wimbledon just after Easter. We figured that was it. But they scraped a 1–0 home win over Sheffield Wednesday and then, quite unexpectedly, Steve Lomas scored the only goal of the game at Aston Villa. It was ten to five on a fine spring Saturday. I had to travel back to Manchester the following weekend because I had been invited to be the chief guest at Bury Grammar School Old Boys' Annual Dinner. The fates were conspiring. I picked up the phone and dialled David's number.

He sounded guarded and defensive. He'd also seen the result. Was he going back to Manchester? He thought so. I got my retaliation in first. I was guest of honour at school, I told him, I've got to be in Manchester anyway . . . David told me he'd tried to get hold of me five weeks before. I wondered why, and was shocked when he told me his father had suddenly died and I was the first person he wanted at the funeral. I would undoubtedly have been there had I known, but we had been on a family holiday and knew nothing of the tragedy. I would certainly go and pay my respects to Evelyn, David's mother. Then David mentioned that Mike Chadwick was over from California and that Jeff Cohen would also be at the City v Liverpool game.

The four of us met again in the Pizza Hut off St Ann's Square in the centre of Manchester. It was almost forty years since we had started that pilgrimage to Maine Road, thirty years since we had celebrated promotion at the start of the legendary Mercer and Allison glory days. The first row was over whose car we were going to take. Then we argued about which way through Manchester was the quickest route to the ground. Then we argued about where we were going to park. A terrible sense of *déjà vu* enveloped us all. We were having these rows thirty years ago. We had families, careers, houses, mortgages, businesses even, but it could have been 1966, not 1996. I was on the verge of tears.

When City came out, the tears arrived. The emotion in the ground was tangible and what followed was a classic illustration of what it takes to be a Manchester City fan. The packed house showed admirable restraint during the minute's silence for Peter Swales, who had passed away that week. Reportedly his final words were, 'Tell them the last thing I want is for them to go down.' Bearing in mind the nature of the hostile takeover which the Lee–Barlow consortium had mounted against Swales, it required only a slight change of emphasis in the phrasing of that line, from *last* to *want*, to give it an entirely different meaning.

It was obvious from the kick-off that Liverpool would have been quite happy to have handed City the three points. They were due to play United the following week in the FA Cup final and a frantic Lancashire derby was not the preparation they were looking for. Since Liverpool seemed reluctant to help themselves, City did it for them. After six minutes, Steve Lomas miskicked into his own net. All twenty-two players and 36,000 people watched in silence as the ball trickled unerringly past the transfixed Eike Immel into the

City goal: 0–1. Every time McManaman sprinted effortlessly clear of the City defence, he contrived to screw the ball wide. Rush aimed a speculative shot from a cross. The ball sliced off his shin and looped over Immel: 0–2.

In the second half, City managed to get the ball to Kinkladze where he does his real damage, on the edge of the opposition's penalty area. He jinked past two men and was brought down. Rösler banged the ball in from the penalty spot: 1–2. With just over ten minutes left, Kit Symons poked the ball home from a scramble in the area: 2–2, and salvation was in sight. So what did City do? Acting on erroneous information received, Lomas took the ball out to the corner flag and wasted time. Twenty thousand radios were tuned into BBC Radio 5 Live to hear the clear news that both Coventry and Southampton were drawing 0–0. If the results there and at Maine Road remained the same, City would go down. Alan Ball was the only man on the ground with his radio tuned to the wrong station.

Thus came the end. The referee blew for time, Liverpool slunk away sheepishly, apologetically; they had, after all, done their best to make the party go with a swing. Lomas looked genuinely upset – as he had every right to be. Most of the others were probably wondering what their contracts said about the effects of relegation. I watched them disappear from view down the tunnel, the same tunnel from which I had watched Summerbee, Bell, Lee, Young, Doyle, Corrigan, Oakes, Book and the rest emerge hundreds of times. I cried for City, and for myself, and for the memories of the heroes I had known so intimately. I watched Rösler and Lomas, but I saw Neil Young and Mike Doyle. I watched a right-winger called Summerbee, but it wasn't the right one. The real Summerbee played with a policeman's helmet on, massaged an opponent's leg when he thought he was feigning injury. This Summerbee drew condemnation from the City crowd, not adoration.

I embraced Jeff Cohen and Michael Chadwick with genuine warmth. In those moments of tears and shared memories, this book was born. It had been an emotional weekend. There had been a return to Bury Grammar School, where my speech ('It can get a little raucous', warned the secretary), a compendium of all the dirty jokes my actor friends had told me over the years, had been received with great glee and a little surprise. 'I remember you as being dead quiet,' was the general consensus, along with, 'You took me to Old Trafford to watch Lancashire.'

As I drove home, I tried to absorb the enormity of the emotions I had experienced in the space of a few hours. Returning to Manchester and to Maine Road is always like coming home, but returning to school, to see David's newly widowed mother, to see another relegation, to see Jeff Cohen again after fifteen years, Mike Chadwick after twenty-five, was to disturb primaeval emotions which had lain in a shallow grave these many years.

I turned on the radio to help me calm down. The airwaves were filled with the gravelly Scottish tones of the Manchester United manager describing the magnificence of his 3–0 victory at Middlesbrough (managed by the former United captain Bryan Robson) which had given him the Premier League title for the third time in four years. I wondered idly if it was in Robson's contract when he left United that he had to lie down in front of them if United needed the points. There was little sadness on the blue side of Manchester when Robson's arrogance and *folie de grandeur* led him and his Boro team of all the talents straight through the trapdoor the following season. These were unhealthy thoughts. I snapped off the radio.

It is bad enough that Manchester United infiltrate their supporters like old-style Soviet agents into every area of British public life. Even my beloved *Guardian* newspaper has taken to hiring columnists who use their pulpit to sell their

Red wares. The late Vincent Hanna, the political commentator, part of the massive Irish United support, once caught me twice in a day, over breakfast in the paper and at night on radio, peddling his loathsome, effusive Red views. United fan Jim White wrote perhaps the laziest article on the post-Coppell, pre-Clark fiasco when his research appeared to amount to talking to one man in a pub about Manchester City's current plight.

We are approaching the millennium, when I shall be fifty years old. For all but a few months of the past half-century, I have been emotionally enveloped in my loyal support for Manchester City and my deep and abiding scepticism for all things that derive from Manchester United. It doesn't matter if Alex Ferguson wins the European Cup with a team composed of the cream of European football or a team composed entirely of Tellytubbies. Manchester United are as alien to me as the Cossacks riding through the *shtetls* of my ancestors in Eastern Europe.

The odd thing is that many of the City players over the past twenty years have left me cold, though their victories have warmed me and their defeats have devastated me. They have gone now, those interlopers like Steve Daley and David Cross, Gordon Dalziel and Tony Cunningham. Where they come from nobody knows and where the wind blows them I don't care. They are the new Roy Gratrixes. My sole comfort is that after Roy Gratrix and Dave Bacuzzi came the Great Ones, Corrigan, Book, Pardoe, Doyle, Heslop, Oakes, Summerbee, Bell, Lee, Young and Coleman. I can only hope that my children will live to see their own versions of those heroes.

My daughter was born in March 1975, between the League Cup final defeat by Wolves in 1974 and the League Cup final victory over Newcastle in 1976. Amy was a breech birth, left foot sliding out first like a Cliff Sear tackle. It was a sight which even edged out Tommy Booth's goal in the 1969

FA Cup semi-final to claim top spot in the league table of Great Moments in My Life. She was born on Sunday 2 March, leaving the coast clear for her father to travel with David Green to watch City at Leicester on the following Saturday. Corrigan was carried off injured after twenty minutes, which left Summerbee, Doyle and Marsh to throw the goalkeeping jersey at each other for five minutes. Doyle lost – and so did we.

Amy's first match was at Maine Road in April 1978. It ended in a 1–1 draw. Channon scored the goal. She emitted no great emotion, other than a craving for more sweets than I had brought with us. When she was twelve years old, she was stricken by a rare cancer. I thought of all the terrible things I had done in my life, and none of them individually or collectively seemed to add up to this devastating punishment.

Although my faith disappeared with my mother's death, I like to think of myself as a good Jew, because I believe that being a good Jew means being a *mensch*, being a man, the sort of man my mother would still respect. I am not ashamed to say that my daughter's life-threatening illness produced the kind of contractual discussions with God that are entirely different from those conducted during derby matches against United. Although the cancer was diagnosed as malignant, Amy made a brave and total recovery.

The first Saturday after the surgeon removed the tumour, City beat Huddersfield 10–1. It was such a freakish result, I couldn't but believe that He had reached for the yellow, not the red card. When she won her way through sheer hard work to admission to Gonville & Caius College, Cambridge, she made her father very happy by pinning to the noticeboard in her room a Colin Bell pennant bought in the Maine Road souvenir shop in 1968. It had travelled round the world with me only to return to its first home, twenty-eight years later. It was what psychotherapists call 'closure'.

My son David was born on 23 July 1977, a few weeks after City had again missed out on the First Division Championship by a single point. Since the moment of his birth, David has known little but defeat and disaster. At his school in London, he remained isolated as the only Manchester City supporter, although one of his teachers, Brendan, amazingly enough is the real thing and accompanies us to matches now. I keep hoping for David's sake that the wheel of fortune will turn again. He has now reached the point in his life when the Mercer/Allison miracle has become due. In my first year at Caius College, we won the League and in the second year, we won the Cup. In David's first year in the same college, scarcely a dozen rooms away from where I had taped MERCER'S MARVELS across my front door, he heard the news that City had been relegated. In his second year, he saw five City managers and the lowest position in the club's history. I'm sorry, Dave, I'm really sorry.

It's been like that for all our children. Howard Davies's two sons, George and Archie, have been confirmed in the faith for many years now. Howard and I used to play badminton every week before his shoulder went and my knee disintegrated. One day, he came in looking very solemn. George must have been about five or six. On my enquiring what the reason was for his grim visage, Howard revealed that George was showing an unhealthy interest in Nottingham Forest. Fortunately, it transpired that the principal appeal of the City Ground club was in its scansion. George is now back safe and sound, none the worse for his experience, and has taken over as the Keeper of the Statistics. On the day of the Liverpool defeat, it was Howard who was vainly searching the City shop for the letter 'K' to give the boys a Kinkladze shirt. They had to settle for 'Gio'.

When David Green returned from Hollywood, Sam, his elder son, was seven years old. David gave him the choice of supporting Spurs, Arsenal or City. The unmentionable remained unmentioned. Brave Sam opted for City. At a recent Parents' Day at his London school, the headmaster was talking about the morality of Cantona's kung fu assault at Crystal Palace. He asked if there were any Manchester United supporters in the Hall. Something like 80 percent of those assembled raised their hands. Before beginning his sermon the head asked as an afterthought if there were any Manchester City fans present. Slowly, slowly, Sam raised his hand. The entire body of pupils and parents turned to stare. He kept his hand steadfastly aloft. He was the only one. His father, displaying all the fortitude of Captain Pugwash, abandoned his son in his moment of public exposure.

I am convinced that David would like to transfer his support to Manchester United. The bitching from him we all have to endure on our travels to Charlton and Watford, Luton and Millwall, is terrible. David now runs September Films, a thriving, very successful production company. The glamour and financial excesses of Manchester United fit precisely the 'millionaire lifestyle' he affects. Marooned in mediocrity in the Nationwide League Division One Manchester City assuredly do not. It is loyal unfaltering Sam who now keeps his father honest.

For my son David, the obsessions of his father also extended to immersing him in Lancashire cricket from an early age. When he was five, I took him to Lord's for the first time to see Lancashire playing Middlesex. Although Fowler and Allott had fought their way to Test recognition, Lancashire were not much of a team and hadn't been since the Clive Lloyd, David Lloyd, Harry Pilling side broke up in the late 1970s. Still, it was important that David got his first sight of the Red Rose at the same age his father did.

I made for my favourite spot, behind the bowler's arm at the Nursery End. I stood at the back, waiting for the end of the over. It was a midweek morning in early May and a pale, watery sun struggled to lighten the overcast sky. A small group of old men sat at the front of the balcony, just about where I would choose to sit. One of them had his shirt off. Of course, it was my Uncle Laurence.

David and I sat quietly as Mike Gatting and Roland Butcher batted Middlesex out of the trouble Allott and Croft had bowled them into. The umpires removed the bails for lunch and we all stood up. Laurence and his cronies started to walk up the gangway towards me.

I clutched my little boy's hand even tighter. As my uncle passed me, I said, 'Hello. Remember me?' He stopped and looked at me. He nodded. 'You're Colin, Florrie's boy.' I looked down at my son. 'This is my little boy, David. This is his first Lancashire match.' Laurence looked at him sadly, and then back at me. 'I see your name now and then. On the television.'

My eyes filled with tears. There was so much I wanted to say. He had meant so much to me. He must have known the significance of my visit to watch Lancashire with my son. And now meeting him again. The two of us here at Lord's watching Lancashire, both of us filled with a passion for the game of cricket, for the county of Lancashire. I thought of everything that he had given me and everything that he had destroyed. I hated him and I loved him. To an extent that neither of us could or would acknowledge, I was very much his creation. Perhaps more than my own parents, he had shaped me, shaped my soul, filled it with a love of music and theatre and politics as well as sport. I don't know how much of this passed through his mind as well at that moment. It was only a moment. The players were still walking off the field towards the pavilion. Laurence suddenly looked very old, very frail, more like my grandfather than my uncle. He looked up at his friends waiting for him at the top of the gangway. Maybe this wasn't the place for a discussion of the rights and wrongs of everything that happened between the time he defected to London and the time he refused to talk to me when I moved there and needed him so badly.

Laurence walked slowly up the steps to join his friends. I waited until he disappeared from sight and then David and I went to McDonald's for lunch. There was a train in the Swiss Cottage branch. David liked to sit in it while he ate his cheeseburger. I never saw Uncle Laurence again. He died a couple of years later. But I still go to Lord's with my son to watch Lancashire when they play there. And I still think about Uncle Laurence. And about Brian Statham and Noddy Pullar, about Cyril Washbrook and Roy Tattersall.

For the field is full of shades as I near the shadowy coast
And a ghostly batsman plays to the bowling of a ghost,
And I look through my tears on a soundless-clapping host
As the run stealers flicker to and fro
To and fro
O my Hornby and my Barlow long ago!

Postscript

A nd so the torch has been passed to a new generation of Manchester City supporters, one born in this century but who will take their commitment into the next millennium.

That last meeting with Uncle Laurence is seared into my mind partly because of its emotional content and partly because of its symbolism. It seemed the right place to finish a book that is about more than sport. It is about what sport does to people, to their friendships, to their family relationships. When I am gone and the physical memory of me has faded even from my children whom I love so deeply, there will only be the emotional triggers left to evoke my existence.

For my daughter Amy, it will be almost any piece of music by Mozart, but particularly *The Marriage of Figaro*. For my son David, it will be there every Saturday between three o'clock and five o'clock. Every time he picks up a newspaper (rare enough, I have to say) and looks at the football results, or hears the close of play scores and wonders how Lancashire have managed to collapse from a comfortable 74 for 1 overnight to 138 all out, there will come into his head the voice of his father, bewailing the unfairness of the world.

It won't be the same for him and his children as it was for me. I was a Manchester boy; he was born in Welwyn Garden City. I grew up in an Orthodox Jewish household and mixed mostly with Jewish kids; he has celebrated Christmas as well as Chanukah, Easter as well as Pesach. I made a conscious, if somewhat capricious choice to support Manchester City; he was indoctrinated before he had the chance to defend himself. His children, God forbid, depending on their school and neighbourhood, might show an inclination towards Chelsea or Middlesex. But I know that as long as I am alive, the Great Betrayal will never happen: Manchester United may have ruined my life, but it won't ruin theirs.

A verbal contract to support a football team may not, in Sam Goldwyn's memorable phrase, be worth the paper it's written on, but in the minds of millions of us, it is as binding as one written in blood.